JESUS
IS COMING

The Second Advent

Lo! He comes, with clouds descending,
Once for favored sinners slain;
Thousand thousand saints attending,
Swell the triumph of his train;
Hallelujah!
God appears on earth to reign.

Every eye shall now behold him
Robed in dreadful majesty;
Those who set at naught and sold him,
Pierced and nailed him to the tree,
Deeply wailing
Shall the true Messiah see.

All the tokens of his passion
Still his dazzling body bears,
Cause of endless exultation
To his ransomed worshipers;
With what rapture
Gaze we on those glorious scars.

Yea, Amen! let all adore thee,
High on thy eternal throne;
Savior, take the power and glory;
Claim the kingdom for thine own:
Jah! Jehovah!
Everlasting God, come down!
—*Charles Wesley*

JESUS IS COMING

God's HOPE For A Restless World

WILLIAM E. BLACKSTONE

FOREWORD BY JOHN F. WALVOORD

KREGEL PUBLICATIONS
Grand Rapids, Michigan 49501

Jesus Is Coming: God's Hope for a Restless World
by William E. Blackstone

Updated edition with Foreword by John F. Walvoord © 1989 by
Kregel Publications, a division of Kregel, Inc. P.O. Box 2607,
Grand Rapids, MI 49501. All rights reserved.

Cover Design: Brian Fowler
Cover Photo: The Image Bank

Library of Congress Cataloging-in-Publication Data
Blackstone, W. E. (William Eugene), 1841-1935.
   Jesus is coming / by William E. Blackstone; foreword by
John F. Walvoord.
         p.   cm.
   Reprint. Originally published: 3rd rev. ed. New York: F.H.
Revell, 1908.
   Includes index.
   1. Second Advent. I. Title.
BT885.B5   1989   236'.9—dc20   89-2581
                                                     CIP

ISBN 978-0-8254-2275-1

5 6 7 8 9 / 11 10 09 08 07

Printed in the United States of America

CONTENTS

6 Contents

Contents 7

FOREWORD

W. E. Blackstone's book, *Jesus Is Coming*, which had such widespread circulation earlier in the twentieth century, in large measure set the tone for this period of history. More than any other single book, it provided a study in eschatology which served to introduce the twentieth century as a time for intense study of prophecy.

Everyone interested in prophecy should read this and acquaint himself with the hope as expressed by Mr. Blackstone that Jesus is coming and He may be coming soon.

The publication of a new, attractive printing of the book will be welcomed by all who treasure the truth of the Lord's coming. It should be read by those who have not read it before, and it would be a gracious gift to others as an introduction to the doctrine.

JOHN F. WALVOORD

Chancellor
Dallas Theological Seminary

PREFACE

I dedicate this book to those who "love our Lord's appearing." It has been my prayerful desire to furnish, in abbreviated form, a handbook that might serve as a convenient reference in the study of this truth, and as an aid in the presentation of it to others.

I gratefully acknowledge the blessing of God, which has rested upon it so that it has passed through many editions and also been issued in many foreign languages.* I have no desire for controversy, but have only sought to testify of my convictions regarding the scriptural importance of this subject, and to help candid inquirers in obtaining "like precious faith with us." After continued, earnest and prayerful study, I am more than ever confirmed in the faith that Christ's coming will be pre-millennial, and this all-important point we would emphasize, if possible, with the zeal and earnestness manifested by the early disciples, who repeatedly taught us to look for Jesus (Philippians 3:20; Titus 2:13; Hebrews 9:28; 2 Peter 3:14).

I would not be dogmatic concerning the order of events which cluster about our Lord's return and, should any hold views different from what I have set forth, I will cordially shake hands with them if I can agree on the great fact that His return will be premillennial and that the time of it is uncertain and imminent (Matthew 24:42); and further that this hope ("Blessed Hope," Titus 2:13) produces a purifying, separating power in the heart, winning us over to holiness, love and service.

For the kind criticism and helpful suggestions of brethren dearly beloved—we express our sincere thanks, and we humbly pray for the continued blessing of "the Coming One."

WILLIAM E. BLACKSTONE

---

* *Jesus Is Coming* has been translated into over 40 foreign languages and over 500,000 copies have been printed (publisher's note).

FOREWORD TO
FELLOW MINISTERS

Having found in over 40 years' experience the "Blessed Hope" for our Lord's return to be a most precious influence in my Christian life, promoting holiness, consecration of time and substance, and intense activity in our Master's service, I humbly commend it to each of you for personal comfort, and as meat in due season to preach to your congregations.

Let me emphasize the plain exhortation of the Holy Spirit—"These things speak" (Titus 2:15); "Comfort one another with these words" (1 Thessalonians 4:18). Oh! Brethren! There are tens of thousands sitting under your ministries who would be comforted by the simple testimony of the Scriptures on this all important subject.

Thank God there are many who do exalt this truth, but how it must grieve the Master to see the multitude of preachers who are indifferent to His promised return, and eliminate the "comfort" which He has commanded and which the masses need.

Thirty-nine years ago (1878) I was providentially led to issue the first edition of *Jesus Is Coming*, which has been followed by numerous editions with translations into many languages encircling the world. I rapturously praise our coming Bridegroom that He has let His "errand boy" have so wide a testimony.

With all my heart in this my seventy-sixth year I implore you to read this book. Many have testified that it has made the Bible a new book to them. May it be so to you, and may we all, some day, rejoice together with Luther, Melanchthon, Calvin, Knox, and the Wesleys, singing Charles' beautiful hymns as a welcome to our descending Lord.

WM. E. BLACKSTONE

January, 1917

1

JESUS IS COMING AGAIN

Do you know that Jesus is coming again?

Christ said, "I will come again" (John 14:3) and His word endures forever,[1] for His is the truth.[2]

The angels said He would come again. "The same Jesus," "and in like manner,"[3] and they were not mistaken when they announced His first coming.[4]

The Holy Spirit, by the mouth of the apostles, has repeatedly said Christ would come again.[5] Is not such an event, stated with such authority, of vital importance to

---

1. *1 Peter 1:25*. But the word of the Lord endureth for ever. And this is the word which by the gospel is preached unto you.

2. *John 14:6*. Jesus saith unto him, I am the way, the truth, and the life: no man cometh unto the Father, but by me.

3. *Acts 1:11*. Which also said, Ye men of Galilee, why stand ye gazing up into heaven? This same Jesus, which is taken up from you into heaven, shall so come in like manner as ye have seen him go into heaven.

4. *Luke 1:26-28, 30-31*. And in the sixth month the angel Gabriel was sent from God unto a city of Galilee, named Nazareth. To a virgin espoused to a man whose name was Joseph, of the house of David; and the virgin's name was Mary. And the angel came in unto her, and said, Hail, thou art highly favored, the Lord is with thee: blessed art thou among women. And the angel said unto her, Fear not, Mary: for thou hast found favor with God. And, behold, thou shalt conceive in thy womb, and bring forth a son, and shalt call his name JESUS. He shall be great, and shall be called the Son of the Most High; and the Lord God shall give unto him the throne of his father David. And he shall reign over the house of Jacob for ever and of his kingdom there shall be no end. See also *Luke 2:8-18*.

5. *1 Thessalonians 4:16*. For the Lord himself shall descend from heaven with a shout, with the voice of the archangel, and with the trump of God: and the dead in Christ shall rise first.

Hebrews 9:28. So Christ was once offered to bear the sins of many; and unto them that look for him shall he appear the second time without sin unto salvation.

Hebrews 10:37. For yet a little while, and he shall come will come, and will not tarry.

us? At His first coming, the world rejected Him. He was the despised Nazarene. But when He comes again, He will appear as "the blessed and only Potentate, the King of Kings and Lord of Lords."[6]

He is coming to sit upon the throne of His glory,[7] and to be admired by all those that believed,[8] and to rule all the nations of the earth[9] in judgment and equity.

How glorious it will be to see the King in His beauty![10]

Perhaps you are not a Christian, and say,

"I Don't Care Anything About it"

Then, dear friend, I point you to the crucified Savior as *the only hope of salvation.*

I beg of you to "kiss the Son," lest you perish from the way. Blessed are all who put their trust in Him.[11] What will it profit you if you gain the whole world but lose your

---

6. *1 Timothy 6:13-15.* I give thee charge in the sight of God, who quickeneth all things, and before Christ . . . that thou keep this commandment without spot, unrebukable, until the appearing of our Lord Jesus Christ: which in his times he shall show, who is the blessed and only Potentate, the King of kings, and Lord of lords.

7. *Matthew 25:31.* When the Son of man shall come in his glory, and all the holy angels with him, then shall he sit upon the throne of his glory.

8. *2 Thessalonians 1:10.* When he shall come to be glorified in his saints, and to be admired in all them that believe (because our testimony among you was believed) in that day.

9. *Psalm 2:9.* Thou shalt break them with a rod of iron; thou shalt dash them in pieces like a potter's vessel.

Isaiah 9:6-7. For unto us a child is born, unto us a son is given: and the government shall be upon his shoulder: and his name shall be called Wonderful, Counsellor, The mighty God, The everlasting Father, The Prince of Peace. Of the increase of his government and peace there shall be no end, upon the throne of David, and upon his kingdom, to order it, and to establish it with judgment and with justice from henceforth even for ever. The zeal of the Lord of hosts will perform this.

Revelation 2:25-27. But that which ye have already, hold fast till I come. And he that overcometh, and keepeth my works unto the end, to him will I give power over the nations: and he shall rule them with a rod of iron; as the vessels of a potter shall they be broken to shivers: even as I received of my Father.

10. *Isaiah 33:17.* Thine eyes shall see the King in his beauty; they shall behold the land that is very far off.

11. *Psalm 2:12.* Kiss the Son, lest he be angry, and ye perish from the way, when his wrath is kindled but a little. Blessed are all they that put their trust in him.

own soul?[12] Christ is coming, and we don't know the day, or the hour, when He may come.[13] What if He should come now? Would you be found resting in His peace,[14] or would you be left behind to endure the terrible things which will come upon the world,[15] while the church is with Christ in the air?[16] At His appearing[17] will you be mourning[18] and praying to the mountains and rocks to hide you from His face?[19]

"Prepare to meet thy God," was the solemn injunction to Israel (Amos 4:12), and every one of us, both Jew and Gentile, must meet Him, either in *grace* or in *judgment*.

As an ambassador for Christ, I implore you: be reconciled to God[20] *now,* in the accepted time, in the day

---

12. *Matthew 16:26-27.* For what is a man profited, it he shall gain the whole world, and lose his own soul? or what shall a man give in exchange for his soul? For the Son of man shall come in the glory of his Father with his angels; and then he shall reward every man according to his works.

13. *Matthew 25:13.* Watch therefore; for ye know neither the day nor the hour wherein the Son of man cometh.

14. *2 Peter 3:14.* Wherefore, beloved, seeing that ye look for such things, be diligent that ye may be found of him in peace, without spot, and blameless.

15. *Luke 21:25-26.* And there shall be signs in the sun, and in the moon, and in the stars; and upon the earth distress of nations, with perplexity; the sea and the waves roaring; men's hearts failing them for fear, and for looking after those things which are coming on the earth: for the powers of heaven shall be shaken.

16. *Luke 21:36.* Watch ye therefore, and pray always, that ye may be accounted worthy to escape all these things that shall come to pass, and to stand before the Son of man.

   1 Thessalonians 4:17. Then we which are alive and remain shall be caught up together with them in the clouds, to meet the Lord in the air: and so shall we ever be with the Lord.

17. *2 Thessalonians 1:7-10.* And to you who are troubled rest with us, when the Lord Jesus shall be revealed from heaven with his mighty angels, in flaming fire taking vengeance on them that know not God, and that obey not the gospel of our Lord Jesus Christ: who shall be punished with everlasting destruction from the presence of the Lord, and from the glory of his power; when he shall come to be glorified in his saints, and to be admired in all them that believe (because our testimony among you was believed) in that day.

18. *Matthew 24:30.* And then shall appear the sign of the Son of man in heaven: and then shall all the tribes of the earth mourn, and they shall see the Son of man coming in the clouds of heaven with power and great glory.

19. *Revelation 6:16.* And said to the mountains and rocks, Fall on us, and hide us from the face of him that sitteth on the throne, and from the wrath of the Lamb.

20. *2 Corinthians 5:20.* Now then we are ambassadors for Christ, as though God did beseech you by us: we pray you in Christ's stead, be ye reconciled to God.

of salvation.[21] Repent and be converted, that your sins
may be blotted out.[22] Turn "to serve the living and true
God, and to wait for his Son from Heaven,"[23] and be
unblamable at the coming of our Lord Jesus Christ.[24]

But if you are a Christian, then I point you to *His
coming again,* as

The True Incentive to a Holy Life[25]

Jesus is coming, therefore deny your flesh while you
are on the earth, that you may appear with Him in glory.[26]

Strive and pray for purity of heart, that you may "be
like Him and see Him as He is."[27] Search the Word, that

---

21. *2 Corinthians 6:2.* (For he saith, I have heard thee in a time accepted,
and in the day of salvation have I succored thee: behold, now is the accepted
time; behold, now *is* the day of salvation.)

Luke 14:31-33. Or what king, going to make war against another king,
sitteth not down first and consulteth whether he be able with ten thousand to
meet him that cometh against him with twenty thousand? Or else, while the
other is yet a great way off, he sendeth an ambassage, and desireth conditions
of peace. So likewise, whosoever he be of you that forsaketh not all that he
hath, he cannot be my disciple.

22. *Acts 10:42-43.* And he commandeth us to preach unto the people, and to
testify that it is he which was ordained of God to be the Judge of quick and
dead. To him give all the prophets witness, that through His name whosoever
believeth in him shall receive remission of sins.

Acts 17:30-31. And the time of this ignorance God winked at; but now
commandeth all men every where to repent: because he hath appointed a day,
in the which he will judge the world in righteousness by that man whom he
hath ordained; whereof he hath given assurance unto all men, in that he hath
raised him from the dead.

23. *1 Thessalonians 1:9-10.* For they themselves show of us what manner of
entering in we had unto you, and how ye turned to God from idols to serve the
living and true God; and to wait for his Son from heaven, whom he raised
from the dead, even Jesus, which delivered us from the wrath to come.

24. *1 Thessalonians 3:13.* To the end he may stablish your hearts unblamable
in holiness before God, even our Father, at the coming of our Lord Jesus
Christ with all his saints.

25. *1 John 3:2-3.* Beloved, now are we the sons of God, and it doth not yet
appear what we shall be: but we know that, when he shall appear, we shall be
like him; for we shall see him as he is. And every man that hath this hope in
him purifieth himself, even as he is pure.

26. *Colossians 3:4-5.* When Christ, who is our life, shall appear, then shall ye
also appear with him in glory. Mortify therefore your members which are
upon the earth; fornication, uncleanness, inordinate affection, evil concupis-
cence, and covetousness, which is idolatry.

27. *Matthew 5:8.* Blessed are the pure in heart: for they shall see God.

1 John 3:2-3. Beloved, now are we the sons of God, and it doth not yet
appear what we shall be: but we know that, when he shall appear, we shall be

you may be sanctified and cleansed by it,[28] and that your whole spirit, and soul, and body may be preserved blameless until the coming of our Lord Jesus Christ.[29] But possibly you say, with contempt,

"Oh, That's Second Adventism"

Beloved, have you considered that Moses,[30] David,[31] Isaiah,[32] Jeremiah,[33] Daniel,[34] Zechariah,[35] and all the prophets and apostles,[36] were believers in the *second advent of Christ?* And because some, by setting dates, and others errors, have brought disrepute on this doctrine, should we cast it aside altogether?

---

like him; for we hall see him as he is. And every man that hath this hope in him purifieth himself, even as he is pure.

28. *Ephesians 5:26.* That he might sanctify and cleanse it with the washing of water by the word.

29. *1 Thessalonians 5:23.* And the very God of peace sanctify you wholly; and I pray God your whole spirit and soul and body be preserved blameless unto the coming of our Lord Jesus Christ.

30. *Deuteronomy 33:2.* And he said, The Lord came from Sinai, and rose up from Seir unto them; he shined forth from Mount Paran, and he came with ten thousands of saints: from his right hand went a fiery law for them.

31. *Psalm 102:16.* When the Lord shall build up Zion, he shall appear in his glory.

32. *Isaiah 59:20.* And the Redeemer shall come to Zion, and unto them that turn from transgression in Jacob, saith the Lord.

Isaiah 60:1. Arise, shine; for thy light is come, and the glory of the Lord is risen upon thee.

33. *Jeremiah 23:5-6.* Behold the days come, saith the Lord, that I will raise unto David a righteous Branch, and a King shall reign and prosper, and shall execute judgment and justice in the earth. In his days Judah shall be saved, and Israel shall dwell safely: and this is his name whereby he shall be called, THE LORD OUR RIGHTEOUSNESS.

34. *Daniel 7:13.* I saw in the night visions, and, behold, one like the Son of man came with the clouds of heaven, and came to the Ancient of days, and they brought him near before him.

35. *Zechariah 14:4-5.* And his feet shall stand in that day upon the mount of Olives, which is before Jerusalem on the east; and the mount of Olives shall cleave in the midst thereof toward the east and toward the west, and there shall be a very great valley; and half of the mountain shall remove toward the north, and half of it toward the south. And ye shall flee to the valley of the mountains; for the valley of the mountains shall reach unto Azal: yea, ye shall flee, like as ye fled from before the earthquake in the days of Uzziah king of Judah: and the Lord my god shall come, and all the saints with thee.

36. *Acts 15:15-17.* And to this agree the words of the prophets; as it is written, after this I will return, and will build again the tabernacle of David, which is fallen down; and I will build again the ruins thereof, and I will set it up: that the residue of men might seek after the Lord, and all the Gentiles, upon whom my name is called, saith the Lord, who doeth all these things.

But it may be you say (as I have been dissappointed to hear from so many even earnest Christians),

"Well, I Don't Think It Concerns Me Much, Anyway"

"I've always thought that in most cases it meant death, and if I'm prepared for death, that's enough; there is too much speculation about it to suit me; I don't believe it's a practical doctrine; and, more than that, I think it's a mistake to pay so much attention to it."

Yes, this shows many Christians—who profess to be members of the body of Christ,[37] and who have been espoused unto one husband, that they may be presented to Him,[38]—summarily dispose of this precious truth: that Jesus is coming, to take to Himself His bride.[39]

O, beloved, do not deprive yourself of this comforting truth. Please take your pencil and mark in your Bible the passages that relate to it; and see

How Large a Portion of the Word Is Devoted to It

If the Holy Spirit considered it so important, is it not worthy of our attention? The Word exhorts us[40] to give attention to it;[41] and the danger of condemnation is to those who do not.[42]

---

37. *1 Corinthians 12:27.* Now ye are the body of Christ, and members in particular.

38. *2 Corinthians 11:2.* For I am jealous over you with godly jealousy: for I have espoused you to one husband, that I may present you as a chaste virgin to Christ.

39. *John 14:3.* And if I go and prepare a place for you, I will come again, and receive you unto myself; that where I am, there ye may be also.

Ephesians 5:23, 32. For the husband is the head of the wife, even as Christ is the head of the church: and he is the Savior of the body. This is a great mystery: but I speak concerning Christ and the church.

40. *1 Thessalonians 4:18.* Wherefore comfort one another with these words.

1 Corinthians 1:7. So, that ye come behind in no gift; waiting for the coming of our Lord Jesus Christ.

41. *Revelation 1:3.* Blessed is he that readeth, and they that hear the words of this prophecy, and keep those things which are written therein: for the time is at hand.

42. *Luke 12:45-46.* But and if that servant say in his heart, My lord delayeth his coming; and shall begin to beat the menservants and maidens, and to eat

Please examine the passages cited in chapter 17, "A Practical Doctrine," on page 181 and see how Jesus and the apostles used this doctrine to stimulate us to watchfulness, repentance, patience, ministerial faithfulness, brotherly love, etc., and then decide whether anything else could be more practical.

Surely no other doctrine in the Word of God presents a deeper motive for crucifying the flesh, for separation to God, to work for souls, and as our hope and joy and crown of rejoicing,[43] than this does.

For the whole teaching of it is, that our citizenship is in heaven. From there also, we look for our Savior, the Lord Jesus Christ, who will change our lowly bodies, that they may be like His glorious body.[44] The truth of His coming awakens our inner groaning for our adoption as sons and the redemption of our bodies.[45]

---

and drink, and to be drunken; the lord of that servant will come in a day when he looketh not for him, and at an hour when he is not aware, and will cut him in sunder, and will appoint him his portion with the unbelievers.

Luke 21:34-36. And take heed to yourselves, lest at any time your hearts be overcharged with surfeiting, and drunkenness, and cares of this life, and *so* that day come upon you unawares. For as a snare shall it come on all them that dwell on the face of the whole earth. Watch ye therefore, and pray always, that ye may be accounted worthy to escape all these things that shall come to pass, and to stand before the Son of man.

1 Thessalonians 5:1-7. But of the times and the seasons, brethren, ye have no need that I write unto you. For yourselves know perfectly that the day of the Lord so cometh as a thief in the night. For when they shall say, Peace and safety; then sudden destruction cometh upon them, as travail upon a woman with child; and they shall not escape. But ye, brethren, are not in darkness, that the day should overtake you as a thief. Ye are all the children of light, and the children of the day: we are not of the night, nor the darkness. Therefore let us not sleep, as do others; but let us watch and be sober. For they that sleep sleep in the night; and they that be drunken are drunken in the night.

43. *1 Thessalonians 2:19.* For what is our hope, or joy, or crown of rejoicing? *Are* not even ye in the presence of our Lord Jesus Christ at his coming?

Daniel 12:3. And they that be wise shall shine as the brightness of the firmament; and they that turn many to righteousness as the stars for ever and ever.

44. *Philippians 3:20-21.* For our conversation is in heaven; from whence also we look for the Savior, the Lord Jesus Christ: who shall change our vile body, that it may be fashioned like unto his glorious body, according to the working whereby he is able even to subdue all things, unto himself.

45. *Romans 8:23.* And not only they, but ourselves also, which have the first

It gives us a view of the world as a wrecked vessel,[46] and stimulates us to work with all our strength that we might save some.[47] Most, if not all, of the evangelists of our day are empowered by this doctrine, and surely their work is practical.

---

fruits of the Spirit, even we ourselves groan within ourselves, waiting for the adoption, to wit, the redemption of our body.

Luke 21:28. And when these things begin to come to pass, then look up, and lift up your heads; for your redemption draweth nigh.

46. *Matthew 7:13-14.* Enter ye in at the strait gate: for wide is the gate, and broad is the way, that leadeth to destruction, and many there be which go in thereat: because strait is the gate, and narrow is the way, which leadeth unto life, and few there be that find it.

1 Thessalonians 5:3. For when they shall say, Peace and safety; then sudden destruction cometh upon them, as travail upon a woman with child; and they shall not escape.

2 Peter 2:3-9. And through covetousness shall they with feigned word make merchandise of you: whose judgment now of a long time lingereth not, and their damnation slumbereth not. For if God spared not the angels that sinned, but cast them down to hell, and delivered them into chains of darkness, to be reserved unto judgment; and spared not the old world, but saved Noah the eighth person, a preacher of righteousness, bringing in the flood upon the world of the ungodly; and turning the cities of Sodom and Gomorrah into ashes condemned them with an overthrow, making them as ensample unto those that after should live ungodly; and delivered just Lot, vexed with the filthy conversation of the wicked: (for that righteous man dwelling among them, in seeing and hearing, vexed his righteous soul from day to day with their unlawful deeds;) the Lord knoweth how to deliver the godly out of temptation, and to preserve the unjust unto the day of judgment to be punished.

2 Peter 3:5-12. For this they willingly are ignorant of, that by the word of God the heavens were of old, and the earth standing out of the water and in the water: whereby the world that then was, being overflowed with water, perished: but the heavens and the earth, which are now, by the same word are kept in store, reserved unto fire against the day of judgment and perdition of ungodly men. But, beloved, be not ignorant of this one thing, that one day is with the Lord as a thousand years, and a thousand years as one day. The Lord is not slack concerning his promise, as some men count slackness; but is longsuffering to us-ward, not willing that any should perish, but that all should come to repentance. But the day of the Lord will come as a thief in the night: in the which the heavens shall pass away with a great noise, and the elements shall melt with fervent heat, the earth also and the works that are therein shall be burned up. Seeing then that all these things shall be dissolved, what manner of persons ought ye to be in all holy conversation and godliness, looking for and hasting unto the coming of the day of God, wherein the heaven being on fire shall be dissolved, and the elements shall melt with fervent heat?

47. *1 Corinthians 9:22.* To the weak became I weak; that I might gain the weak: I am made all things to all men, that I might by all means save some.

Again, Peter says, "We have a more sure word of prophecy,* whereunto ye do well that ye *take heed* (as unto a light that shineth in a dark place, until the day dawn, and the day star arise) in your hearts."48** He exhorts us to be mindful of these words.49 Therefore, *we are not speculating* when we prayerfully study prophecy.

---

* Greek: "We have the prophetic word more confirmed."
** See Tregelles' punctuation.

---

48. *2 Peter 1:19*. We have also a more sure word of prophecy; whereunto ye do well that ye take heed, as unto a light that shineth in a dark place, until the day dawn, and the daystar arise in your hearts.

49. *2 Peter 3:1-2*. This second epistle, beloved, I now write unto you; in both which I stir up your pure minds by way of remembrance: that ye may be mindful of the words which were spoken before by the holy prophets, and of the commandment of us the apostles of the Lord and Savior.

2

LITERAL INTERPRETATION

Perhaps you ask, "Shouldn't these prophecies be interpreted 'spiritually'? And doesn't this 'coming' mean our acceptance of Him at conversion, and the witness of the spirit? Or doesn't it refer to His reign over the Church?" etc.

No! Not at all. Think a moment. Do you condemn the Jews for rejecting Christ, when He came in such literal fulfillment of prophecy, and yet you reject the same literalness about His second coming? If so, you are not consistent. While we believe Luke 1:31 to be literally true, let us also believe the literalness of verses 32 and 33.

Luke 1:31-33

31. And, behold, thou shalt conceive in thy womb, and bring forth a son, and shall call his name Jesus.
32. He shall be great, and shall be called the Son of the Highest: and the Lord God shall give unto Him the throne of His Father, David.
33. And He shall reign over the house of Jacob forever; and of His kingdom there shall be no end.

The inconsistency of accepting literally verse 31 and "spiritualizing" verses 32 and 33, is clearly illustrated by the following account of a conversation between a Christian minister and a Jew:

Taking a New Testament and opening it at Luke 1:32, the Jew asked: "Do you believe that what is written here shall be literally accomplished—'The Lord God shall give unto Him the throne of His Father, David; and He shall reign over the house of Jacob forever'?

"I do not," answered the clergyman, "but rather take it to be figurative language, descriptive of Christ's spiritual reign over the church."

"Then," replied the Jew, "neither do I believe literally the preceding words, which say that this Son of David would be born of a virgin; but take them to be merely a figurative description of the remarkable purity of the one who is the subject of the prophecy. But why, continued the Jew, "do you refuse to believe literally verses 32 and 33, while you believe implicitly the far more incredible statement of verse 31?"

"I believe it," replied the clergyman, "because it is a fact."

"Ah!" exclaimed the Jew, with an attitude of scorn and triumph, "*You* believe Scripture because it is a *fact;* I believe it because it is the *Word of God*."

Now wasn't the argument of the Jew honest and compelling? There are *symbols, figures* or *types, metaphors,* etc., used in Scripture and there are also *allegories*. But, unless they are so stated in the text, or plainly indicated in the context, we should hold only to the literal sense.

The words of Christ in John 7:38, we are told in the very next verse, were spoken "of the Spirit, which they that believe on him should receive."[1]

The *allegory* in Galatians 4:24-31[2] in no way detracts from the literal sense of Scripture, but on the contrary it confirms it. We know that both Hagar and Sarah had a literal physical existence. Mount Sinai and Jerusalem are literal.

---

1. *John 7:38-39*. He that believeth on me, as the Scripture hath said, out of his belly shall flow rivers of living water. (But this spake he of the Spirit, which they that believe on him should receive: for the Holy Spirit was not yet given; because that Jesus was not yet glorified.)

2. *Galatians 4:24-26*. Which things are an allegory: for these are the two covenants; the one from the mount Sinai, which gendereth to bondage, which is Agar. For this Agar is mount Sinai in Arabia, and answereth to Jerusalem which now is, and is in bondage with her children. But Jerusalem which is above is free, which is the mother of us all.

We have a literal Christ, the mediator of the new covenant.[3] And so we believe that the "Jerusalem which is above," of which Sarah is typical—"the heavenly Jerusalem,"[4] "the new Jerusalem which cometh down out of heaven from God,"[5] is also literal, tangible and real. How then, are we authorized, from such examples as these (which are most the prominent among those cited by postmillennialists as authority for "spiritualizing"), to do away with the literal sense of Luke 1:32-33, or of the multitude of passages which predict the restoration of Israel, the coming of Christ, or which describe His glorious Kingdom? There is no warrant for it. It subverts the authority and power of the Word of God, and postmillennialists, by so doing, open wide the door for skeptics and liberals of all descriptions. They likewise spiritualize Old Testament prophecies and have therefore ceased to look for any literal Messiah. That even Jews would join with Gentiles in *spiritualizing* Scripture, is a discouraging sign of the times in which we live. ("When the Son of Man cometh shall He find [the] faith on the earth?" Luke 18:8.) Why! the same process of *spiritualizing* away the literal sense of these plain texts of Scripture will sap the foundation of every Christian doctrine and leave us to drift into absolute infidelity or other forms of heresy.

What is the purpose of language, if not to convey definite ideas? Surely the Holy Spirit could have chosen

---

3. *Hebrews 12:24*. And to Jesus the mediator of the new covenant, and to the blood of sprinkling, that speaketh better things than that of Abel.

4. *Hebrews 12:22*. But ye are come unto mount Sion, and unto the city of the living God, the heavenly Jerusalem, and to an innumerable company of angels.

5. *Revelation 3:12*. Him that overcometh will I make a pillar in the temple of my God, and he shall go no more out: and I will write upon him the name of my God, and the name of the city of my God, *which is* new Jerusalem, which cometh down out of heaven from my God: and *I will write upon him* my new name.

Revelation 21:2, 10. And I John saw the holy city, new Jerusalem, coming down from God out of heaven, prepared as a bride adorned for her husband. And he carried me away in the spirit to a great and high mountain, and showed me that great city, the holy Jerusalem, descending out of heaven from God.

words to convey His thoughts correctly. Indeed it is all summed up in the question of a little child, "If Jesus didn't mean what He said, why didn't He say what He meant?" But we believe that He did mean what He said, and that His words will "not pass away" (Matthew 24:35).

Christ said He came "not to destroy the law or the prophets, but to fulfill," and "till heaven and earth pass, one jot or one tittle shall in no wise pass from the law, till all be fulfilled" (Matthew 5:17-18).

Prophecies Literally Fulfilled at the First Coming

If Christ came and literally fulfilled the prophecies of a suffering Messiah (Psalm 22, Isaiah 53, etc.), will He not just as surely come and also fulfill the prophecies of a glorified Messiah reigning in victory and majesty? (Psalm 2; 72; Daniel 7:13-14, Isaiah 9; 11; 60, etc.) Think of the many prophecies descriptive of a suffering Messiah which we have seen literally fulfilled. We rest on these as strong evidence for the truth and inspiration of the Word:

Isaiah 7:14—Born of a virgin.
Micah 5:2—At Bethlehem.
Jeremiah 31:15—Slaughter of the children.
Hosea 11:1—Called out of Egypt.
Isaiah 11:2—Anointed with the Spirit.
Zechariah 9:9—Entry into Jerusalem.
Psalm 41:9; 55:12-14—Betrayed by a friend.
Zechariah 13:7—Disciples forsake Him.
Zechariah 11:12—Sold for thirty pieces of silver.
Zechariah 11:13—Potter's field bought.
Isaiah 50:6—Spit on and scourged.
Exodus 12:46; Psalm 34:20—Not a bone broken.
Psalm 69:21—Gall and vinegar.
Psalm 22—Hand and feet pierced. Garments parted; lots cast.
Isaiah 53—Poverty, suffering, patience, and death.

Many other passages could be mentioned.

All these were literally fulfilled when Christ came. Do not, then, reject the literal fulfillment of those numerous prophecies which describe His future coming, and His glorious reign upon the earth. Namely:

Prophecies to Be Literally Fulfilled at the Second Coming

Then He will come Himself ....1 Thessalonians 4:16
That He will shout ....1 Thessalonians 4:16
That the dead will hear His voice ....John 5:28
That the raised and changed believers will be
    caught up to meet Him in the air ....1 Thessalonians 4:17
That He will receive them unto Himself ....John 14:3
That He will minister unto His watching servants ....Luke 12:37
That He will come to the earth again ....Acts 1:11
    To the same Mount Olivet from which
      He ascended ....Zechariah 14:4
      In flaming fire ....2 Thessalonians 1:8
    In the clouds of heaven with power
      and great glory ....Matthew 24:30; 1 Peter 1:7; 4:13
    And stand upon the earth ....Job 19:25
    That His saints (the Church) will come
      with Him ...Deuteronomy 33:2; 1 Thessalonians 3:13; Jude 14
That every eye will see Him ....Revelation 1:7
That He will destroy the Antichrist ....2 Thessalonians 2:8
That He will sit on His throne ....Matthew 25:31; Revelation 5:13
That all nations will be gathered before Him,
    and He will judge them ....Matthew 25:32
That He will have the throne of David ....Isaiah 9:6-7; Luke 1:32;
                       Ezekiel 21:25-27
That it will be upon the earth ....Jeremiah 23:5-6
That He will have a kingdom ....Daniel 7:13-14
And rule over it with His saints ...Daniel 7:18-22-27; Revelation 5:10
That all kings and nations will serve Him ....Psalm 72:11;
                  Isaiah 49:6-7; Revelation 15:4
That the kingdoms of this world will become
    His kingdom ....Zechariah 9:10; Revelation 11:15
That the people will gather unto Him ....Genesis 49:10
That every knee will bow to Him ....Isaiah 45:23
That they will come and worship the King ....Zechariah 14:16;
                              Psalm 86:9
That He will build up Zion ....Psalm 102:16
That His throne will be in Jerusalem ....Jeremiah 3:17;
                            Isaiah 33:20-21

That the apostles will sit upon twelve thrones, judging
    the twelve tribes of Israel . . . . Matthew 19:28; Luke 22:28-30
That He will rule all nations . . . . Psalm 2:8-9; Revelation 2:27
That He will rule with judgment and justice . . . . Isaiah 9:7
That the Temple in Jerusalem will be rebuilt
    and the glory of the Lord will come into it . . . . Ezekiel 40—48;
                                                                    43:2-5; 44:4
That the glory of the Lord will be revealed . . . . Isaiah 40:5
That the wilderness will be a fruitful field . . . . Isaiah 32:15
That the desert will blossom as the rose . . . . Isaiah 35:1-2
And His rest will be glorious . . . . Isaiah 11:10

And there are many more we might mention.

Surely, these plain prophecies are not mere symbolism, which gives us any authority to spiritualize them. Rather let us expect that He will fulfill these Scriptures just as literally as He did those predicting His first coming.

3

CHRIST'S COMING DOES NOT MEAN DEATH

Christ's *first* coming did not mean death to the Jews, and they did not understand it that way; neither does His *second* coming mean death to Christians, nor should they so understand this way.

Jesus makes a clear distinction between *death* and *His coming* in John 21.[1] He tells Peter how he would die, and then, by contrast, He speaks of John, saying: "If I will that he tarry till I come, what is that to thee?" That is, that John might not die, but live until Jesus would come again. The disciples understood that John would not die.

Death is an enemy,[2] and at Christ's coming we are raised from the dead, and shout victory over death and the grave. "O Death, where is thy sting? O Hades, where is thy victory?"[3]

---

1. *John 21:18-23*. Verily, verily, I say unto thee, When thou wast young, thou girdedst thyself, and walkedst whither thou wouldest: but when thou shalt be old, thou shalt stretch forth thy hands, and another shall gird thee, and carry thee whither thou wouldest not. This spake he, signifying by what death he should glorify God. And when he had spoken this, he saith unto him, Follow me. Then Peter, turning about, seeth the disciple whom Jesus loved following; which also leaned on his breast at supper, and said, Lord, which is he that betrayeth thee? Peter seeing him saith to Jesus, Lord, and what shall this man do? Jesus saith unto him, If I will that he tarry till I come, what is that to thee? Follow thou me. Then went this saying abroad among the brethren, that the disciple should not die: yet Jesus said not unto him, He shall not die; but, If I will that he tarry till I come, what is that to thee?

2. *1 Corinthians 15:26*. The last enemy that shall be destroyed is death.

3. *1 Corinthians 15:23, 54-55*. But every man in his own order: Christ the firstfruits; afterward they that are Christ's at his coming. So when this corruptible shall have put on incorruption, and this mortal shall have put on

If we are faithful unto death (that is, even though faithfulness costs us our lives), Christ has promised us a crown;[4] but we do not receive it until He comes.[5]

Nothing is promised us at death, except to be at rest[6] in paradise.[7] But we are promised all things in the resurrection, when Jesus comes.[8]

Therefore, we find Paul yearning for this resurrection.[9] He did not want to be unclothed by death but clothed by the resurrection.[10]

---

immortality, then shall be brought to pass the saying that is written, Death is swallowed up in victory. O death, where *is* thy sting? O grave, where *is* thy victory?

4. *Revelation 2:10*. Fear none of those things which thou shalt suffer: behold, the devil shall cast *some* of you into prison, that ye may be tried; and ye shall have tribulation ten days: be thou faithful unto death, and I will give thee a crown of life.

5. *2 Timothy 4:8*. Henceforth there is laid up for me a crown of righteousness, which the Lord, the righteous judge, shall give me at that day: and not to me only, but unto all them also that love his appearing.

1 Peter 5:4. And when the chief Shepherd shall appear, ye shall receive a crown of glory that fadeth not away.

6. *2 Thessalonians 1:7*. And to you who are troubled rest with us, when the Lord Jesus shall be revealed from heaven with his mighty angels.

Revelation 14:13. And I heard a voice from heaven saying unto me, Write, Blessed *are* the dead which die in the Lord from henceforth. Yes, saith the Spirit, that they may rest from their labors; and their works do follow them.

7. *Luke 16:22*. And it came to pass, that the begger died, and was carried by the angels into Abraham's bosom: the rich man also died, and was buried.

Luke 23:43. And Jesus said unto him, Verily I say unto thee, Today shalt thou be with me in paradise.

8. *Luke 14:14*. And thou shalt be blessed; for they cannot recompense thee: for thou shalt be recompensed at the resurrection of the just.

Luke 20:35-36. But they which shall be accounted worthy to obtain that world, and the resurrection from the dead, neither marry, nor are given in marriage: Neither can they die any more: for they are equal unto the angels; and are the children of God, being the children of the resurrection.

Romans 8:32. He that spared not his own Son, but delivered him up for us all, how shall he not with him also freely give us all things?

9. *Philippians 3:11*. If by any means I may attain unto the resurrection from the dead.

10. *2 Corinthians 5:4*. For we that are in this tabernacle do groan, being burdened: not for that we would be unclothed, but clothed upon, that mortality might be swallowed up of life.

1 Corinthians 15:51-54. Behold, I show you a mystery; we shall not all sleep, but we shall all be changed, in a moment, in the twinkling of an eye, at the last trump: for the trumpet shall sound, and the dead shall be raised incorruptible, and we shall be changed. For this corruptible must put on incorruption, and this mortal must put on immortality. So when this corruptible shall have put on incorruption, and this mortal shall have put on immortality, then shall be brought to pass the saying that is written, Death is swallowed up in victory.

Let anyone insert "death" in the passages which speak of Christ's coming and he will see that it doesn't fit. For instance:

> For "death" shall come in the glory of His Father (Matthew 16:27).
> When "death" shall sit in the throne of His glory (Matthew 19:28).
> Hereafter shall ye see "death" sitting on the right hand of power, and coming in the clouds of heaven (Matthew 26:64).
> Behold he [death] cometh with clouds and every eye shall see Him (Revelation 1:7).
> For our conversation is in heaven, from whence, also, we look for "death" (Philippians 3:20).

If you think these are exceptional passages, try it in other Scriptures referring to His coming. The only possible similarity consists in analogy—in the fact that we do not know the time when we will die. But thanks be to God, we may not die at all, for "we shall not all sleep" (1 Corinthians 15:51).

There will be one generation, at least, who will realize that the coming of our Lord is not death.

And if it is not admissible to say "for death, himself, shall descend from heaven with a shout" (1 Thessalonians 4:16), neither is it admissible to say, "Watch, therefore; for ye know not what hour "death" doth come" (Matthew 24:42). For, by such twisting of Scripture, we jostle this prominent truth of our Lord's advent into the background, and substitute it with the "grim monster," death.

Physical Death Is Not "the Coming of the Lord"

It is assuming too much to say that physical death is what is meant by "the coming of the Lord." For Scriptures do not teach this. On the contrary, the events which occur—as the Scriptures teach us—when the Lord comes, do not occur at the death of a Christian. The dead are not then raised, nor are the living believers changed, as they will be when the Lord comes. We know very little about hades or the intermediate state of the dead. It is probably true that, since the resurrection of our Lord, the souls of believers, at death, go to a paradise above, so that Paul could say, "absent from the body, present with the Lord" (2 Corinthians 5:8). But it would appear, from Revelation 6:9-11,[11] that some of the departed souls yearn for the execution of judgment, which occurs when the Lord comes.[12] Spiritually, the believer is with Christ now and is always,[13] but, to be bodily with Christ[14] is only accomplished by the resurrection, at His coming.[15] Therefore, it is entirely unscriptural to instruct the believer to look for death, as being equivalent to the Lord's coming.

---

11. *Revelation 6:9-11.* And when he had opened the fifth seal, I saw under the altar the souls of them that were slain for the word of God, and for the testimony which they held: and they cried with a loud voice, saying, How long; O Lord, holy and true, dost thou not judge and avenge our blood on them that dwell on the earth? And white robes were given unto every one of them; and it was said unto them, that they should rest yet for a little season, until their fellow servants also and their brethren, that should be killed as they were, should be fulfilled.

12. *1 Corinthians 4:5.* Therefore judge nothing before the time, until the Lord come, who both will bring to light the hidden things of darkness and will make manifest the counsels of the hearts: and then shall every man have praise of God.

2 Timothy 4:1. I charge thee in the sight of God, and of Christ Jesus, who shall judge the living and the dead, and by his appearing and his kingdom.

Revelation 11:18. And the nations were angry, and thy wrath is come, and the time of the dead, that they should be judged, and that thou shouldest give reward unto thy servants the prophets, and to the saints, and them that fear thy name, small and great: and shouldest destroy them which destroy the earth.

See also *Matthew 25:31-40.*

13. *John 14:23.* Jesus answered and said unto him, If a man love me, he will keep my words: and my Father will love him, and we will come unto him, and make our abode with him.

Matthew 28:20. Teaching them to observe all things whatsoever I have commanded you: and, lo, I am with you alway, even unto the end of the world. Amen.

14. *John 12:26.* If any man serve me, let him follow me; and where I am, there shall also my servant be: if any man serve me, him will my Father honor.

John 17:24. Father, I will that they also, whom thou hast given me, be with me where I am; that they may behold my glory, which thou hast given me: for thou lovedst me before the foundation of the world.

15. *John 14:3.* And if I go and prepare a place for you, I will come again, and receive you unto myself; that where I am, there ye may be also.

1 Thessalonians 4:17. Then we which are alive and remain shall be caught up together with them in the clouds, to meet the Lord in the air: and so shall we ever be with the Lord.

Dr. David Brown's Testimony

Rev. David Brown, although a prominent postmillennialist, recognized this and said, "The coming of Christ to individuals at death—however warrantably we may speak so, and whatever profitable considerations it may suggest—is not fitted for taking that place in the view of the believer which Scripture assigns to the Second Advent." And he very properly illustrates this with the following passages:

> "Let not your heart be troubled [Jesus said to his sorrowing disciples]: In my Father's house are many mansions . . . I go to prepare a place for you." And if I go away—What then? You will soon follow me? Death will shortly bring us together? No, rather "If I go away, *I will come again and receive you unto myself;* that where I am there ye may be also" (John 14:3).

> "And while they looked steadfastly toward heaven as He went up, behold, two men stood by them in white apparel; which also said, Ye men of Galilee, why stand ye gazing up into heaven? This same Jesus, which is taken up from you into heaven shall . . ."—What? Take you home soon to himself at death? No, He will *"so come* in like manner as ye have seen Him *go* into heaven" (Acts 1:10-11).

And Dr. Brown adds, "how know we that by jostling this event (the Advent) out of its scriptural place in the expectations of the Church, we are not, in a great degree, destroying its character and power as a practical principle? Can we not believe, though unable to trace it, that God's methods are ever best; and that as in nature, so perhaps in revelation, a modification by us of the divine arrangements, apparently slight, and attended even with some seeming advantages, may be followed by a total and unexcepted change of results, the opposite of what is anticipated and desired? So we fear it to be here."*

We would that we had space to quote more, for we admire this frank admission—that physical death is not the coming of our Lord—from one who labors so hard to support postmillennialism. Again, *the equation of physical death with the coming of the Lord degrades the grand*

---

* David Brown, *Second Advent*, pages 21, 22.

doctrine of the resurrection from its prominence in Scripture to almost an unnecessary appendage.

But we believe in the preaching of Jesus and the resurrection,[16] and we look forward with joyous anticipation to the resurrection from the dead, as the time when Jesus will give us the victory over death.[17]

Oh, that Christians would realize "the grace that is to be brought unto" us (not at death but) "at the revelation of Jesus Christ."[18]

Nowhere in the Savior's teachings are we commanded to watch or prepare for death. But we are commanded to watch and prepare for Christ's coming. Therefore, let us not be deceived by the thought that our great enemy, *Death*, is the precious *coming of Jesus*.

Therefore, this glorious doctrine *does* concern you.

Search the Scriptures

Perhaps, you say: "I don't know much about it, and I can't understand it." But do you *want* to understand it? If so, God's Word is open to you. The Holy Spirit will teach you.[19] He will show you things to come,[20] and these pages are written with the earnest desire to help you in the study of this truth.

---

16. *Acts 4:2*. Being grieved that they taught the people, and preached through Jesus the resurrection from the dead.

　　Acts 17:18. Then certain philosophers of the Epicureans, and of the Stoics, encountered him. And some said, What will this babbler say? other some, He seemeth to be a setter forth of strange gods: because he preached unto them Jesus, and the resurrection.

17. *1 Corinthians 15:54-55*. But when this corruptible shall have put on incorruption, and this mortal shall have put on immortality, then shall come to pass the saying that is written, Death is swallowed up in victory. O death, where is thy victory? O death, where is thy sting?

18. *1 Peter 1:13*. Wherefore gird up the loins of your mind, be sober, and hope to the end for the grace that is to be brought unto you at the revelation of Jesus Christ.

19. *John 14:26*. But the Comforter, which is the Holy Spirit, whom the Father will send in my name, he shall teach you all things to your remembrance, whatsoever I have said unto you.

20. *John 16:13*. Howbeit when he, the Spirit of truth, is come, he will guide you into all truth: for he shall not speak of himself; but whatsoever he shall hear, that shall he speak: and he will show you things to come.

Will you study it? Will you search for yourself, as did the noble Bereans?[21] Don't merely read though this little book, but to use it as an index, for your study of the Word of God. Search out the passages referred to, and read them prayerfully until the Holy Spirit guides you into the truth. If you do this, I believe you will see the light, and find great comfort concerning Christ's return.

A Christian, who had long opposed the truth of the premillennial coming of Christ said, "I have spent the happiest night of my life, for last evening I saw the truth concerning the second coming." It filled him with joy, and he is one who has been greatly used in leading souls to Christ. May God also bless and use you this way!

---

21. *Acts 17:10-11*. And the brethren immediately sent away Paul and Silas by night unto Berea: who coming thither went into the synagogue of the Jews. These were more noble than those in Thessalonica, in all readiness of mind, and searched the Scriptures daily, whether those things were so.

4

THE THREE APPEARINGS

The greatest fact in all of history is that Jesus Christ, the Lord of Glory, has been in this world. The most important fact today is that He is now in heaven making intercession for us.[1] And the greatest prophesied event of the future is that He is coming again.

These three appearings are beautifully described in the ninth chapter of Hebrews:[2]

His appearing upon earth "to put away sin by the sacrifice of Himself" (v. 26).

His entering "into Heaven itself, now to appear in the presence of God for us" (v. 24).

"And unto them that look for Him shall He appear the second time, without sin unto salvation" (v. 28).

---

1. *Hebrews 7:25*. Wherefore he is able also to save them to the uttermost that come unto God by him, seeing he ever liveth to make intercession for them.

Romans 8:34. Who is he that condemneth? It is Christ that died, yea rather, that is risen again, who is even at the right hand of God, who also maketh intercession for us.

1 John 2:1. My little children, these things write I unto you, that ye may sin not. And if any man sin, we have an advocate with the Father, Jesus Christ the righteous.

2. *Hebrews 9:24, 26, 28*. For Christ is not entered into the holy places made with hands, which are the figures of the true; but into heaven itself, now to appear in the presence of God for us. For then must he often have suffered since the foundation of the world: but now once in the end of the world hath he appeared to put away sin by the sacrifice of himself. So Christ was once offered to bear the sins of the many; and unto them that look for him shall he appear the second time without sin unto salvation.

While Christ was on earth He said, "It is expedient for you that I go away,"[3] and He went away.[4] He said, "I go to prepare a place for you." But "if I go and prepare a place for you, I will come again, and receive you unto myself; that where I am, there ye may be also" (John 14:2-3). He gave us this promise as our *hope* and *comfort* while He is away.

He said: "In the world ye shall have tribulation" (John 16:33), "ye shall weep and lament, and . . . be sorrowful . . . but I *will see you again,* and your heart shall rejoice" (vv. 20, 22).

Nothing can be more comforting to the church, the bride of Christ,[5] than this precious promise which our absent Lord has left us—that He will come and receive us unto Himself, and that we will be with Him, to behold His glory.[6]

He has given us the Lord's Supper that we should take the bread and the cup in remembrance of Him,[7] and to proclaim His death, until He comes.[8] We have this simple and loving memorial as a continual sign of this *promise*

---

3. *John 16:7.* Nevertheless I tell you the truth; it is expedient for you that I go away: for if I go not away, the Comforter will not come unto you; but if I depart, I will send him unto you.

4. *Acts 1:9.* And when he had spoken these things, while they beheld, he was taken up, and a cloud received him out of their sight.

5. *Ephesians 5:25-32.* Husbands, love your wives, even as Christ also loved the church, and gave himself for it: that he might sanctify and cleanse it with the washing of water by the word. That he might present it to himself a glorious church, not having spot, or wrinkle, or any such thing; but that it should be holy and without blemish. So ought men to love their wives as their own bodies. He that loveth his wife loveth himself. For no man ever yet hated his own flesh; but nourisheth and cherisheth it, even as the Lord the church: for we are members of his body, of his flesh, and of his bones. For this cause shall a man leave his father and mother, and shall be joined unto his wife, and they two shall be one flesh. This is a great mystery; but I speak concerning Christ and the church.

6. *John 17:24.* Father, I will that they also, whom thou hast given me, be with me where I am; that they may behold my glory, which thou hast given me; for thou lovedst me before the foundation of the world.

7. *Luke 22:19.* And he took bread, and gave thanks, and brake it, and gave unto them, saying, This is my body which is given for you: this do in remembrance of me.

8. *1 Corinthians 11:26.* For as often as ye eat this bread, and drink this cup, ye do show the Lord's death till he come.

during the entire earthly pilgrimage of the church.[9] Through it we look forward from the cross to His coming, when He will drink the cup anew with us in His Father's kingdom,[10] at the marriage feast of the Lamb.[11]

It is a constant reminder of His promise, pointing our eye of faith to His coming again. "He is faithful that promised"[12] and we are exhorted to have confidence and patience, that we may "receive the promise," for "yet a little while, and He that shall come, will come, and will not tarry" (Hebrews 10:36-37).

Someone has insightfully said that the coming of Christ is the very "pole star" of the church,* and the apostle Paul calls it "that *blessed hope.*"[13]

Jesus and the apostles and the prophets have given great prominence in the Scriptures to this inspiring theme. The Early Fathers and the Christian church, for the first two centuries of our era, found in it their chief source of hope and comfort. The belief that Jesus was coming in glory to reign with His saints on the earth, during the Millennium, was almost universal with them.

---

* Rev. David Brown, D.D.

---

9. *Hebrews 11:13.* These all died in faith, not having received the promises, but having seen them afar off, and were persuaded of them, and embraced them, and confessed that they were strangers and pilgrims on the earth.

1 Peter 2:11. Dearly beloved, I beseech you as strangers and pilgrims, abstain from fleshly lusts, which war against the soul.

10. *Matthew 26:29.* But I say unto you, I will not drink henceforth of this fruit of the vine, until that day when I drink it new with you in my Father's kingdom.

11. *Matthew 22:2.* The kingdom of heaven is like unto a certain king, which made a marriage for his son.

Revelation 19:9. And he saith unto me, Write, Blessed are they which are called unto the marriage supper of the Lamb. And he saith unto me, These are the true sayings of God.

See also *Luke 14:16-24.*

12. *Hebrews 10:22-25.* Let us draw near with a true heart in fullness of faith, having our hearts sprinkled from an evil conscience: and having our body washed with pure water, let us hold fast the confession of our hope that it waver not; for he is faithful that promised: and let us consider one another to provoke unto love and good works; not forsaking our own assembling together, as the custom of some is, but exhorting one another; and so much the more, as ye see the day drawing nigh.

13. *Titus 2:13.* Looking for that blessed hope, and the glorious appearing of the great God and our Savior Jesus Christ.

But in the third century there arose a school of interpreters, headed by Origen, who so "spiritualized" the Scriptures that they ceased to believe in any literal Millennium whatsoever. Their system of interpretation has been severely condemned by Martin Luther, Adam Clarke and other commentators.

When Constantine was converted and the Roman empire became nominally Christian, it appeared to many that the Millennium had come, and that they had the kingdom on earth. The church, hand in hand with the world, plunged into the dark ages, until awakened by the great reformers of the sixteenth century, who again began to proclaim the comforting hope and blessed promise of the coming of Christ. Since that time the subject—so long neglected—has been studied and preached with increasing interest. Indeed, in the last two centuries, it seems to have risen (with the doctrine of salvation by simple faith in a crucified Savior) into somewhat the same prominence which it occupied in the early church. God be praised for it!

5

THE MILLENNIUM

Millennium (Latin) is the same as *Chiliad* (Greek), and both mean a thousand years. Both terms stand for the doctrine of a future era of righteous government on the earth, to last a thousand years.

Jewish writers throughout the Talmud hold that this Millennium will be chiefly characterized by the deliverance of the Jews from all their enemies, the recovery of Palestine and the literal reign of their Messiah in unequaled splendor therein.

Premillennial Christians hold much in common with the Jews, but also that our Lord Jesus Christ is the Messiah; that He is to return to the earth and overthrow Satan, all ungodly government and lawlessness. He will establish a kingdom of righteousness, including the church; Himself as sovereign; Jerusalem as the capital; regathered and converted Israel as the center, and all nations included in a universal, worldwide kingdom of pure and blessed government.

Postmillennialists, for the most part, hold that the present preaching of the gospel will result in the conversion of the world and usher in a golden era of righteousness and a government of justice and peace to last a thousand years, after which the Lord will return for a "general judgment" and introduction of an eternal state. It is helpful to have these distinctive views of the Millennium clearly in mind.

Contrary to the postmillennial view, the literal reign of Christ, with His saints, for a thousand years is plainly stated in chapter 20 of Revelation.[1] Six times the expression "a thousand years" is repeated (verses 2, 3, 4, 5, 6 and 7). The teaching is so plain that "wayfaring men shall not err therein" (Isaiah 35:8).

But those who oppose this "blessed hope" of the premillennial coming of our Lord usually begin their arguments by the assertion that the doctrine of the Millennium is nowhere taught in Scripture except in this chapter of Revelation. They say that the symbolical character of this book forbids our establishing a literal view. Yet it is glaringly apparent that the Jews had fully developed the doctrine of the Millennium as the teaching of the Old Testament scriptures long before the book of Revelation or any portion of the New Testament was written. It was the view most frequently expressed in the Talmud that "the Messianic kingdom would last for *one thousand years,"* and this was commonly believed among the Jews. It is easy to discern on what they established this doctrine. It is the *Sabbath* of God's weeks.

The division of time into *sevens,* or *weeks,* permeates the Scriptures. A fundamental enactment of the Mosaic

---

1. *Revelation 20:1-9.* And I saw an angel come down from heaven, having the key of the bottomless pit and a great chain in his hand. And he laid hold on the dragon, that old serpent, which is the Devil, and Satan, and bound him a thousand years, and cast him into the bottomless pit, and shut him up, and set a seal upon him, that he should deceive that nations no more, till the thousand years should be fulfilled: and after that he must be loosed a little season. And I saw thrones, and they sat upon them, and judgment was given unto them: and I saw the souls of them that were beheaded for the witness of Jesus, and for the word of God, and which had not worshiped the beast, neither his image, neither had received his mark upon their foreheads, or in their hands; and they lived and reigned with Christ a thousand years. But the rest of the dead lived not again until the thousand years were finished. This is the first resurrection. Blessed and holy is he that hath part in the first resurrection: on such the second death hath no power, but they shall be priests of God and of Christ, and shall reign with him a thousand years. And when the thousand years are expired, Satan shall be loosed out of his prison, and shall go out to deceive the nations which are in the four quarters of the earth, Gog and Magog, to gather them together to battle: the number of whom is as the sand of the sea. And they went up on the breadth of the earth, and compassed the camp of the saints about, and the beloved city: and fire came down from God out of heaven and devoured them.

law was the keeping of the *Sabbath* (Exodus 20:8). This was based upon God's great rest day in Genesis 2. Upon this is founded not only the *week* of days, but also the *week of weeks* leading to Pentecost (Leviticus 23:15-16); the *week* of months, with the Atonement and *seven* days' feast of Tabernacles in the *seventh* month (Leviticus 23:27-28); the *week* of years, ending with the *Sabbatic* year (Leviticus 25:4); and the *week* of *weeks* of years, ending with the *seventh Sabbatic* year, and followed by the year of Jubilee (Leviticus 25:8-12).

Even the duration of Israel's great punishments was based upon this law of the *sevens*. Their captivity in Babylon was for *seventy* years (Jeremiah 25:11-12; Daniel 9:2). The great period revealed to Daniel (chapter 9), leading to the coming of the Messiah was divided into *seventy sevens*. The unequaled period of Israel's punishment and dispersion in the lands of their enemies, prophesied by Moses, is, with four-fold emphasis, specified to be for *seven times* (Leviticus 26:18, 21, 24, 28). This sacred *seven* is woven into the laws, life and history of the chosen people, with whom God established His theocracy. And notwithstanding all of Israel's rebellion and sinfulness and consequent chastisement, there still remains for them and the whole world a keeping of the *Sabbath* (Hebrews 4:9, margin). With God a day is as a thousand years (Psalm 90), and a thousand years as one day (2 Peter 3:8).

On this rock of the sacred *sevens* we can consistently, with the Jews, base our conclusion that as we have the scriptural *week, week* of *weeks, week* of months, *week* of years, *week* of *weeks* of years, *week* of *seventy* years, *week* of times, *week* of olams or aiōns (ages; see page 229), so we also have the great *week* of Millenniums. Six thousand-year days of labor and then the Millennium, or blessed *seventh* thousand-year of rest.

This scriptural doctrine of the Millennium can't be shaken. Its root is in the *Sabbath* of Genesis, and its fruit is in the thousand-year kingdom of Revelation. It shines throughout the Word of God as a glorious hope for the nations, whom God has promised to bless (Genesis 12:3). Shine on, O blessed Revelation of God, and the Lord stamp on our hearts the warning that, "if any man shall take away from the words of the book of this prophecy, God shall take away his part from the Tree of Life" (Revelation 22:19).

6

POSTMILLENNIALISM

About the year 1700 a new error called postmillennialism crept into the church. It was instituted by Daniel Whitby, an English divine. He proclaimed a new hypothesis that the church would prosper and extend until the world would be converted, and this triumph of the church would constitute the Millennium; and that Jesus Christ would not come until after the Millennium.

No wonder that he calls it a "new hypothesis," for he himself testifies in his *Treatise on Traditions* that the doctrine of the Millennium, or the reign of saints on earth a thousand years, passed among the best of Christians for 250 years. It was an *apostolic* tradition, and as such was stated by many fathers of the second and third centuries, who speak of it as the tradition of our Lord and His apostles.

For lack of space I would refer you to *The Voice of the Church*, by D. T. Taylor, which shows the long line of eminent witnesses, including Hermas, Justin and the Martyrs, Martin Luther, Philip Melanchton, Joseph Mede, John Milton, Burnett, Isaac Newton, Isaac Watts, Charles Wesley, Augustus Toplady, and a host of others, illustrious in the annals of the church. Through all the past centuries, they have borne overwhelming testimony to the truth of the premillennial coming of Christ.*

---

* See also page 67.

It is strange that the church, in the face of such evidence, would drift away from the simple teaching of the Word and the faith of the fathers. And yet, though of such recent origin, this error of postmillennialism has not only crept into the church, but has been accepted by many Christians, both pastors and people.

This, is the principle point of the question: Will the coming of Christ occur before the Millennium, and can it therefore happen at any moment, as premillennialists believe, or will it occur after the Millennium, and thus be at least a thousand years in the future, as postmillennialists believe?

7

PREMILLENNIAL ARGUMENTS

I now invite your prayerful attention to the following scriptural arguments, which, I believe show that the coming of our Lord will be premillennial.

1. Antichrist

In 2 Thessalonians 2:8,[1] Antichrist, whose existence is on all sides confessed to be premillennial, is to be destroyed with the brightness of Christ's coming, or more literally the epiphany (appearing*) of His own presence. This fixes the coming of Christ as premillennial. Bishop McIlvaine says of this argument that "it is wholly unanswerable."

Even David Brown, the great champion of postmillennialism, admits that this is an apparent evidence for the premillennial advent, and he has been forced to answer it by that process of "spiritualizing" Scripture which has been so condemned by John Pye Smith, Martin Luther, Sir Isaac Newton, Bishop Hooker, Adam Clarke, and others. On this argument alone we could rest, but we have others just as conclusive.

---

* See Greek ἐπιφάνεια, the same word used in 1 Timothy 6:14; 2 Timothy 1:10; 4:1; 4:8; and Titus 2:13; in each place translated "appearing."

---

1. *2 Thessalonians 2:8*. And then shall that Wicked be revealed, whom the Lord shall consume with the spirit of his mouth, and shall destroy with the brightness of his coming.

2. Immediately After the Tribulation

In Matthew 24:29-31,[2] the coming of the Son of Man* is said to be *immediately* after the Tribulation. But this Tribulation is premillennial, or before the reign of peace.[3] See also the diagram on page 73. Therefore the coming is premillennial.

3. A Persecuted Church

The true church is a persecuted, suffering, cross-bearing people.[4] This is its calling,[5] as the Scripture says, "all that will live godly in Christ Jesus shall suffer persecution" (2 Timothy 3:12). And this will continue until Christ comes,[6] which precludes any Millennium until after His coming.

---

* This is His coming at the Revelation; see diagram, page 73.

---

2. *Matthew 24:29-30*. Immediately after the tribulation of those days shall the sun be darkened, and the moon shall not give her light, and the stars shall fall from heaven, and the powers of the heavens shall be shaken: and then shall appear the sign of the Son of man in heaven: and then shall all the tribes of the earth mourn, and they shall see the Son of man coming in the clouds of heaven with power and great glory.

3. *Matthew 24:21*. For then shall be great tribulation, such as was not since the beginning of the world to this time, no, nor ever shall be.

   Isaiah 24:20-23. The earth shall reel to and fro like a drunkard, and shall be removed like a cottage; and the transgression thereof shall be heavy upon it; and it shall fall, and not rise again. And it shall come to pass in that day, that the Lord shall punish the host of the high ones that are on high, and the kings of the earth upon the earth. And they shall be gathered together, as prisoners are gathered in the pit, and shall be shut up in the prison, and after many days shall they be visited. Then the moon shall be confounded, and the sun ashamed, when the Lord of hosts shall reign in mount Zion, and in Jerusalem, and before his ancients gloriously. See also *Luke 21:24*, etc.

4. *John 15:19-21*. If ye were of the world, the world would love his own; but because ye are not of the world, but I have chosen you out of the world, therefore the world hateth you. Remember the word that I said unto you, The servant is not greater than his lord. If they have persecuted me, they will also persecute you; if they have kept my saying, they will keep yours also. But all these things will they do unto you for my name's sake, because they know not him that sent me. See also *John 16:33*.

5. *1 Thessalonians 3:3*. That no man should be moved by these afflictions: for yourselves know that we are appointed thereunto.

6. *2 Thessalonians 1:7-10*. And to you that are afflicted rest with us, at the revelation of the Lord Jesus from heaven with the angels of his power in flaming fire, rendering vengeance to them that know not God, and to them that obey not the gospel of our Lord Jesus: who shall suffer punishment, even eternal destruction from the face of the Lord and from the glory of his might, when he shall come to be glorified in his saints, and to be marvelled at in all them that believed (because our testimony unto you was believed) in that day.

4. Tares and Wheat

We are nowhere in the New Testament directed to look for the Millennium before the coming of Christ. But we are clearly taught that the tares and the wheat will grow together until the end (of this age); that evil men and seducers will grow worse and worse; that as it was in the days of Noah and Lot, so shall it be at the coming of the Son of man.[7] And such is the character and number of the *tares* that their destruction, before the harvest, would endanger the children of the kingdom (Matthew 13:29). This absolutely precludes the idea of a millennial reign of righteousness in this dispensation.

From the time that the first Adam surrendered the kingdom to Satan, the effort to re-establish it with man has been a continual failure, though it was given to Noah,[8] Saul (1 Samuel 9:16; 13:13), Nebuchadnezzar[9] and others.

---

7. *Matthew 13:29-30.* But he said, Nay; lest while ye gather up the tares, ye root up also the wheat with them. Let both grow together until the harvest: and in the time of harvest I will say to the reapers, Gather ye together first the tares, and bind them in bundles to burn them: but gather the wheat into my barn.

2 Peter 3:3-4. Knowing this first, that there shall come in the last days scoffers, walking after their own lusts, and saying, Where is the promise of his coming? for since the fathers fell asleep, all things continue as they were from the beginning of the creation.

1 Timothy 4:1. Now the Spirit speaketh expressly, that in the latter times some shall depart from the faith, giving heed to seducing spirits, and doctrines of devils.

2 Timothy 3:13. But evil men and seducers shall wax worse and worse, deceiving, and being deceived.

Luke 17:26-30. And as it was in the days of Noe, so shall it be also in the days of the Son of man. They did eat, they drank, they married wives, they were given in marriage, until the day that Noe entered into the ark, and the flood came, and destroyed them all. Likewise also as it was in the days of Lot; they did eat, they drank, they bought, they sold, they planted, they builded; but the same day that Lot went out of Sodom it rained fire and brimstone from heaven, and destroyed them all. Even thus shall it be in the day when the Son of man is revealed. See also *2 Timothy 4:3-4; Matthew 24:37-51.*

8. *Genesis 9:1-2.* And God blessed Noah and his sons, and said unto them, Be fruitful, and multiply, and replenish the earth. And the fear of you and the dread of you shall be upon every beast of the earth, and upon every fowl of the air, upon all that moveth upon the earth and upon all the fishes of the sea; into your hand are they delivered.

9. *Daniel 2:37-38.* Thou, O king, art a king of kings: for the God of heaven hath given thee a kingdom, power, and strength, and glory. And wheresoever the children of men dwell, the beasts of the field and the fowls of the heaven hath he given into thine hand, and hath made thee ruler over them all. Thou art this head of gold.

And it will be a failure in this sin-cursed earth until the second Adam, who has overcome Satan, returns to purify the earth and establish the kingdom on resurrection ground. Therefore, there will be no Millennium until Christ comes.

But while we are not told to look for the Millennium, we are repeatedly urged to look faithfully for the return of our Lord. So we again conclude that His return must be premillennial.

5. The Literal Reign of Christ

The millennial kingdom will be a literal reign of Christ on the earth, and not simply a spiritual exaltation of the church.

"A king shall reign in righteousness" (Isaiah 32:1; Jeremiah 23:1-6), "upon the throne of David"[10] "in Jerusalem."[11] The apostles will sit on the 12 thrones (Matthew 19:28), and the saints will reign on the earth (Revelation 5:10).

Speaking of the kingdom, or crown of Israel, the Lord God says: "I will overturn, overturn, overturn it, and it shall be no more, until He come whose right it is; and I will give it Him" (Ezekiel 21:27).

The multitude of passages which support this fact are too many to even refer to. John Pye Smith says that they are far more numerous than those which describe the humiliation and suffering of Christ. And they are so spe-

---

10. *Isaiah 9:7.* Of the increase of his government and peace there shall be no end, upon the throne of David, and upon his kingdom, to order it, and to establish it with judgment and with justice from henceforth even for ever. The zeal of the LORD of hosts will perform this.

Luke 1:32-33. He shall be great, and shall be called the Son of the Highest: and the LORD God shall give unto him the throne of his father David: and he shall reign over the house of Jacob for ever; and of his kingdom there shall be no end.

11. *Jeremiah 3:17.* At that time they shall call Jerusalem the throne of the LORD; and all the nations shall be gathered unto it, to the name of the LORD, to Jerusalem: neither shall they walk any more after the imagination of their evil heart.

Zechariah 14:16. And it shall come to pass, that every one that is left of all the nations which come against Jerusalem shall even go up from year to year to worship the King, the LORD of hosts, and to keep the feast of tabernacles.

cific, so full of detail, so like the prophecies concerning the first coming, in their literalness, that our postmillennial brethren are compelled to do great violence to the laws of interpretation in the "spiritualizing" way they respond to this argument.

I believe we have the *word of prophecy* spoken by "holy men of God . . . as they were moved by the Holy Spirit" (2 Peter 1:21), and that we should direct our first efforts to understanding the literal sense "which alone," as Martin Luther says, "is the substance of faith and of Christian theology."

Jesus is in heaven, at "the right hand of God" (1 Peter 3:22), "upon the throne with the Father" (Psalm 110:1; Revelation 3:21), in the Holy of Holies, or true Holy Place (Hebrews 9:24), making intercession (Romans 8:34), for those that come to God through Him (Hebrews 7:25). But Heaven has only received Him until the time of restitution of all things—which God has spoken by the mouth of all His holy prophets (Acts 3:21)—when He will come again, to sit on the throne of His Father David.[12] This again proves His coming to be premillennial.*

6. Argument From the Order of the Resurrection

I believe there is also a conclusive argument based on the resurrection. All the dead will be raised, but, as Jesus was raised out of the dead and the rest of the dead were left, so the dead in Christ that are His at His coming, will be raised out of the dead, and the rest of the dead will be left until another and final resurrection, and the Millennium will occur between these two resurrections, thus clearly showing Christ's coming to be premillennial.

We believe that any unprejudiced mind will be convinced of this by simply reading the following passages:

---

* For further evidence of the distinction between the Church and the Kingdom, see page 85ff.

12. *Acts 3:20-21.* And he shall send Jesus Christ, which before was preached unto you; whom the heaven must receive until the times of restitution of all things, which God hath spoken by the mouth of all his holy prophets since the world began.

Order of the Resurrection

1 Corinthians 15:22-26. For as in Adam all die, even so in Christ shall all be made alive. But every man in his own order: Christ the firstfruits; afterwards they that are Christ's at His coming. Then [or afterwards] cometh the end* . . . The last enemy that shall be destroyed is death.

Dead in Christ Rise First

1 Thessalonians 4:13-17. But I would not have you to be ignorant, brethren, concerning them which are asleep, that ye sorrow not, even as others which have no hope. For IF WE BELIEVE that Jesus died and rose again, even so them also which sleep in Jesus will God bring with Him . . . For the Lord Himself shall descend from Heaven with a shout, with the voice of the archangel, and with the trump of God, and the dead in Christ shall rise first.

The First Resurrection

Revelation 20:4-14. And I saw thrones, and they sat upon them . . . and I saw the souls of them that were beheaded for the witness of Jesus, and for the Word of God, and which had not worshiped the beast . . . and they lived and reigned with Christ a thousand years. BUT THE REST OF THE DEAD LIVED NOT AGAIN UNTIL THE THOUSAND YEARS WERE FINISHED. THIS IS THE FIRST RESURRECTION. Blessed and holy is he that hath part in the FIRST RESURRECTION, on such the second death hath no power, but they shall be priests of God and of Christ, and shall reign with Him a thousand years. And when the thousand years are expired Satan will be loosed out of his prison, and shall go out to deceive the nations . . . And I saw a GREAT WHITE THRONE, and Him that sat in it, from whose face the earth and the heavens fled away; . . . And I saw the dead, small and great, stand before God; . . . and the sea gave up the dead which were in it, and death and hell [Hades] delivered up the dead which were in them. . . .

---

* The Greek εἶτα (*eita*) here signifies next in order but not necessarily immediate, as will be seen by the use of the same word in Mark 4:17, 28; 1 Timothy 2:13. And in this same chapter (vv. 5-7), it is used interchangeably with ἔπειτα (*epeita*). This fact seems to have been overlooked altogether by postmillennialists who have therefore entirely misconstrued the passage.

When the Holy Spirit means "immediately" He uses ἐξαυτῆς εὐθέω or παραχρῆμα. See *Acts 10:33; Matthew 4:22; Luke 1:64*, etc.

These three passages are so clear that anyone can see this truth in them.

In the first passage we are told the order of the resurrection—each "in his own order" (Greek "band"). The image is that of troops moving by band or regiments. First, Christ ("the first born from the dead," Colossians 1:18): next, the godly, who die in Christ and who are His at His coming; next, the end, when "the rest of the dead" (who are not Christ's) will come forth and death itself be destroyed.

The second passage reiterates the fact that the dead in Christ will rise *first* and at the time when the Lord descends from Heaven with a shout. The resurrection of the ungodly is not mentioned, for they have no part in this blessed *first resurrection.*

In the third passage we have the first resurrection completed by the resurrection of the Tribulation saints (see page 102) and the reign with Christ for a thousand years is stated to occur before the rest of the dead are raised. And after the thousand years the rest of the dead, who lived not again until the thousand years were finished, stand before God, and death and Hades deliver up the dead in them.

This one thousand years is the Millennium (Latin, *mille annum*). What could be plainer than this proof that Christ's coming is to be premillennial? The dead in Christ are raised at His coming and they are raised *before the millennium.* Therefore, His coming must be premillennial.

Objections Considered

The Use of Scripture Passages

It is objected that we have no right to bring together these passages from different parts of the Word. We answer, Why not? Are they not all inspired?[13] Are they

---

13. 2 *Timothy 3:16.* All Scripture is given by inspiration of God, and is profitable for doctrine, for reproof, for correction, for instruction in righteousness. That the man of God may be complete, furnished complete, unto every good work. Or, *every scripture is inspired of God and is profitable.*

not all the product of one mind? See how plainly we are taught that they are all the utterances of the Holy Spirit.[14] And it is clear that they all relate to the same subject— the resurrection.

Paul uses quotations in the same manner in Romans 3 to prove that all have sinned, and again in Romans 10 to prove the righteousness which is of faith, and in Hebrews 11 to show the fruits of faith. We must certainly acknowledge the propriety of following *his* example.

Indeed, the same method of aggregating proof texts is used and relied on to show the divinity of Christ and every evangelical doctrine.

Only Souls Mentioned

It is objected that only the souls are mentioned in Revelation 20 and therefore it cannot be a literal resurrection, but is only the regeneration, or spiritual resurrection and present life of believers in Christ.

The fallacy of this is easily seen, for these holy dead enjoyed the spiritual resurrection before they "were beheaded for the witness of Jesus" (Revelation 20:4). Clearly, it was because of this spiritual life in Christ and their faith in the Word of God, that they became witnesses for Jesus and refused to worship the beast or his image, or receive his mark, and therefore they were beheaded (see 13:11-15). Besides, ψυχὰς (*psuchas*—souls) also means life, person, or individual. The same word is used in Acts 2:41, "there were added unto them about three thousand souls [persons]," and in Acts 7:14; 27:10-37; 1 Corinthians 15:45; 1 Peter 3:20; Revelation 12:11; 16:3, it unmistakably

---

14. *John 14:26*. But the Comforter, which is the Holy Spirit, whom the Father will send in my name, he shall teach you all things, and bring all things to your remembrance, whatsoever I have said unto you.

John 16:13. Howbeit when he, the Spirit of truth, is come, he will guide you into all truth: for he shall not speak of himself; but whatsoever he shall hear, that shall he speak: and he will show you things to come.

1 Corinthians 2:10. But God hath revealed them unto us by his Spirit: for the Spirit searcheth all things, yea, the deep things of God.

2 Peter 1:21. For the prophecy come not in old time by the will of man: but holy men of God spake as they were moved by the Holy Spirit.

means persons.[15] A spirit could not be beheaded. Only a person having body and spirit could be beheaded, and it is evident these were. But they suffered physical death; that is, separation of soul and body, and became part of the great company of *the dead*. The fifth verse emphatically confirms this—these being that portion of the dead ones (νεκρῶν) who *lived,* while "the rest of the dead *lived not again* until the thousand years were finished," and "this is the *first resurrection*" (Revelation 20:5).

In this objection postmillennialists manifest one of their most remarkable inconsistencies. They persistently attempt to disprove the literalness of the first resurrection, described in verses 4-6, where ζάω—*zaō* (to live) and ἀνάστασις—*anastasis* (resurrection) are each twice used, while they hold that verses 12 and 13 do describe a literal resurrection, though neither *zaō* nor *anastasis* are used there. Consistency requires that, if either is spiritual, it should be the latter. How much better to accept both as literal!

Spiritual Life in Paradise

Equally fallacious is the interpretation that claims the first resurrection is the spiritual life of believers with Christ in paradise (the intermediate place of the holy dead). For this spiritual life begins, not at death, but at the resurrection. It beings with the first exercise of faith in Christ. "He that believeth on the Son *hath* everlasting life." John 3:36. He has it *now*; is quickened already (Colossians 2:13), and has been raised (Ephesians 2:6; Colossians 3:1), and lives the life he now lives by faith in the Son of God (Galatians 2:19, 20). This spiritual

---

15. *Acts 7:14*. Then sent Joseph, and called his father Jacob to him, and all his kindred, threescore and fifteen souls.

Acts 27:37. And we were in all in the ship two hundred threescore and sixteen souls.

1 Peter 3:20. Which sometimes were disobedient, when once the longsuffering of God waited in the days of Noah, while the ark was preparing, wherein few, that is, eight souls were saved by water.

Revelation 16:3. And the second angel poured out his vial upon the sea; and it became as the blood of a dead man: and every living soul died in the sea.

resurrection spoken of in Ephesians 2:6; Colossians 2:12, 13; 3:1, is expressed by words entirely different from *anastasis*, which is used in Revelation 20:5-6, and which everywhere in the New Testament expresses a literal resurrection.

Only the Beheaded Mentioned

Again it is objected that only the beheaded are mentioned along with those who have specially to do with the beast and His image.

This is true of the latter part of the verse only. We believe that these are the Tribulation saints who accept Christ and become His martyrs under the reign of Antichrist,[16] after the church has been caught up to meet Christ in the air[17] (see page 102). But notice that the first

---

16. *2 Thessalonians 2:1-9.* Now we beseech you, brethren, by the coming of our Lord Jesus Christ, and by our gathering together unto him. That ye be not soon shaken in mind, or be troubled, neither by spirit, nor by word, nor by letter as from us, as that the day of Christ is at hand. Let no man deceive you by any means: for that day shall not come, except there come a falling away first, and that man of sin be revealed, the son of perdition; who opposeth and exalteth himself above all that is called God, or that is worshiped; so that he as God sitteth in the temple of God, showing himself that he is God. Remember ye not, that, when I was yet with you, I told you these things? And now ye know what withholdeth that he might be revealed in his time. For the mystery of iniquity doth already work: only he who now letteth will let, until he be taken out of the way. And then shall that Wicked be revealed, whom the Lord shall consume with the spirit of his mouth, and shall destroy with the brightness of his coming: even him, whose coming is after the working of Satan with all power and signs and lying wonders.

Revelation 13:11-18. And I beheld another beast coming up out of the earth; and he had two horns like a lamb, and he spake as a dragon. And he exerciseth all the power of the first beast before him, and causeth the earth and them which dwell therein to worship the first beast, whose deadly wound was healed. And he doeth great wonders, so that he maketh fire come down from heaven on the earth in the sight of men, and deceiveth them that dwell on the earth by the means of those miracles which he had power to do in the sight of the beast; saying to them that dwell on the earth, that they should make an image to the beast, which had the wound by a sword, and did live. And he had power to give life unto the image of the beast, that the image of the beast should both speak, and cause that as many as would not worship the image of the beast should be killed. And he causeth all, both small and great, rich and poor, free and bond, to receive a mark in their right hand, or in their foreheads: and that no man might buy or sell, save he that had the mark, or the name of the beast, or the number of his name. Here is wisdom. Let him that hath understanding count the number of the beast: for it is the number of a man; and his number is Six hundred threescore and six.

17. *1 Thessalonians 4:16-18.* For the Lord himself shall descend from heaven with a shout, with the voice of the archangel, and with the trump of God: and

part of verse 4 speaks of some as though they had already been raised. "And I saw thrones, and they sat upon them, and judgment was given unto them." Nothing is said about the resurrection of these because they had already been raised at the Rapture prior to the Tribulation.

They are all ready to occupy the thrones and reign on the earth according to the promises.[18] But John sees the Tribulation saints also raised to take part in this reign with Christ, which is in perfect accord with the order of the first resurrection.

Christ ....*The Firstfruits*

Next,
they who
are
Christ's
at His
Coming

{

The Church and the Old Testament saints who are raised at the Rapture when Christ comes in the air.

_____

The Tribulation saints who are raised at the Revelation when Christ comes to the earth.

The Last Day

Again we hear it objected that Christ said He would raise up those who believe in Him at the last day (John 6:39, 40, 44, 54), and if it is at the last day there can't follow a thousand years before the unbelievers are raised. But Peter says, "one day is with the Lord as a thousand years and a thousand years as one day" (2 Peter 3:8).

---

the dead in Christ shall rise first: then we which are alive and remain shall be caught up together with them in the clouds, to meet the Lord in the air: and so shall we ever by with the Lord. Wherefore comfort one another with these words.

18. *Matthew 19:28.* And Jesus said unto them, Verily I say unto you, That ye which have followed me, in the regeneration when the Son of man shall sit in the throne of his glory, ye also shall sit upon twelve tribes of Israel.

1 Corinthians 6:2-3. Do ye not know that the saints shall judge the world? and if the world shall be judged by you, are ye unworthy to judge the smallest matters? Know ye not that we shall judge angels? How much more things that pertain to this life?

Revelation 3:21. To him that overcometh will I grant to sit with me in my throne, even as I also overcame, and am set down with my Father in his throne.

This is the great Millennial day ushered in and ending with resurrection and judgment, and during which Christ shall rule the nations and judge the world in righteousness.[19]

It is "the day of an age" as the Holy Spirit designates it in 2 Peter 3:18. See the Greek ἡμέραν αἰῶνος (*hēmeran aiōnos*). In harmony with this we find that the same word ἡμέρα (*hēmera*—day) signifies "a long period," in John 8:56; 9:4; Romans 10:21, 2 Corinthians 6:2; and Hebrews 4:7-8.

"That Day"

"That day" is the key to the book of Isaiah and many of the other prophets. Note how frequently it occurs: Isaiah 2:11; 3:7, 18; 4:1, 2; 5:30; 7:18, 20, 21, 23; 10:27, etc.; Jeremiah 25:33; Ezekiel 38:14, 16; 39:11; 48:35; Joel 3:18; Amos 9:11; Micah 4:6; 7:11, 12; Zephaniah 3:11, 16; Haggai 2:23; Zechariah 9:16; 12:3, 4, 6, 8, 9, 11; 13:1, 2, 4; 14:6, 8, 13, 21; Malachi 3:17; Matthew 7:22; 24:36; Mark 13:32; Luke 21:34.

See how clearly it is identified with the Day of the Lord. Compare Isaiah 2:12 with 20. "For the day of the Lord of hosts shall be upon every one that is proud and lofty . . . In that day a man shall cast his idols . . . to the moles and bats." Also Zephaniah 1:14, 15. "The great day of the Lord is near . . . that day is a day of wrath." See the same in Zechariah 14:1-4.

In Hosea 6:2 we read, "After two days will He revive us; in the third day He will raise us up." These are evidently three days of one thousand years each, for "one

---

19. *Acts. 17:31.* Because he hath appointed a day, in the which he will judge the world in righteousness by that man whom he hath ordained; whereof he hath given assurance unto all men, in that he hath raised him from the dead.

Isaiah 11:9-11. They shall not hurt nor destroy in all my holy mountain: for the earth shall be full of the knowledge of the LORD, as the waters cover the sea. And in that day there shall be a root of Jesse, which shall stand for an ensign of the people; to it shall the Gentiles seek: and his rest shall be glorious. And it shall come to pass in that day, that the Lord shall set his hand again the second time to recover the remnant of his people, which shall be left from Assyria, and from Egypt, and from Pathros, and from Cush, and from Elam, and from Shinar, and from Hamath, and from the islands of the sea. See also *Revelation 2:27.*

day is with the Lord as a thousand years." So "that day" is undoubtably the last thousand year day of God's great week of *aiōns* (ages; see page 225).

Mentioned in Same Verse

It is also objected that, while there will be a great difference in the character of the resurrection of the just and of the unjust, yet they must be simultaneous in time, for both are mentioned in conjunction in the same verse.[20]

But Jesus has taught us that this objection has no force, by giving us a remarkable example otherwise. In Luke 4:16-21 we read that He opened the book, found the place and read from Isaiah 61,[21] to the comma (or division of clauses) in verse 2, and closed the book, saying: "This day is this Scripture fulfilled in your ears." Why did He stop there? Because the time had not come to proclaim "the day of vengeance." That comma has lasted many centuries and will continue until Christ (having gathered His saints, 1 Thessalonians 4:16-17) shall appear with them executing vengeance on the ungodly (2 Thessalonians 1:7-10; Jude 14, 15). Therefore, Jesus Himself has taught us that the two events, stated consecutively in Isaiah 61:2, are separated. Surely we should respect God's Word, when it so plainly states that there will be a period of a thousand years between the resurrection of the "blessed and holy,"—and that of "the rest of the dead."

20. *Daniel 12:2*. And many of them that sleep in the dust of the earth shall awake, some to everlasting life, and some to shame and everlasting contempt.

John 5:29. And shall come forth; they that have done good, unto the resurrection of life; and they that have done evil, unto the resurrection of damnation.

Acts 24:15. And have hope toward God, which they themselves also allow, that there shall be a resurrection of the dead, both of the just and unjust.

21. *Isaiah 61:1-3*. The Spirit of the LORD God is upon me; because the LORD hath anointed me to preach good tidings unto the meek; he hath sent me to bind up the broken-hearted, to proclaim liberty to the captives, and the opening of the prison to them that are bound; to proclaim the acceptable year of the LORD, and the day of vengeance of our God; to comfort all that mourn; to appoint unto them that mourn in Zion, to give unto them beauty for ashes, the oil of joy for mourning, the garment of praise for the spirit of heaviness; that they might be called Trees of righteousness, The planting of the LORD, that he might be glorified.

Luke 4:16-21. And he came to Nazareth, where he had been brought up: and, as his custom was, he went into the synagogue on the sabbath day, and

The word ὥρα (*hōra*—hour) which Jesus used in John 5:28 is the same word as that used in verse 25.[22] The latter we all believe has lasted many centuries. Why then can't the former be at least a thousand years long and thus perfectly harmonize with Revelation 20? See also John 4:21, 23 and Romans 13:11 (high time—ὥρα—it is already the hour) in each of which *hour* signifies a long period.

Samuel Tregelles—who is supported by the Jewish commentators—renders Daniel 12:2 as follows: "And many *from among* the sleepers of the dust of the earth shall awake; *these* shall be unto everlasting life; but *those* (the rest of the sleepers who do not awake at this time) shall be unto shame." (See Jamieson, Fausset and Brown on this passage.) This intensely confirms the doctrine of the first resurrection.

Only One Text

Lastly, it is objected that a difference in time for the resurrection of the just from that of the unjust is stated in only one place in the Word: Revelation 20, and that this is a book so symbolical that we must not rely on it for such an important fact.

Only one place indeed! But is that not enough? Why, the existence of all light rests on a single sentence in Genesis 1:3,[23] and it rests safely, because God spoke those words! The most marvelous fact in connection with our

---

stood up for to read. And there was delivered unto him the book of the prophet Esaias. And when he had opened the book, he found the place where it was written, the Spirit of the Lord is upon me, because he hath anointed me to preach the gospel to the poor; he hath sent me to heal the broken-hearted, to preach deliverance to the captives, and recovering of sight to the blind, to set at liberty them that are bruised, to preach the acceptable year of the Lord. And he closed the book, and he gave it again to the minister, and sat down. And the eyes of all them that were in the synagogue were fastened on him. And he began to say unto them, This day is this Scripture fulfilled in your ears.

22. *John 5:25, 28.* Verily, verily, I say unto you, The hour is coming and now is, when the dead shall hear the voice of the Son of God: and they that hear shall live. Marvel not at this: for the hour is coming, in the which all that are in the graves shall hear his voice.

Lord's first appearing, was the immaculate conception. It has caused suspicion of Mary's character, and it calls for the greatest exercise of faith to believe in the Holy Spirit Fatherhood of her Son. It professes the holiest purity where the world can see only fornication and shame. And yet this astonishing event rested for centuries upon a single passage of prophecy, "Behold a virgin shall conceive and bear a son" (Isaiah 7:14). And although it was given by the Lord to the Jews as a special and important sign they don't rely on it, because it occurs in a poetical book, and so they reject the Babe of Bethlehem.

But will we—who believe that Isaiah 7:14 has been literally fulfilled—condemn the Jews for not accepting it, and yet justify ourselves in rejecting the literal fulfillment of this plain statement in Revelation 20? God forbid! Remember that He says, "Behold I come quickly; blessed is he that keepeth the saying of the prophecy of this book" (Revelation 22:7; 1:3). Then let me earnestly urge you to comprehend this *one passage* even though it may pierce through your established opinions.[24] Don't reject it. Don't pervert its simple teaching, for it is God's holy Word of prophecy and is as immovable as the rocky security of the mountains—even more—for these will pass away "but the Word of the Lord endureth forever."

Dean Alford's Comments

Let me invite your careful attention to Dean Alford's comment upon this passage, "this is the first resurrection." He says:

> It will have been long ago anticipated by the readers of this commentary, that I cannot consent to distort its words from their plain sense and chronological place in the prophecy, on account of any consideration of difficulty, or any risk of abuses which the doctrine of the Millennium may bring with it. Those who lived next

---

23. *Genesis 1:3.* And God said, Let there be light: and there was light.

24. *Hebrews 4:12.* For the word of God is quick, and powerful, and sharper than any twoedged sword, piercing even to the dividing asunder of soul and spirit, and of the joints and marrow, and is a discerner of the thoughts and intents of the heart.

to the apostles, and the whole church for three hundred years, understood them in the plain literal sense; and it is a strange sight in these day to see expositors who are among the first in reverence of antiquity, complacently casting aside the most cogent instance of unanimity which primitive antiquity presents. As regards the text itself, no legitimate treatment of it will extort what is known as the spiritual interpretation now in fashion. If, in a passage where *two resurrections* are mentioned, where certain *souls lived* at the first, and the rest of the *dead lived* only at the end of a specified period after that first, if in such a passage, the first resurrection may be understood to mean *spiritual* rising with Christ, while the second means literal rising from the grave; then there is an end of all significance in language, and Scripture is wiped out as a definite testimony to anything. If the first resurrection is spiritual, then so is the second, which I suppose no one will be hardy enough to maintain. But if the second is literal, then so is the first, which in common with the whole primitive church and many of the best modern expositors, I do maintain and receive as an article of faith and hope.*

Resurrection From the Dead

Now if Christ is coming to raise the righteous a thousand years before the ungodly, it would be natural and imperative that the former should be called a resurrection *from,* or *out of the dead,* the rest of the dead being left until after the thousand years. I rejoice that this is just what is carefully done in the Word, and in this I believe we have another comprehensive and definite proof of the premillennial coming of Christ. It consists in the use made, *in the Greek text* in the use of the words ἐκ νεκρῶν (*ek nekron*). These words signify "from the dead" or, "out of the dead," implying that the other dead are left. The resurrection νεκρῶν or τῶν νεκρῶν (*nekron,* or *tōn nekron*—of the dead) is applied to both classes because all will be raised. But the resurrection ἐκ νεκρῶν (*ek nekron*—out of the dead) is not once applied to the ungodly.**

* See also the quotations from distinguished authorities, both English and German given as critical testimonies in the appendix to *Premillennial Essays.*
** Matthew 22:31; Acts 17:32; 23:6; 24:15, 21; 1 Corinthians 15:12, 13, 21, 42 and especially John 5:28-29 (R.V.): Marvel not at this: for the hour cometh, in

The latter phrase is used altogether 49 times: 34 times, to express Christ's resurrection, whom we know was thus raised *out of the dead;*[*] 3 times, to express John's supposed resurrection, who, as Herod thought, had been thus raised *out of the dead;*[**] 3 times, to express the resurrection of Lazarus, who was also raised *out of the dead;*[***] 3 times it is used figuratively, to express spiritual life *out of the* deadness of sin: Romans 6:13, "As those that are alive from the dead;" 11:15: "Life from the dead." Ephesians 5:14: "Arise from the dead." It is used in Luke 16:31; in the parable of the rich man: "Though one rose *from the dead;*" and in Hebrews 11:19: Abraham's faith that God could raise Isaac *from the dead.*

And the remaining four times it is used to express a future resurrection *out of the dead,* namely, in Mark 12:25, where Jesus says: "When they shall *rise from the dead* [ἐκ νεκρῶν] they neither marry, nor are given in marriage; but are as the angels which are in heaven," and in Luke 20:35-36: "But they which shall be accounted worthy to obtain that world, and the *resurrection which is from among (the) dead* [τῆς ἀναστάσεως τῆς ἐκ νεκρῶν], neither marry, nor are given in marriage; neither can they die any more; for they are equal unto the angels; and are the children of God, being the children *of the resurrection.*"

Acts 4:1-2 says that the Sadducees were grieved because Peter and John "preached, through Jesus, *the resurrection which is from among (the) dead*" [τὴν ἀνάστασιν τὴν ἐκ νεκρῶν]. And in Philippians 3:11 it is used in a remarkably significant manner. My version renders it, "resurrection of the dead," which is especially wrong, for the Greek preposition ἐκ occurs here in a duplicate form in all the

---

which all that are in the tombs shall hear his voice, and shall come forth; they that have done good, unto the resurrection of life; and they that have done evil, unto the resurrection of judgment.

[*] Matthew 17:9; Mark 9:9-10; Luke 24:46; John 2:22; 20:9; 21:14; Acts 3:15; 4:10; 10:41; 13:30; 13:34; 17:3; 17:31; 26:23; Romans 1:4; 4:24; 6:4-9; 7:4; 8:11; 10:7, 9; 1 Corinthians 15:12, 20; Galatians 1:1; Ephesians 1:20; Colossians 1:18; 2:12; 1 Thessalonians 1:10; 2 Timothy 2:8; Hebrews 13:20; 1 Peter 1:3, 21.

[**] Mark 6:14, 16; Luke 9:7.

[***] John 12:1, 9, 17.

oldest manuscripts.* The phrase is τὴν ἐξανάστασιν τὴν ἐκ νεκρῶν** (*tēn exanastasin tēn ek nekrōn*), and the literal translation is *the out resurrection from among the dead,* which peculiar construction of language gives a special emphasis to the idea that this is a resurrection *out from among the dead.*

These passages clearly show that there is yet to be a resurrection out of the dead; that is, that part of the dead will be raised, before all are raised. Olshausen declares that the "phrase would be inexplicable if it were not derived from the idea that out of the mass of the dead some would rise first."***

That no unrighteous have part in this "first resurrection" is evident from Luke 20:36: they "are the children of God" and are "equal unto the angels."

It is the resurrection of a select class only: the righteous, and therefore Jesus calls it the resurrection *of the just.* Luke 14:14 says, "And thou shalt be blessed; for they cannot recompense thee: for thou shalt be recompensed at the *resurrection of the just.*"

Paul calls it the *better resurrection.*[25] It is the resurrection of those that are Christ's at His coming,[26] "the dead in Christ," who will "rise first."[27]

The First Resurrection

"Blessed and holy is he that hath part in the first resurrection" (Revelation 20:6).

---

* See the discussion in Jamieson, Fausset and Brown, Alford, and Adam Clarke.

** Greek text, Tischendorf and Alford.

*** Vol. 2, p. 183, American edition.

25. *Hebrews 11:35.* Women received their dead raised to life again; and others were tortured, not accepting deliverance; that they might obtain a better resurrection.

26. *1 Corinthians 15:23.* But every man in his own order: Christ the firstfruits; afterward they that are Christ's at his coming.

27. *1 Thessalonians 4:16.* For the Lord himself shall descend from heaven with a shout, with the voice of the archangel, and with the trump of God: and the dead in Christ shall rise first.

Paul, as a Pharisee, believed in the general fact of the resurrection.[28] But we see from the above references why he counted all things but loss that he might win Christ ". . . and know Him, and the power of His resurrection, and the fellowship of His sufferings, . . ." if by any means he might attain unto the *out* resurrection *from among the dead* (Philippians 3:8-11).

And we also see why the three favored disciples were "questioning one with another what the rising *from* the dead should mean."[29] They understood perfectly what the resurrection *of* the dead meant, for this was a commonly accepted Jewish doctrine.[30] But the resurrection *from* the dead was a new revelation to them. And it is an important revelation to us, for it is "the resurrection of *life*."[31]

But there is also to be a resurrection of *judgment* (so the Greek; John 5:29). It is the resurrection of the unjust,[32] and completes the resurrection (νεκρῶν or τῶν νεκρῶν) of the dead. Therefore we see a difference in time as well as in character in the order of the resurrection; the first being that of the just, and the second that of the unjust. This difference in time is in perfect accordance with the

---

28. *Acts 23:6-8*. But when Paul perceived that the one part were Sadducees, and the other Pharisees, he cried out in the council, Men and brethren, I am a Pharisee, the son of a Pharisee: of the hope and resurrection of the dead I am called in question. And when he had so said, there arose a dissension between the Pharisees and the Sadducees; and the multitude was divided. For the Sadducees say that there is no resurrection, neither angel, nor spirit: but the Pharisees confess both.

29. *Mark 9:10*. And they kept that saying with themselves, questioning one with another what the rising from the dead should mean.

30. *Hebrews 6:2*. Of the doctrine of baptisms, and of laying on of hands, and of resurrection of the dead, and of eternal judgment.

31. *John 5:29*. And shall come forth, they that have done good, unto the resurrection of life; and they that have done evil, unto the resurrection of damnation [judgment].

Daniel 12:2. And many of them that sleep in the dust of the earth shall awake, some to everlasting life, and some to shame and everlasting contempt.

32. *Acts 24:15*. And have hope toward God, which they themselves also allow, that there shall be a resurrection of the dead, both of the just and unjust.

Revelation 20:12-13. And I saw the dead, small and great, stand before God; and the books were opened; and another book was opened, which is the book of life: and the dead were judged out of those things which were written in the books, according to their works. And the sea gave up the dead which were in it; and death and hell delivered up the dead which were in them: and they were judged every man according to their works.

account in Revelation 20, where the interval is stated to be the 1000 years of the Millennial kingdom. And as Christ comes at the resurrection of the just, or those who sleep in Him (1 Thessalonians 4:13-16), His coming must be premillennial.*

7. Watching

We are commanded to *watch* for Christ's coming. Again and again Jesus told His disciples to *watch!* He said: "Watch therefore, for ye know not what hour your Lord doth come" (Matthew 24:42). "Watch therefore, for ye know neither the day nor the hour" (Matthew 25:13). Adding, "And, what I say unto you, I say unto all, Watch" (Mark 13:35-37). He places special emphasis on the word *Watch*, particularly in Revelation 16:15, "Blessed is he that watcheth." (See the Greek text.)

Now it is absolutely inconsistent with the make up of the human mind, that we are to watch for an event we believe to be one thousand years or more in the future. And yet this is just the position which postmillennialists are forced to take.

Matthew Henry, commenting on Luke 12:45, says: "Our looking at Christ's second coming as a thing at a distance is the cause of all those irregularities which render the thought of it terrible to us." And on watching, he says: "To watch implies not only to believe that our Lord will come, but to desire that He would come, to be often thinking of His coming, and always looking for it as sure and near, and the time of it uncertain."

As followers of Christ we are compared to soldiers, fighting the fight of faith (1 Timothy 1:18; 6:12; 2 Timothy 2:3; 4:7), and perhaps no better illustration of watching could be given than that of picket duty in the army.

---

* I humbly invite a candid and prayerful consideration of the above argument by Greek students. Dr. David Brown quite superficially disposes of it by the erroneous presumption that premillenarians apply the resurrection (νεκρῶν or τῶν νεκρῶν) *of the dead*, only to the ungodly. Whereas, we hold that it embraces all, even Christ Himself, but the (ἐκ νεκρῶν) *from the dead*, applies only to the select class who have part in the first resurrection. Again he is wrong in his citation of the texts Mark 9:9-10; Acts 10:41; 13:34; 26:23, and Romans 1:4, each of which, according to Griesbach, have ἐκ νεκρῶν or ἐξ ανα-στάσεως νεκρὼν. *Second Advent,* p. 198.

Old soldiers know that out on the skirmish line it is full of life and excitement, because they are watching for something immediately possible. But in camp it is a dull, lifeless drudgery, because they are expecting nothing until the outer pickets, perhaps five or six miles away, are driven in. How intensely do we increase this difference in watching, if we separate the pickets by a thousand years. And this is what postmillennialism does.

I believe this argument appeals to the common sense of every person, and I pray to God that these seven arguments may be blessed to the perfecting of that which is lacking in your faith.[33]

> He is faithfu' that hath promised, an' He'll surely come again,
> He'll keep his tryst wi' me, at what hour I dinna ken;
> But he bids me still to wait, an' ready aye to be,
> To gang at ony moment to my ain countrie.
>
> So I'm WATCHING aye, and singing o' my hame as I wait,
> For the soun'ing o' His footfa' this side the gowden gate,
> For His bluid hath made me white, and His hand shall dry my e'e
> When He brings me hame at last to my ain countrie.

True watching is an attitude of mind and heart which would joyfully and quickly turn from any occupation to meet our Beloved, rapturously exclaiming "this is the Lord; we have waited for Him (Isaiah 25:9).

Continue to Watch

But perhaps you say: "The church has been watching for many centuries and He has not come, and He may not come for many centuries more." Well, possibly He may not; but do we know He will not? And will we set a date for His coming and cease to watch?

Postmillennialists say that He will not come for a thousand years or more, which is equivalent to setting a date, as it places His coming out of all possibility in our

---

33. *1 Thessalonians 3:9-10*. For what thanks can we render to God again for you, for all the joy wherewith we joy for your sakes before our God; night and day praying exceedingly that we might see your face, and might perfect that which is lacking in your faith?

life-time. Notice how quickly we give up our watching
with this faulty understanding.

The principle condemnation pronounced in the
Scripture, in regard to the Lord's return, is to those who
say, "My Lord delayeth His coming."[34] It is immeasurably
better to be *ready* than to be *late*.[35] Premillennialists
believe that He may come any moment, and that we
should always be found watching and waiting, dressed
and ready for service, our lights burning, and like men
that wait for their Lord (Luke 12:35). The many centuries
that have passed only make "our salvation" much "nearer
than when we believed," and it is "high time to awake
out of sleep" (Romans 13:11).

A Little While

There is no prophesied event which has to be fulfilled
before His coming in the air to receive the church.
Therefore, we have need of patience that we might receive
the promise: "For yet a little while" (Greek—*very, very
little while*) "and He that shall come will come, and will
not tarry" (Hebrews 10:37).

"But," you say, "it is not a little while." My friends,
does it seem long to you from creation to the flood, or
from the flood to Christ? The "little while" of Haggai 2:6-
7,[36] I believe, has not ended yet,[37] and it certainly covered
the 500 years up to Christ's first coming. Remember that
God addresses you as an immortal soul.

---

34. *Matthew 24:48-51*. But and if that evil servant shall say in his heart, My
lord delayeth his coming; and shall begin to smite his fellow servants, and to
eat and drink with the drunken; the lord of that servant shall come in a day
when he looketh not for him, and in an hour he is not aware of, and shall cut
him asunder, and appoint him his portion with the hypocrites: there shall be
weeping and gnashing of teeth. See also *Luke 12:45*.

35. *Matthew 25:10*. And while they went to buy, the bridegroom came; and
they that were ready went in with him to the marriage: and the door was
shut.

36. *Haggai 2:6-7*. For thus saith the LORD of hosts; Yet once, it is a little
while, and I will shake the heavens, and the earth, and the sea, and the dry
land; and I will shake all nations, and the Desire of all nations shall come:
and I will fill this house with glory, saith the LORD of hosts.

37. *Joel 3:16-17*. The LORD also shall roar out of Zion, and utter his voice
from Jerusalem; and the heavens and the earth shall shake: but the LORD will

Wait until you have realized a few of the mighty cycles of eternity, and then these centuries will indeed appear to be "a very, very little while."

Oh! Let us focus our eyes on Jesus. Let us watch and wait for the Eternal King.[38]

The Faith of the Early Church

It is admitted on all sides that the postmillennial coming of Christ, and His reign with His saints on the earth a thousand years, was the faith of the early church. Indeed, this is substantiated by such an abundance of evidence, that it cannot be denied.

I wish there was space to quote at length from the many authorities on this point, but I must be content to select a few:

Johann Mosheim says: "The prevailing opinion that Christ was to come and reign a thousand years among men before the final dissolution of the world had met with *no opposition previous to the time of Origen.*"[*]

Geisler says: "In all the works of this period [the first two centuries] millenarianism is so prominent that *we cannot hesitate to consider it as universal.*"[**]

Chillingworth, with his characteristic invulnerable logic, argues: "Whatever doctrine is believed and taught by the most eminent Fathers of any age of the church and by none of their contemporaries opposed or condemned, *that* is to be esteemed the Catholic doctrine of the church of those times. But the doctrine of the millenaries was believed and taught by the most eminent Fathers of the

---

[*] Vol. 1, p. 89.
[**] Geisler, *Church History.* Vol. 1, p. 215.

---

be the hope of his people, and the strength of the children of Israel. So shall ye know that I am the LORD your God dwelling in Zion, my holy mountain: then shall Jerusalem be holy, and there shall no strangers pass through her any more.

Hebrews 12:26-27. Whose voice then shook the earth; but now he hath promised, saying, Yet once more I shake not the earth only, but also heaven. And this word, Yet once more, signifieth the removing of those things that are shaken, as of things that are made, that those things which cannot be shaken may remain.

38. *1 Timothy 1:17.* Now unto the King eternal, immortal, invisible, the only wise God, be honor and glory for every and ever. Amen.

age next after the apostles, and by none of that age opposed or condemned; therefore, *it was the Catholic doctrine of those times."* *

Stackhouse, in his *Complete Body of Divinity* (Vol. 1, p. 597), says: "It cannot be denied but that this doctrine [Millenarianism] has its antiquity, and *was once the general opinion of all orthodox Christians."*

Bishop Newton says: "The doctrine of the Millennium [as held by Millenarians] *was generally believed in the first three and purest ages."* **

Bishop Russell, though an anti-millenarian, says: "Down to the beginning of the fourth century, *the belief was universal and undisputed."* ***

Edward Gibbon, who is at least an unprejudiced witness, says: "The ancient and popular doctrine of the Millennium was carefully inculcated by a succession of Fathers from Justin Martyr and Irenæus, who conversed with the immediate disciples of the apostles, down to Lactantius, who was the preceptor of the son of Constantine. It appears to have been *the reigning sentiment of orthodox believers."* He also says: "As long as this error [as he calls it] was permitted to subsist in the church, it was productive of the *most salutary effects* on the faith and practice of Christians." ****

Dr. Daniel Whitby, the father of the modern postmillennial theory, in his *Treaties on Traditions*, candidly acknowledges that "the doctrine of the Millennium passed among the best of Christians, for two hundred and fifty years, for a tradition apostolical, and as such is delivered by many Fathers of the second and third centuries, who speak of its as *a tradition of our Lord and His apostles, and of all the ancients who lived before them,* who tell us the very words in which it was delivered, the Scriptures which were so interpreted, and say that *it was held by all Christians that were exactly orthodox."*

---

* Chillingworth's *Works*, 1844, p. 730.
** *Dissertations on the Prophecies*, p. 527.
*** *Discourse on the Millennium*, p. 236.
**** Henry Hart Milman Gibbon's *Rome*, Vol. 1, p. 262.

Lest anyone should lose the full force of these quotations, it may be proper to state that this *"ancient and popular doctrine of the Millennium,"* as Gibbon styles it, was the belief in the premillennial coming of Christ and His reign on the earth for a thousand years. It was commonly called chiliasm as in Webster's *Dictionary*.

Such, in brief, is the testimony of historians, both ecclesiastical and secular, concerning this subject. And some of the early Fathers of whom they speak were very nearly, contemporaries with the apostles.

Papias, Bishop of Hierapolis in Phrygia, who was a disciple of John, or who at least received his doctrines from the immediate followers of the Apostle, was an extreme Millennialist, and has been called the father of millenarianism. (See McClintock and Strong's *Cyclopedia of Biblical, Theological & Ecclesiastical Literature*) Irenaeus, as a disciple of Polycarp, Bishop of Smyrna, was directly connected with John. And Justin Martyr was also one of the earliest of the Fathers.

Is it not solemnly incumbent upon us to respect and heed this doctrine, which these eminent Christian Fathers so undisputedly taught as being the "tradition of our Lord and His apostles"? Why is it that on every other subject connected with our holy religion, such as baptism, church government, forms of worship, articles of faith, etc., we go back and search diligently to ascertain the doctrine of the Fathers, placing so much stress upon what we *think* they believed and taught, and yet upon this most important theme, we cast aside what we *know* was their faith and testimony? Is it consistent?

We must here emphasize Paul's exhortation to the Thessalonians: "Brethren, stand fast and hold the traditions [teachings] which ye have been taught whether by word or by our epistle."[39] That is, whether taught in writing or orally (see also verse 5). Now, what were these traditions (teachings) if not the coming of Christ and the reign of the saints, of which Paul and the other apostles wrote so freely? Being thus exhorted, it is reasonable to believe that they did hold them, and that they are the very traditions which Whitby and the other authorities clearly prove were held by the early church. Then let us also hold not the comparatively modern postmillennial theory of Whitby, but the aged faith of the Fathers.

The Apostles Were Not Mistaken

We cannot believe (as some assert) that the apostles were mistaken, and consequently not inspired on this theme, nor that they and all the early Christians mocked themselves with false hopes in regard to the premillennial coming of Christ. They watched and waited for the return of our Lord as a sure event, the time of which none but the Father knew, but which had been enjoined on them as uncertain[40] and imminent.[41] And as they passed away to the unseen domain of paradise, they left us the written Word, their reiterated traditions (teachings handed down), and their great hope. So we take up their vigil, hopefully watching, not daring to say that He will come tomorrow, nor a thousand years from now, but only this are we sure of—He may come *now*.

Expectancy

God has held this glorious hope constantly before the church to keep her in her proper attitude of expectancy and longing until the Bridegroom comes. Like Israel in the wilderness, we should realize that we are pilgrims

---

39. *2 Thessalonians 2:5, 15.* Remember ye not, that, when I was yet with you, I told you these things? So then, brethren, stand fast and hold the traditions which ye were taught whether by word, or by epistle as of ours.

40. *Matthew 24:42-44.* Watch therefore; for ye know not what hour your Lord doth come. But know this, that if the goodman of the house had known in what watch the thief would come, he would have watched, and would not have suffered his house to be broken up. Therefore be ye also ready: for in such an hour as ye think not the Son of man cometh.

41. *Luke 12:35-40.* Let your loins be girded about, and your lights burning; and ye yourselves like unto men that wait for their lord, when he will return from the wedding; that, when he cometh and knocketh, they may open unto him immediately. Blessed are those servants, whom the lord when he cometh shall find watching: verily I say unto you, that he shall gird himself, and make them to sit down to meat, and will come forth and serve them. And if he shall come in the second watch, or come in the third watch, and find them so, blessed are those servants. And this know, that if the goodman of the house had known what hour the thief would come, he would have watched, and not have suffered his house to be broken through. Be ye therefore ready also: for the Son of man cometh at an hour when ye think not.

and strangers, seeking a *Land,* a *City,* and a *King,* which are beyond our Jordan of death and resurrection.

Death and resurrection is the common lot of the great mass of the church. But, of course, there will be some living when Christ comes,[42] who will not die but be changed in a moment,[43] and be caught up, like Elijah, with the raised saints to meet the Lord in the air (1 Thessalonians 4:16-17).

It may be at morn, when the day is awakening,
When sunlight thro' darkness and shadow is breaking,
That Jesus will come in the fullness of glory,
    To receive from the world "His own."

It may be at midday, it may be at twilight,
It may be perchance, that the blackness of midnight,
Will burst into light in the blaze of His glory,
    When Jesus receives "His own."

While its hosts cry Hosanna, from heaven descending,
With glorified saints and the angels attending,
With grace on His brow, like a halo of glory,
    Will Jesus receive "His own."

Oh, joy! Oh delight! should we go without dying;
No sickness, no sadness, no dread, and no crying;
Caught up thro' the clouds, with our Lord, into glory,
    When Jesus receives "His own."

Hebrews 10:37. For yet a little while, and he that shall come will come, and will not tarry.

42. *1 Thessalonians 4:15-18.* For this we say unto you by the word of the Lord, that we which are alive and remain unto the coming of the Lord shall not prevent them which are asleep. For the Lord himself shall descend from heaven with the voice of the archangel, and with the trump of God: and the dead in Christ shall rise first: then we which are alive and remain shall be caught up together with them in the clouds, to meet the Lord in the air: and so shall we ever be with the Lord. Wherefore comfort one another with these words.

43. *1 Corinthians 15:51-52.* Behold, I show you a mystery; We shall not all sleep, but we shall all be changed, in a moment, in the twinkling of an eye, at the last trump: for the trumpet shall sound, and the dead shall be raised incorruptible, and we shall be changed.

Matthew 23:37-39. O Jerusalem, Jerusalem, thou that killest the prophets, and stonest them which are sent unto thee, how often would I have gathered thy children together, even as a hen gathereth her chickens under her wings, and ye would not! Behold, your house is left unto you desolate. For I say unto you, Ye shall not see me henceforth, till ye shall say, Blessed is he that cometh in the name of the Lord.

8

DIAGRAM

The following diagram, is presented merely as an outline of the order of events in connection with our Lord's return. I exhort (1 Thessalonians 4:18, Greek) a faithful study of it, together with the references and explanations appended, believing that it will be a great help as an object lesson in understanding these mighty questions.

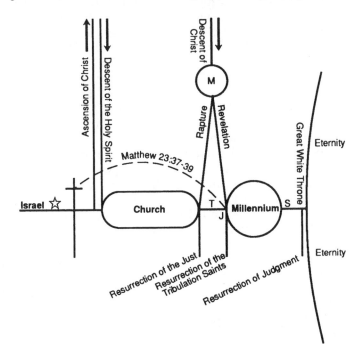

Diagram Key

☆ —The birth of Christ, the King of the Jews (Matthew 2:2).

✝ —The death and resurrection of Christ.

Ascension of Christ—(Acts 1:9).

Descent of the Holy Spirit—(Acts 2).

Church—Mystical body of Christ (Ephesians 1:22-23; 3:3-6; Romans 12:4-5; Colossians 1:24-27; 1 Corinthians 12:12-27; and the Bride of Christ, Ephesians 5:21-23).

Descent of Christ—(1 Thessalonians 4:16) to receive His Bride (John 14:3).

Resurrection of the Just—(Luke 14:14; Acts 24:15; 1 Thessalonians 4:15-16; and change of living believers. 1 Corinthians 15:23, 51, 52).

Rapture—Translation of the saints who (like Enoch) are caught up to meet Christ in the air (1 Thessalonians 4:17).

M—The meeting of Christ and His Bride (1 Thessalonians 4:17; Ephesians 5:21-32; 2 Corinthians 11:2).

This is our gathering together unto Him (2 Thessalonians 2:1) and the marriage of the Lamb (Matthew 22:2-10; 25:10; Luke 14:15-24; Revelation19:7-8). So shall we ever be with the Lord (John 12:26; 14:3; 17:24; 1 Thessalonians 4:17). It is the Hope of the Church (Philippians 3:20-21; Titus 2:13; 1 John 3:2-3). And the redemption mentioned in Luke 21:28; Romans 8:23; Ephesians 4:30. Wherefore, comfort one another with these words (1 Thessalonians 4:18). Thus the Church escapes the tribulation (Luke 21:36; 2 Peter 2:9; Revelation 3:10).

T—Period of unequaled tribulation to the world (Daniel 12:1; Matthew 24:21; Luke 21:25-26) during which—the Church having been taken out—God begins to deal with Israel again (Acts 15:13-17; Psalm 51:18; 102:16), and will restore them to their own land (Isaiah 11:11; 60; Jeremiah 30:3; 31; 32:36-44; Amos 9:15; Zechariah 8:10; Romans 11). Antichrist will be revealed (2 Thessalonians 2:8). The vials of God's wrath are poured out (Psalm 2:1-5; Revelation 6:16-17; 14:10; 16). But men only blaspheme God (Revelation 16:11-21). Israel accepts Christ (Zechariah 12:10-14; 13:6), and are brought through the fire (Zechariah 13:9). They do not pass away (Mattthew 24:34; Psalm 22:30).

Revelation—The revelation of Christ and His saints (Colossians 3:4; 1 Thessalonians 3:13), in flaming fire (2 Thessalonians 1:7-10) to execute judgment on the earth (Jude 14-15). This is Christ's second coming to the earth (Acts 1:11; Deuteronomy 33:2; Zechariah 14:4-5; Matthew 16:27; 24:29–30).

J—Judgment of the nations, or the living (Matthew 25:31-46; 19:28; Acts 10:42; 1 Peter 4:5). Antichrist is destroyed (2 Thessalonians 2:8). The Beast and the False Prophet are taken (Revelation 19:20). Gog and his allies are smitten (Ezekiel 38 and 39). Satan is bound (Revelation 20:1-3; Romans 16:20).

Resurrection of the Tribulation Saints—Completes the First Resurrection (Revelation 20:4-6).

Millennium—Christ's glorious reign on the earth for 1,000 years (Revelation 20:4) with His Bride (2 Timothy 2:12; Revelation 5:10; Isaiah 2:2-5; 4; 11:1-12; 25:6-9; Isaiah 65:18-25; Micah 4:1-4; Zephaniah 3:14-20; Zechariah 8:3-8; 8:20-23; 14:16-21).

S—Satan loosed for a little season, and destroyed with Gog and Magog (Revelation 20:7-10; Hebrews 2:14).

Resurrection of Judgment—(Revelation 20:12-15; John 5:29; Daniel 12:2).

Great White Throne—Judgment at the Great White Throne of all the remaining dead (Revelation 20:11-15). Death and Hell destroyed (Revelation 20:14; 1 Corinthians 15:26).

Eternity—or rather, The *aions* to come (Ephesians 2:7).*

---

* These events, we believe, are plainly foretold in the Word, though we would not be dogmatic as to the precise order in which they are given above (see preface). But we trust it will enable the reader to apprehend, in some degree, the extent to which the future has been revealed to us by the Spirit (2 Peter 1:21; John 16:13; 1 Corinthians 2:10) and to realize that ETERNITY ITSELF will not be a blank, or statue-like condition, but a continually unfolding manifestation of God to us throughout the "ages to come" (Ephesians 2:7), even the "AGES OF AGES." See Greek text of Galatians 1:5; Ephesians 3:21; Philippians 4:21; 1 Timothy 1:17; 2 Timothy 4:18; Hebrews 13:21; 1 Peter 4:11; Revelation 1:6, 18; 4:9, 10; 5:13; 7:12; 10:6; 11:15; 14:11; 15:7; 19:3; 20:10; 22:5. See also page 221.

9

RAPTURE AND REVELATION

Two things are of vital importance for the right understanding of this subject. First is the distinction between the Rapture and the Revelation. The second is the distinction between the church and the Millennial Kingdom (see chapter 10). *Rapture* means to be caught up, or away. *Revelation* (ἀποκάλυψις—*apokalupsis*) means appearing or shining forth or manifestation.[1] The *Rapture* occurs when the church is caught up to meet Christ in the air[2] before the Tribulation; and the *Revelation* occurs when Christ comes, with His saints, to end the Tribulation, by the execution of righteous judgment upon the earth.[3]

At the Rapture, Christ comes in the air *for* his saints.[4]

---

1. *Romans 8:19*. For the earnest expectation of the creature waiteth for the manifestation of the sons of God.

2. *1 Thessalonians 4:14, 17*. For if we believe that Jesus died and rose again, even so them also which sleep in Jesus will God bring with him. Then we which are alive and remain shall be caught up together with them in the clouds, to meet the Lord in the air, so shall we ever be with the Lord.

3. *2 Thessalonians 1:7-10*. And to you who are troubled rest with us, when the Lord Jesus shall be revealed from heaven with his mighty angels, in flaming fire taking vengeance on them that know not God, and that obey not the gospel of our Lord Jesus Christ: who shall be punished with everlasting destruction from the presence of the Lord, and from the glory of his power; when he shall come to be glorified in his saints, and to be admired in all them that believe.

Jude 14-15. And Enoch also, the seventh from Adam, prophesied of these, saying, Behold, the Lord cometh with ten thousand of his saints, to execute judgment upon all, and to convince all that are ungodly among them of all their ungodly deeds which they have ungodly committed, and of all their hard speeches which ungodly sinners have spoken against him.

4. *John 14:3*. And if I go and prepare a place for you, I will come again, and receive you unto myself; that where I am, there ye may be also.

At the Revelation, He comes to the earth *with* them.[5] He certainly must come for them before He can come with them. The assurance that God will bring them (Greek— *lead them forth*) with Jesus (1 Thessalonians 4:14) is evidence that He will first come for them, they being caught up to meet him in the air (v. 17). The Greek word here rendered "to meet" signifies *a going forth, in order to return with*. The same word is used in Acts 28:15,[6] where the brethren came out to meet Paul and had a time of thanksgiving with him at Appii Forum and the Three Taverns, when he was on his way to Rome. This accords exactly with our being caught up to meet Christ and afterward returning to the earth with Him.

Again, at the Rapture Christ comes as the Bridegroom[7] to take unto Himself His bride, the church.[8] At the Revelation, He comes with His bride to rule the nations.[9]

At the Rapture He comes only to meet the saints in the *air* (1 Thessalonians 4:17). At the Revelation, He comes

---

5. *1 Thessalonians 3:13*. To the end he may stablish your hearts unblamable in holiness before God, even our Father, at the coming of our Lord Jesus Christ with all his saints.

Zechariah 14:15. And ye shall flee to the valley of the mountains; for the valley of the mountains shall reach unto Azal: yea, ye shall flee, like as ye fled from before the earthquakes in the days of Uzziah king of Judah: and the LORD my God shall come, and all the saints with thee.

6. *Acts 28:15*. And from thence, when the brethren heard of us, they came to meet us as far as Appii Forum, and the Three Taverns; whom when Paul saw, he thanked God, and took courage.

7. *Matthew 25:10*. And while they went to buy, the bridegroom came; and they that were ready went in with him to the marriage: and the door was shut.

8. *Ephesians 5:25-32*. Husbands, love your wives, even as Christ also loved the church, and gave himself for it; that he might sanctify and cleanse it with the washing of water by the word. That he might present it to himself a glorious church, not having spot, or wrinkle, or any such thing; but that it should be holy and without blemish. So ought men to love their wives as their own bodies. He that loveth his wife loveth himself. For no man ever yet hated his own flesh; but nourisheth and cherisheth it, even as the Lord the church: for we are members of his body. For this cause shall a man leave his father and mother, and shall be joined unto his wife, and they two shall be one flesh. This is a great mystery: but I speak concerning Christ and the church.

9. *Revelation 2:26-27*. And he that overcometh, and keepeth my works unto the end, to him will I give power over the nations: and he shall rule them with a rod of iron; as the vessels of a potter shall they be broken to shivers: even as I received of my Father.

Revelation 5:10. And madest them to be unto our God a kingdom and priests; and they reign upon the earth.

to the *earth,*[10] and His feet stand upon the same Mount Olivet from which He ascended.[11]

At the Rapture, the church, like Enoch, is taken out of the world.[12] In Luke 21:28, the Rapture is referred to at the beginning of the Tribulation. "When these things *begin* to come to pass, then look up, and lift up your heads; for your redemption draweth nigh." (Redemption here means the first resurrection, the same as in Romans 8:23.)[13]

In Luke 21:31, the Revelation is referred to when "these things" (the Tribulation) have *come to pass,* and the kingdom of God draws near. The Rapture may occur any moment.[14] The Revelation cannot occur until the Antichrist is revealed, and all the times and seasons (which point to the day of the Lord) in Leviticus 26, Daniel and Revelation are fulfilled. The Revelation ushers in the Day of the Lord.[15] The failure to make this distinction has led to great confusion among commentators on this subject.

Revelation 19:15. And out of his mouth goeth a sharp sword, that with it he should smite the nations; and he shall rule them with a rod of iron: and he treadeth the winepress of the fierceness and wrath of Almighty God. See also *Revelation 12:5.*

10. *Acts 1:11.* Which also said, Ye men of Galilee, why stand ye gazing up into heaven? this same Jesus, which is taken up from you into heaven, shall so come in like manner as ye have seen him go into heaven.

11. *Zechariah 14:4-5.* And his feet shall stand in that day upon the mount of Olives, which is before Jerusalem on the east; and the mount of Olives shall cleave in the midst thereof toward the east and toward the west, and there shall be a very great valley; and half of the mountain shall remove toward the north, and half of it toward the south . . . And the LORD my God shall come and all the saints with thee.

12. *Acts 15:13-17.* And after they had held their peace, James answered, saying, Men and brethren, hearken unto me: Simeon hath declared how God at the first did visit the Gentiles, to take out of them a people for his name. And to this agree the words of the prophets; as it is written. After this I will return, and will build again the tabernacle of David, which is fallen down; and I will build again the ruins thereof, and I will set it up: that the residue of men might seek after the Lord, and all the Gentiles, upon whom my name is called, saith the Lord, who doeth all these things.

13. *Romans 8:23.* And not only they, but ourselves also, which have the first-fruits of the Spirit, even we ourselves groan within ourselves, waiting for the adoption, to wit, the redemption of our body.

14. *Matthew 24:42.* Watch therefore; for ye know not what hour your Lord doth come.

15. *1 Thessalonians 5:2.* For yourselves know perfectly that the day of the Lord so cometh as a thief in the night.

For instance, in 2 Thessalonians 2:1, the apostle speaks of the Rapture, that is, the coming of the Lord and our gathering together unto Him, of which He had written so fully in the previous epistle, especially in the fourth chapter. In verse 2 he speaks of the Revelation, or Day of the Lord,* which could not come except there be a falling away first, and the "man of sin" (verse 3) and "that Wicked" (verse 8), or the Antichrist, is revealed.

And yet most commentators have argued that the apostle, in both of these verses, referred to one and the same event, and thus they have made Scripture contradict itself.

But we see plainly that Paul had no intention of contradicting Christ's admonitions, given to all, to watch for His imminent coming (Mark 13:35-37; Luke 12:35-40). He only made the distinction, as above stated, between the Rapture and the Revelation. The persecuted Thessalonians thought that they were *in* the Tribulation, and that the Day of the Lord had set in.** But Paul corrects them, first by reminding them that the Lord had not come for *them yet,* as He had said that He would (1 Thessalonians 4:15-17), and then by adding certain other things which must occur before the Day of the Lord would come. He had told them that the Day of the Lord would come as a thief in the night (1 Thessalonians 5:2), but that they were not of the night, and therefore He exhorts them to watch and be sober (see also Luke 21:36).[16]

Another evidence of the difference between the Rapture and Revelation consists in the fact that the church is to

---

* Greek, the oldest MSS. read κυρίου = Lord, not χριστοῦ = Christ. See John Bengel, *New Testament Commentary* (Kregel Publications, 2 vols.), and others.

** ἐνέστηκεν (*enesteken*) which the Authorized version renders "at hand," means to be present, or to have set in. See the same word in Romans 8:38; 1 Corinthians 3:22; 7:26; Galatians 1:4; Hebrews 9:9, where in each place it is rendered "present."

Luke 17:30. Even thus shall it be in the day when the Son of man is revealed. See also 2 *Thessalonians 1:7-10; 2 Peter 3:10-12,* etc.

16. *Luke 21:36.* Watch ye therefore, and pray always, that ye may be accounted worthy to escape all these things that shall come to pass, and to stand before the Son of man.

escape the Tribulation, which precedes the Revelation (Matthew 24:29-30). Enoch, a type of the church, by his rapture,—that is by being caught away or translated (Hebrews 11:5)—escaped the flood.

In keeping with Christ's injunction in Luke 21:36, He gave a blessed promise to the church in Revelation 3:10: "Because thou hast kept the word of my patience, I also will keep thee from the hour of temptation, which shall come upon all the world, to try them that dwell upon the earth. Behold I come quickly. . . ." A special hour, or time, of temptation—i.e., trial—is here mentioned, which will come upon all the world (οἰκουμένη-*oikoumenē—the whole habitable*—which is the same word as in Matthew 24:14—*all the world.*)

It is a time of trouble not limited to Judea, but as extensive as the inhabited earth. This accords with the Great Tribulation described in Matthew 24:21, a "tribulation, such as was not since the beginning of the world . . . nor ever shall be."

Jesus promises to keep the church from, or (ἐκ) *out* of this tribulation, or hour of temptation; that is, the watchful and prayerful believers will escape it (Luke 21:36). Now since it covers the whole earth, there is no way of escape from it but to be taken out of the world, and this is accomplished by the Rapture (Acts 15:14, and 1 Thessalonians 4:17, which present a glorious deliverance for the church).

The elect,[17] a portion of Israel,[18] will be gathered back to Jerusalem[19] and pass through the fire, or great

---

17. *Matthew 24:22.* And except those days should be shortened, there should no flesh be saved: but for the elect's sake those days shall be shortened.

18. *Isaiah 65:9.* And I will bring forth a seed out of Jacob, and out of Judah an inheritor of my mountains: and mine elect shall inherit it, and my servants shall dwell there. See also verses 15 and 22, and *Romans 11:5-7.*

19. *Isaiah 1:26-27.* And I will restore thy judges as at the first, and thy counsellors as at the beginning: afterward thou shalt be called, The city of righteousness, The faithful city. Zion shall be redeemed with judgment, and her converts with righteousness.

Zechariah 10:6-10. And I will strengthen the house of Judah, and I will save the house of Joseph, and I will bring them again to place them: for I have mercy upon them: and they shall be as though I had not cast them off: for I am the LORD their God, and will hear them. And they of Ephraim shall be like a mighty man, and their heart shall rejoice as through wine: yea, their children

trial.[20] Like Enoch, the church escapes from it. Like Noah, Israel passes through it.

So the church should humble herself to walk with God (Micah 6:8), as Enoch did (Genesis 5:24), having the testimony that she pleases God,[21] and should watch for the Rapture at any moment.

The Jews, through their dates and seasons, may look for the Revelation, or day of the Lord, a day of thick darkness to them, in which there is no light at all.[22] Yet, in it they will accept Christ[23] and "at evening time it

shall see it, and be glad; their heart shall rejoice in the Lord. I will hiss for them, and gather them; for I have redeemed them: and they shall increase as they have increased. And I will sow them among the people: and they shall remember me in far countries; and they shall live with their children, and turn again. I will bring them again also out of the land of Egypt, and gather them out of Assyria; and I will bring them into the land of Gilead and Lebanon; and place shall not be found for them.

20. *Zechariah 13:8-9*. And it shall come to pass, that in all the land, saith the Lord, two parts therein shall be cut off and die; but the third shall be left therein. And I will bring the third part through the fire, and will refine them as silver is refined, and will try them as gold is tried: they shall call on my name, and I will hear them: I will say, It is my people; and they shall say, The Lord is my God.

Psalm 57:1. Be merciful unto me, O God, be merciful unto me; for my soul trusteth in thee: yea, in the shadow of they wings will I make my refuge, until these calamities be overpast.

Isaiah 26:20-21. Come, my people, enter thou into thy chambers, and shut thy doors about thee: hide thyself as it were for a little moment, until the indignation be overpast. For, behold, the Lord cometh out of his place to punish the inhabitants of the earth for their iniquity: the earth also shall disclose her blood, and shall no more cover her slain. See also *Psalm 27:5; 31:20*.

21. *Hebrews 11:5*. By faith Enoch was translated that he should not see death; and was not found, because God had translated him: for before his translation he had this testimony, that he pleased God.

22. *Amos 5:18-20*. Woe unto you that desire the day of the Lord! to what end is it for you? the day of the Lord is darkness, and not light. As if a man did flee from a lion, and a bear met him; or went into the house, and leaned his hand on the wall, and a serpent bit him. Shall not the day of the Lord be darkness, and not light? even very dark, and no brightness in it?

22. *Zechariah 12:9-10*. And it shall come to pass in that day, that I will seek to destroy all the nations that come against Jerusalem. And I will pour upon the house of David, and upon the inhabitants of Jerusalem, the spirit of grace and of supplications; and they shall look upon me whom they have pierced, and they shall mourn for him, as one mourneth for his only son, and shall be in bitterness for him, as one that is in bitterness for his first-born.

23. *Revelation 6:12-17*. And I beheld when he had opened the sixth seal, and, lo, there was a great earthquake; and the sun became black as sackcloth of hair, and the moon became as blood; and the stars of heaven fell unto the earth, even as a fig tree casteth her untimely figs, when she is shaken of a

shall be light," and "living waters shall go out from Jerusalem" (Zechariah 14:6-8).

The Rapture, or being caught away, at the coming of the Bridegroom, is full of the sweetest comfort for the believer, and therefore Paul says, "Comfort one another with these words" (1 Thessalonians 4:18). But the Revelation of Christ with His saints, to take vengeance on the ungodly, is full of solemnity and terror to take those who do not obey the gospel of our Lord Jesus Christ.[24]

---

mighty wind. And the heaven departed as a scroll when it is rolled together; and every mountain and island were moved out of their places. And the kings of the earth, and the great men, and the rich men, and the chief captains, and the mighty men, and every bond man, and every free man, hid themselves in the dens and in the rocks of the mountains; and said to the mountains and rocks, Fall on us, and hide us from the face of him that sitteth on the throne, and from the wrath of the Lamb: for the great day of his wrath is come; and who shall be able to stand? See also *2 Thessalonians 1:7-10*.

10

THE CHURCH AND THE MILLENNIAL KINGDOM

The second point of vital importance for a right understanding of premillennialism is the distinction between the church and the millennial kingdom.

The Christian church (ἐκκλησία-*ekklēsia*), meaning assembly or congregation, is distinct from the congregation of the Mosaic dispensation, or the church in the wilderness.[1] For, until after Christ came, it was a thing of the future. This is proved by His assertion in Matthew 16:18, "On this rock *will* I build my church," showing that it had not yet been built. And, it is likewise distinct from the millennial kingdom, which is to follow it.

The church is a companion of Christ in His humiliation, manifesting His sufferings and filling up the afflictions which are lacking.[2] *The kingdom is the manifestation of the glory of Christ* which will follow,[3] when He "shall sit in the throne of His glory," and when they who have suffered with Him during this time of trial will also be

---

1. *Acts 7:38*. This is he, that was in the church (*ekklēsia*—congregation) in the wilderness with the angel which spake to him in the mount Sinai, and with our fathers: who received the lively oracles to give unto us.

2. *Colossians 1:24*. Who now rejoice in my suffeings for you, and fill up that which is behind of the afflictions of Christ in my flesh for his body's sake, which is the church. See also *2 Corinthians 1:5-6*; *Philippians 3:10*; *2 Timothy 1:8*.

3. *1 Peter 1:11*. Searching what, or what manner of time the Spirit of Christ which was in them did signify, when it testified beforehand the sufferings of Christ, and the glory that should follow.

exalted to regal power and authority.[4] This kingdom was at hand,[5] that is, it came near[6] (or *approached*: same Greek word),[7] when Jesus the King came. So much so, that the three favored disciples witnessed a foretaste of its glory and power on the Mount of Transfiguration.[8]

But the Jews rejected this kingdom and killed their King, Jesus Christ. They were not willing to have this man reign over them, and therefore the kingdom did not "immediately appear." It became like a nobleman who "went into a far country, to receive for himself a kingdom and to return" (see Luke 19:11-27). By this parable Jesus distinctly taught that the kingdom was in the future.

---

4. *Matthew 19:28.* And Jesus said unto them, Verily I say unto you, That ye which have followed me, in the regeneration when the Son of man shall sit in the throne of his glory, ye also shall sit upon twelve thrones, judging the twelve tribes of Israel. See also *Luke 22:28-30.*

5. *Matthew 3:2.* And saying, Repent ye: for the kingdom of heaven is at hand. See also *Matthew 4:17* and *Matthew 10:7.*

6. *Luke 10:9-11.* And heal the sick that are therein, and say unto them, The kingdom of God is come nigh unto you. But into whatsoever city ye enter, and they receive you not, go your ways out into the streets of the same, and say, Even the very dust of your city, which cleaveth on us, we do wipe off against you: notwithstanding, be ye sure of this, that the kingdom of God is come nigh unto you.

7. *Hebrews 10:25.* Not forsaking the assembling of ourselves together, as the manner of some is: but exhorting one another: and so much the more, as ye see the day approaching. See also *Luke 12:33.*

8. *Matthew 17:1-9.* And after six days Jesus taketh Peter, James, and John his brother, and bringeth them up into a high mountain apart, and was transfigured before them: and his face did shine as the sun, and his raiment was white as the light. And, behold, there appeared unto them Moses and Elias talking with him. Then answered Peter, and said unto Jesus, Lord, it is good for us to be here: if thou wilt, let us make here three tabernacles; one for thee, and one for Moses, and one for Elias. While he yet spake, behold, a bright cloud overshadowed them: and behold a voice out of the cloud, which said, This is my beloved Son, in whom I am well pleased; hear ye Him. And when the disciples heard it, they fell on their face, and were sore afraid. And Jesus came and touched them, and said, Arise, and be not afraid. And when they had lifted up their eyes, they saw no man, save Jesus only. And as they came down from the mountain, Jesus charged them, saying, Tell the vision to no man, until the Son of man be risen again from the dead. See also *Mark 9:1-10*; *Luke 9:27-36.*

2 *Peter 1:16-18.* For we have not followed cunningly divised fables, when we made known unto you the power and coming of our Lord Jesus Christ, but were eyewitnesses of his majesty. For he received from God the Father honor and glory, when there came such a voice to him from the excellent glory, This is my beloved Son, in whom I am well pleased. And this voice which came from heaven we heard, when we were with Him in the holy mount.

The Kingdom Still Future

It was concerning the future that Christ said: "I say unto you, I will not any more eat thereof [the passover] until it be fulfilled in the kingdom of God," and again, "For I say unto you, I will not drink of the fruit of the vine until the kingdom of God shall come" (Luke 22:16-18; also Matthew 26:29; Mark 14:25).

It was concerning the future that the thief cried, "Lord, remember me when Thou comest into Thy kingdom" (Luke 23:42). Joseph of Arimathea, who laid Jesus' body in the sepulcher, "waited for the kingdom of God," which also indicates that it was still in the future (Mark 15:43).

It was still future when Paul exhorted the disciples to continue in the faith, and said "that we must through much tribulation enter into the kingdom of God" (Acts 14:22). It was in the future while the persecuted Thessalonians suffered, that they might "be counted worthy of the kingdom of God" (2 Thessalonians 1:4-5).

It was most assuredly future when, years afterward, Peter gave his exhortations as follows: "Wherefore the rather, brethren, give diligence to make your callling and election sure; for if ye do these things ye shall never fall. For so an entrance shall be ministered unto you abundantly into the everlasting kingdom of our Lord and Savior, Jesus Christ" (2 Peter 1:10-11). And it has been future during the long, sad history of the faithful and godly church, while she has suffered the terrible persecutions of fire, inquisition, banishment, ridicule and false accusation.[9]

And it will be future until Jesus, "having received the kingdom,"[10] will return to recompense tribulation to those

---

9. *2 Timothy 3:12*. Yea, and all that will live godly in Christ Jesus shall suffer persecution.

10. *Luke 19:15*. And it came to pass, that when he was returned, having received the kingdom, then he commanded these servants to be called unto him, to whom he had given the money, that he might know how much every man had gained by trading.

who have troubled the church,[11] and He will "sit in the throne of His glory."[12] Then the kingdom, which for these centuries has been *hidden in mystery,*[13] shall be manifested in power and glory.[14] Then the kingdom of this world will become our Lord's and His Christ's,[15] and then the kingdom will be given unto the saints of the Most High.[16] Therefore we pray as Jesus taught us, "thy kingdom come."

---

11. *2 Thessalonians 1:6-10*. Seeing it is a righteous thing with God to recompense tribulation to them that trouble you. And to you who are troubled rest with us, when the Lord Jesus shall be revealed from heaven with his mighty angels, in flaming fire taking vengeance on them that know not God, and that obey not the gospel of our Lord Jesus Christ: who shall be punished with everlasting destruction from the presence of the Lord, and from the glory of his power; when he shall come to be glorified in his saints, and to be admired in all them that believe. See also *Luke 19:27*.

12. *Matthew 19:28*. And Jesus said unto them, Verily I say unto you, That ye which have followed me, in the regeneration when the Son of man shall sit in the throne of his glory, ye also shall sit upon twelve thrones, judging the twelve tribes of Israel.

13. *Matthew 13:11*. He answered and said unto them, Because it is given unto you to know the mysteries of the kingdom of heaven, but to them it is not given. See also *Mark 4:11*; *Luke 8:10*.

14. *Matthew 13:43*. Then shall the righteous shine forth as the sun in the kingdom of their Father. Who hath ears to hear, let him hear. See also *Luke 13:25-29*.

Romans 8:17-23. And if children, then heirs; heirs of God, and joint-heirs with Christ; if so be that we suffer with him, that we may be also glorified together. For I reckon that the sufferings of this present time are not worthy to be compared with the glory which shall be revealed in us. For the earnest expectation of the creature waiteth for the manifestation of the sons of God. For the creature was made subject to vanity, not willingly, but by reason of him who hath subjected the same in hope; because the creature itself also shall be delivered from the bondage of corruption into the glorious liberty of the children of God. For we know that the whole creation groaneth and travaileth in pain together until now. And not only they, but ourselves also, which have the firstfruits of the Spirit, even we ourselves, waiting for the adoption, to wit, the redemption of our body.

15. *Revelation 11:15*. And the seventh angel sounded; and there followed great voices in heaven, and they said, The kingdom of this world is become the kingdom of our Lord, and of his Christ: and he shall reign for ever and ever.

Daniel 7:14. And there was given him dominion, and glory, and a kingdom, that all people, nations, and languages, should serve him: his dominion is an everlasting dominion, which shall not pass away, and his kingdom that which shall not be destroyed.

16. *Daniel 7:27*. And the kingdom and dominion, and the greatness of the kingdom under the whole heaven, shall be given to the people of the saints of the Most High, whose kingdom is an everlasting kingdom, and all dominions shall serve and obey him.

The church militant, which was begun on the day of Pentecost (Acts 2) ends at the Rapture, before the Tribulation. The kingdom begins with the Revelation, at the close of the Tribulation:

- It is the personal reign of Christ on earth.
- He was prophesied to be King of the Jews (Isaiah 9:6).
- He was born King of the Jews (Matthew 2:2).
- He said He was the King of the Jews (Matthew 27:11).
- He was crucified as King of the Jews (Matthew 27:37).
- He came preaching the gospel of the kingdom, saying, "The time is fulfilled, the kingdom of God *is at hand*" (Mark 1:14-15).
- He said the kingdom was *among them* (Luke 17:21, margin).
- He came to His own, but His own did not receive Him (John 1:11).
- He would have set up the kingdom (Matthew 23:37-39), but they rejected and crucified Him.
- However, God raised Him from the dead and set Him on high.[17]

He sent the Holy Spirit into the world, and under His power and guidance the apostles went out preaching the good news of the kingdom (Acts 2, etc.) to the *Jews first,* [18] but they rejected it, and the disciples turned to the Gentiles.[19] Therefore the kingdom came near to the Jews,

17. *Hebrews 10:12-13.* But this man, after he had offered one sacrifice for sins for ever, sat down on the right hand of God; from henceforth expecting till his enemies be made his footstool.

Acts 2:31, 35-36. For David is not ascended into the heavens: but he saith himself, The Lord said unto my Lord, Sit thou on my right hand, until I make thy foes thy footstool. Therefore let all the house of Israel know assuredly, that God hath made the same Jesus, whom ye have crucified, both Lord and Christ. See also *Matthew 22:44.*

18. *Acts 3:26.* Unto you first God, having raised up his Son Jesus, sent him to bless you, in turning away every one of you from his iniquities.

Romans 1:16. For I am not ashamed of the gospel of Christ: for it is the power of God unto salvation to every one that believeth; to the Jew first, and also to the Greek. See also *Matthew 10:6.*

19. *Acts 13:46.* Then Paul and Barnabas waxed bold, and said, It was necessary that the word of God should first have been spoken to you: but seeing ye put it from you, and judge yourselves unworthy of everlasting life, lo, we turn to the Gentiles. See also *Acts 18:6* and *28:28.*

who spurned it; while it waits,[*][20] God visits "the Gentiles, to take out of them a people for His name" (Acts 15:14), breaking down the middle wall of partition to make out of both (all Jews and Gentiles who believe in His name) one new man,[21] that is, the church, or mystical body of Christ.[22]

The Mystery

Thus the church came in as a mystery, and was rarely, if at all, spoken of in the Old Testament prophecies. For we read in Romans 16:25 that it is a "mystery, which was kept secret since the world began;" and in Ephesians 3:3–6, "the mystery . . . which in other ages was not made known unto the sons of men;" and in Colos-

---

* This we believe is the true explanation of this subject. The kingdom did come "nigh" when Christ came, and had they received Him, it would have been manifested, but now it is in abeyance, or waiting until He comes again.

However the Greek word ἐνγίζω—engizo, which is translated at hand in Matthew 3:2; 4:17; 10:7, and is come nigh in Luke 10:9-11, does not necessarily mean immediately near. For we find the same word used in Romans 13:12: "The day is at hand," and in Hebrews 10:25, "as ye see the day approaching" and in James 5:8, "the coming of the Lord draweth nigh," and in 1 Peter 4:7, "the end of all things is at hand," each of which passages are yet unfulfilled.

So we see that the word *engizo* (is at hand) covers a period of time expanding beyond our day, and reaching to the second coming of the Lord.

---

20. *Matthew 23:39.* For I say unto you, Ye shall not see me henceforth, till ye shall say, Blessed *is* he that cometh in the name of the Lord.

21. *Ephesians 2:14-15.* For he is our peace, who hath made both one, and hath broken down the middle wall of partition between us; having abolished in his flesh the enmity, even the law of commandments contained in ordinances; for to make in himself of twain one new man, so making peace.

22. *Ephesians 4:12-13.* For the perfecting of the saints, for the work of the ministry, for the edifying of the body of Christ: till we all come in the unity of the faith, and of the knowledge of the Son of God, unto a perfect man, unto the measure of the stature of the fulness of Christ:

Ephesians 5:23-32. For the husband is the head of the wife, even as Christ is the head of the Church; and he is the Savior of the body. Therefore as the Church is subject unto Christ, so let the wives be to their own husbands in everything. Husbands, love your wives, even as Christ also loved the church, and gave himself for it; that he might sanctify and cleanse it with the washing of water by the word. That he might present it to himself a glorious church, not having spot, or wrinkle, or any such thing; but that it should be holy and with out blemish. So ought men to love their wives as their own bodies. He that loveth his wife loveth himself. For no man ever yet hated his own flesh: but nourisheth and cherisheth it, even as the Lord the church: for we are members of his body. For this cause shall a man leave his father and mother, and shall be joined unto his wife, and they two shall be one flesh. This is a great mystery: but I speak concerning Christ and the church.

sians 1:24–27 . . . "Even the mystery which hath been hid from ages and from generations, but now is made manifest . . . the riches of the glory of this mystery among the Gentiles."

It was this *mystery* of the church which so puzzled the prophets and caused them to inquire and search diligently what the Spirit meant when it testified beforehand about the sufferings of Christ.[23] They could understand the glory of the kingdom, which should follow, but could not understand the mystery, which has been revealed unto us, and which interested the angels; that is, a suffering Messiah and a persecuted church.

The church *is to be* the bride of Christ, which He is going to present to Himself (Ephesians 5:23-32). But *now* she is a *virgin of sorrow* and affliction, a companion in suffering with her espoused Husband—the Lord Jesus Christ.[24]

Christ said: "Because ye are not of the world, but I have chosen you out of the world, therefore the world hateth you," and "if they have persecuted me, they will also persecute you" (John 15:19-20), and "in the world ye shall have tribulation" (John 16:33). The apostle says, "yea, and all that will live godly in Christ Jesus shall suffer persecution" (2 Timothy 3:12; see also John 17:14; 1 Thessalonians 3:3).[25] And this is perfectly consistent, for this world has murdered the Son of God, and is guilty of His blood. Yet the Father bears this insult with His

---

23. *1 Peter 1:10-12.* Of which salvation the prophets have inquired and searched diligently, who prophesied of the grace that should come unto you: searching what, or what manner of time the Spirit of Christ which was in them did signify, when it testified before hand the sufferings of Christ, and the glory that should follow. Unto whom it was revealed, that not unto themselves, but unto us they did minister the things, which are now reported unto you by them that have preached the gospel unto you with the Holy Spirit sent down from heaven; which things the angels desire to look into.

24. *2 Corinthians 11:2.* For I am jealous over you with godly jealousy: for I have espoused you to one husband, that I may present you as a chaste virgin to Christ.

25. *John 17:14.* I have given them thy word; and the world hateth them, because they are not of the world, even as I am not of the world.

1 Thessalonians 3:3. That no man should be moved by these afflictions: for yourselves know that we are appointed thereunto.

matchless love and grace, patiently witholding the day of
vengeance, being long suffering and not willing that any
should perish.[26]

If He thus bears with the murderers of His Son, will
He not bear with the persecutors of His church? This
persecution will continue until Jesus comes and takes
the church away,[27] and saves her from the *great hour of
temptation* (or *trial*), which will come upon all the world.[28]
Then He will recompense tribulation to those that have
troubled her.[29] And this spirit of rebellion and persecution
will continue, even through the Tribulation[30] and up to
the very day of the Lord,[31] when Christ will be revealed

---

26. *2 Peter 3:9*. The Lord is not slack concerning his promise, as some men
count slackness; but is longsuffering to usward, not willing that any should
perish, but that all should come to repentance.

27. *1 Thessalonians 4:16-17*. For the Lord himself shall descend from heaven
with a shout, with the voice of the archangel, and with the trump of God: and
the dead in Christ shall rise first; then we which are alive and remain shall be
caught up together with them in the clouds, to meet the Lord in the air: and so
shall we ever by with the Lord.

28. *Revelation 3:10*. Because thou hast kept the word of my patience, I also
will keep thee from the hour of temptation, which shall come upon all the
world, to try them that dwell upon the earth.

29. *2 Thessalonians 1:6*. Seeing it is a righteous thing with God to recompense tribulation to them that trouble you.

30. *Revelation 16:9, 11, 14, 21*. And men were scorched with great heat, and
blasphemed the name of God, which hath power over these. And blasphemed
the God of heaven because of their pains and their sores, and repented not of
their deeds. For they are the spirits of devils, working miracles, which go forth
unto the kings of the earth and of the whole world, to gather them to the
battle of that great day of God Almighty. And there fell upon men a great hail
out of heaven, every stone about the weight of a talent and men blasphemed
God because of the plague of the hail; for the plague thereof was exceeding
great.

31. *2 Peter 3:1-10*. This second epistle, beloved, I now write unto you; in both
which I stir up your pure minds by way of rememberance; that ye may be
mindful of the words which were spoken before by the holy prophets, and of
the commandment of us the apostles of the Lord and Savior: knowing this
first, that there shall come in the last days scoffers, walking after their own
lusts, and saying, Where is the promise of his coming? for since the fathers fell
asleep, all things continue as they were from the beginning of the creation.
For this day they willingly are ignorant of, that by the word of God the
heavens were of old, and the earth standing out of the water and in the water:
whereby the world that then was, being overflowed with water, perished: but
the heavens and the earth which are now, by the same word are kept in store,
reserved unto fire against the day of judgment and perdition of ungodly men.
But, beloved, be not ignorant of this one thing, that one day is with the Lord as
a thousand years, and a thousand years as one day. The Lord is not slack con-

in flaming fire[32] with His saints, to execute judgment upon the earth.[33] So we see that there is no place in the whole earthly history of such a persecuted church, for the millennial kingdom. For in that future time, "righteousness and peace" will kiss each other, "truth shall spring out of the earth, and righteousness shall look out of heaven" (Psalm 85).

"A King shall reign in righteousness, and Princes shall rule in judgment" (Isaiah 32:1). With righteousness He will judge the poor. Judah and Israel shall be restored and dwell safely. There will be no harm or destruction in all of God's holy mountain, and even the animals will be at peace.[34]

---

cerning his promise, as some men count slackness; but is longsuffering to us-ward, not willing that any should perish, but that all should come to repentance. But the day of the Lord will come as a thief in the night; in the which the heavens shall pass away with a great noise, and the elements shall melt with fervent heat, the earth also and the works that are therein shall be burnt up.

32. *2 Thessalonians 1:7-10.* And to you that are afflicted rest with us, at the revelation of the Lord Jesus from heaven with the angels of his power in flaming fire, rendering vengeance to them that know not God, and to them that obey not the gospel of our Lord Jesus: who shall suffer punishment, even eternal destruction from the face of the Lord and from the glory of his might, when he shall come to be glorified in his saints, and to be marvelled at in all them that believed (because our testimony unto you was believed) in that day.

33. *Jude 14-15.* And Enoch also, the seventh from Adam, prophesied of these, saying, Behold, the Lord cometh with ten thousand of his saints. To execute judgment upon all, and to convince all that are ungodly among them of all their ungodly deeds which they have ungodly committed, and of all their hard speeches which ungodly sinners have spoken against him.

34. *Isaiah 11:4-9.* But with righteousness shall he judge the poor, and reprove with equity for the meek of the earth: and he shall smite the earth with the rod of his mouth, and with the breath of his lips shall be slay the wicked. And righteousness shall be the girdle of his loins, and faithfulness the girdle of his reins. The wolf also shall dwell with the lamb, and the leopard shall lie down with the kid; and the calf and young lion and the fatling together; and a little child shall lead them. And the cow and the bear shall feed; their young ones shall lie down together: and the loin shall eat straw like the ox. And the suckling child shall play on the hole of the asp, and the weaned child shall put his hand on the cockatrice' den. They shall not hurt nor destroy in all my holy mountain: for the earth shall be full of the knowledge of the LORD, as the waters cover the sea.

Romans 8:21-23. Because the creature itself also shall be delivered from the bondage of corruption into the glorious liberty of the children of God. For we know that the whole creation groaneth and travalieth in pain together until now. And not only they, but ourselves also, which have the firstfruits of the Spirit, even we ourselves groan within ourselves, waiting for the adoption, to wit, the redemption of our body. See also *Jeremiah 23:3-8* and *32:36-44*; *Ezekiel 34, 36* and *37* and many others.

Again, from all of these passages, and especially Isaiah 60, we see that restored Israel and Jerusalem are to be the very *central glory* of the millennial kingdom. But God does not restore Israel and rebuild Zion, or Jerusalem, until He appears in His glory. "When the Lord shall build up Zion, He shall appear in His glory" (Psalm 102:16). And He does not build up Zion or the tabernacle of David until He has taken out the church.[35]

Thus we see a clear distinction between the suffering church and the glorious kingdom, which are separated by the Tribulation:

THE CHURCH Rapture **Tribulation** Revelation **THE KINGDOM**

See diagram, page 73

The Church Will Be Rewarded

But, do you ask: "Is the church always to suffer and be persecuted?" Surely not. For she will still be married. And her light affliction will result in a far more exceeding and eternal weight of glory in the things which are not yet seen,[36] and the church will be counted worthy of the kingdom of God for which she suffers, when the Lord Jesus is revealed from heaven.[37] Therefore "we glory in

---

35. *Acts 15:13-17.* And after they had held their peace, James answered, saying, Men and brethren, hearken unto me: Simeon hath declared how God at the first did visit the Gentiles, to take out of them a people for his name. And to this agree the words of the prophets; as it is written, after this I will return, and will build again the tabernacle of David, which is fallen down; and I will build again the ruins thereof, and I will set it up: that the residue of men might seek after the Lord, and all the Gentiles, upon whom my name is called, saith the Lord who doeth all these things.

36. *2 Corinthians 4:17-18.* For our light affliction, which is but for a moment, worketh for us a far more exeeding and eternal weight of glory; while we look not at the things which are seen, but at the things which are not seen: for the things which are seen are temporal; but the things which are not seen are eternal.

37. *2 Thessalonians 1:4-10.* So that we ourselves glory in you in the churches of God for your patience and faith in all our persecutions and tribulations that

tribulations also knowing that tribulation worketh patience; and patience, experience; and experience, *hope*" (Romans 5:3-4). And when Christ, who is *our hope* (1 Timothy 1:1) and *our life* appears, then we will also appear with Him in glory.[38] If we suffer with Him we will also reign with Him.[39] We will reign on the earth (Revelation 5:10).

Therefore we conclude that the church will be recompensed in reigning with Christ over the millennial kingdom. "Fear not, little flock, for it is your Father's good pleasure to give you the kingdom" (Luke 12:32; Daniel 7:18-27). Then let us pray as Jesus taught us: *"Thy kingdom come."*

Nominal Christians

But, do you say, "The church is not persecuted, and does, even now enjoys relative peace"? I answer, it is because the professing church (and by this we include Roman Catholics, Greeks and all nominal Christians) has conformed so largely to the world that the world has little, if any, controversy with her.

Of what benefit to God are nominal, cold-hearted, world-conforming Christians? He wants a separate and holy people, and the command is, "Come out and be ye separate" (2 Corinthians 6:14-18).

---

ye endure: which is a manifest token of the righteous judgment of God, that ye may be counted worthy of the kingdom of God, for which ye also suffer: seeing it is a righteous thing with God to recompense tribulation to them that trouble you; and to you who are troubled rest with us, when the Lord Jesus shall be revealed from heaven with his mighty angels. In flaming fire taking vengeance on them that know not God, and that obey not the gospel of our Lord Jesus Christ: who shall be punished with everlasting destruction from the presence of the Lord, and from the glory of his power; when he shall come to be glorified in his saints, and to be admired in all them that believe (because our testimony among you was believed) in that day.

38. *Colossians 3:4.* When Christ, who is our life, shall appear, then shall ye also appear with him in glory.

39. *Romans 8:17.* And if children, then heirs, heirs of God, and joint heirs with Christ; if so be that we suffer with him, that we may be also glorified together.

2 Timothy 2:12. If we suffer, we shall also reign with him, if we deny him, he also will deny us.

I believe that the bride of the air and the leaven in the parables of Matthew 13 represent the children of the wicked one, or hypocrites which have lodged in the church, as well as the false doctrines which have crept in and have so pervaded the professing church that it has, in general, become merely formal and nominal. God wants zealous Christians, in whom the Word of Life burns as it did in Jeremiah's bones. And are not the number of these few today?

The professing church is lukewarm, and I fear it is almost ready to be spued out of the Master's mouth. But thanks be to His name, there are those who are rebuked and chastened, and who are buying gold and white raiment and anointing their eyes that they may see, and who will overcome and sit down with Christ in His throne (Revelation 3:14-22).

The True Church

There is truly a church, and it is the body of Christ,[40] *one and indivisible*,[41] composed of all true believers in Him.[42] It may be called a church within, or among the churches—the wheat among the chaff. And let us remember that this true church of Christ is called to suffer, and that the intervals of rest (Acts 9:31) only strengthen her to endure new and varied forms of persecution. This has been her history, and we may expect it will be her future, amid the scoffers, evil men and seducers of the last times.[43]

---

40. *Ephesians 1:22-23*. And hath put all things under his feet, and gave him to be the head over all things to the church, which is his body, the fulness of him that filleth all in all.

41. *1 Corinthians 12:12-13*. For as the body is one, and hath many members, and all the members of that one body: so also is Christ. For by one Spirit are we all baptized into one body, whether we be Jews or Gentiles, whether we be bond or free; and have been all made to drink into one Spirit.

42. *Ephesians 4:11-12*. And he gave some, apostles; and some, prophets; and some, evangelists; and some pastors and teachers; for the perfecting of the saints, for the work of the ministry, for the edifying of the body of Christ.

43. *2 Peter 3:3*. Knowing this first, that there shall come in the last days scoffers, walking after their own lusts.

1 Timothy 4:1. Now the Spirit speaketh expressly, that in the latter times some shall depart from the faith, giving heed to seducing spirits, and doctrines of devils.

And yet it is her blessed privilege, in all her affliction, to know that she travails in the birth of souls[44] which are born from above by the Holy Spirit (John 3), and that the gospel (good news) of the kingdom, which she preaches, is the power of God to salvation for all who believe.[45]

The Bride of Christ

"Husbands, love your wives, even as Christ also loved the church, and gave Himself for it, that He might sanctify and cleanse it with the washing of water by the word, that He might present it to Himself a glorious church, not having spot or wrinkle, or any such thing; but that it should be holy and without blemish." In this precious passage (Ephesians 5) the church, as the bride of Christ, is typified by the most intimate, tender and sacred relationship known among men.

Abraham's servant went into a far country (Genesis 24) to seek a bride for Issac, who was the honored type of Christ as a sacrifice (Genesis 22). So the Holy Spirit has come into the world to seek a bride for Jesus. Abraham's servant said, "Hinder me not." So the Holy Spirit is striving with the world and pleading with cold-hearted professors, that He may hasten the presentation of the bride to the Bridegroom (see Matthew 22:2-10).

Rebekah said, "I will go." So the bride of Christ should be yearning to go. God has made the wedding and prepared the feast, and all things (except the bride) are ready for the rapturous meeting, and blessed are those who are called to the marriage supper of the Lamb (Revelation 19:9).

---

2 Timothy 3:1-5. This know also, that in the last days perilous times shall come. For men shall be lovers of their own selves, covetous, boasters, proud, blasphemers, disobedient to parents, unthankful, unholy, without natural affection, trucebreakers, false accusers, incontinent, fierce, despisers of those that are good. Traitors, heady, highminded, lovers of pleasures more than lovers of God; having a form of godliness, but denying the power thereof: from such turn away. See also *2 Timothy 4:1-5*.

44. *Galatians 4:19*. My little children, of whom I travail in birth again until Christ be formed in you. See also *1 Corinthians 4:15*; *Philemon 10*.

45. *Romans 1:16*. For I am not ashamed of the gospel of Christ: for it is the power of God unto salvation to every one that believeth; to the Jew first, and also to the Greek.

Oh! that the church would work a hundredfold more earnestly for the conversion of souls and the edifying of the body of Christ! Then the bride would be complete, therefore hastening the coming of her Lord.[46] Let us be ever listening to hear the midnight cry: "Behold the Bridegroom comes!" and "so be ready to go out to meet Him" (Matthew 25:6).

> "O! I am my Beloved's, and my Beloved is mine;
> He brings a poor vile sinner into His 'house of wine.'
> I stand upon His merit—I know no safer stand,
> Not e'en where glory dwelleth in Immanuel's land.
>
> The bride eyes not her garment, but her dear Bridegroom's face;
> I will not gaze at glory, but on my King of Grace;
> Not at the crown He giveth, but on His pierced hand—
> The Lamb is all the glory of Immanuel's land."

---

46. *2 Peter 3:11-12.* Seeing then that all these things shall be dissolved, what manner of persons ought ye to be in all holy conversation and godliness. Looking for and hasting unto the coming of the day of God, wherein the heavens being on fire shall be dissolved, and the elements shall melt with fervent heat?

11

TRIBULATION—
RESURRECTION—JUDGMENT

The Tribulation

The term Tribulation is used to designate the whole period of earthly history, between the Rapture and the Revelation, or between the church and the millennial kingdom. It will not altogether be a time of tribulation, for in it "they shall rejoice and send gifts one to another" (Revelation 11:10), and shall say "peace and safety" (1 Thessalonians 5:3). We believe that it will be comparatively a short season, because the 6,000 years and the times, or year-days, of prophecy have nearly run out. It no doubt embraces that last one of Daniel's seventy weeks,[1] for the reason that then God begins to deal with Israel again after He has taken the church away.[2] And yet it is probable that it includes much more than the seven years of that week.

---

1. *Daniel 9:27*. And he shall confirm the covenant with many for one week: and in the midst of the week he shall cause the sacrifice and the oblation to cease, and for the overspreading of abominations he shall make it desolate, even until the consummation, and that determined shall be poured upon the desolate.

2. *Acts 15:13-17*. And after they had held their peace, James answered, saying, Men and brethren, hearken unto me. Simeon hath declared how God at the first did visit the Gentiles, to take out of them a people for his name. And to this agree the words of the prophets; as it is written, after this I will return, and will build again the tabernacle of David, which is fallen down; and I will build again the ruins thereof, and I will set it up: that the residue of men might seek after the Lord, and all the Gentiles, upon whom my name is called, saith the Lord, who doeth all these things.

It is certain that there will be in it a period of unequalled trial, sorrow and calamity,[3] spiritual darkness and open wickedness.[4] It is the night of the world.[5] But the true church, which is not of the night,[6] being *watchful* and *prayerful,* will be accounted worthy to escape it by the Rapture, and to stand before the Son of Man.[7] Meanwhile a third part of Israel will be brought through it,[8] and for the elect's sake the days of this culminating tribulation will be shortened[9] by the revelation of Christ.[10]

From Isaiah 24—28 an idea may be gained of the terrible character of this period, during which the Antichrist will also be revealed (see p. 108). Some, especially from the remnant of Israel, will accept Christ, become His witnesses, and be killed by Antichrist. These we call the tribulation saints, who are to be raised at the close of the great tribulation, as the gleanings of the great harvest of the first resurrection.

---

3. *Matthew 24:21.* For then shall be great tribulation, such as was not since the beginning of the world to this time, no, nor ever shall be. See also *Daniel 12:1.*

4. *2 Peter 3:3-4.* Knowing this first, that there shall come in the last days scoffers, walking after their own lusts, and saying, Where is the promise of his coming? for since the fathers fell asleep, all things continue as they were from the beginning of the creation. See also *Luke 18:7.*

5. *John 9:4.* I must work the works of him that sent me, while it is day: the night cometh, when no man can work.
   Luke 17:34. I tell you, in that night there shall be two men in one bed; the one shall be taken, and the other shall be left.

6. *1 Thessalonians 5:4-5.* But ye, brethren, are not in darkness, that that day should overtake you as a thief. Ye are all the children of light, and the children of the day: we are not of the night, nor of darkness.

7. *Luke 21:36.* Watch ye therefore, and pray always, that ye may be accounted worthy to escape all these things that shall come to pass, and to stand before the Son of man. See also *Revelation 3:10.*

8. *Zechariah 13:9.* And I will bring the third part through the fire, and will refine them as silver is refined, and will try them as gold is tried: they shall call on my name, and I will hear them: I will say, It is my people; and they shall say, The Lord is my God.

9. *Matthew 24:22.* And except those days should be shortened, there should no flesh be saved: but for the elect's sake those days shall be shortened.

10. *2 Thessalonians 1:7.* And to you who are troubled rest with us, when the Lord Jesus shall be revealed from heaven with his mighty angels.
   2 Thessalonians 2:18. And then shall that Wicked be revealed, whom the Lord shall consume with the spirit of his mouth, and shall destroy with the brightness of his coming.

The Resurrection

In regard to the Resurrection, I would say that the literal rendering of 1 Corinthians 15:23 is "but each one in his own band."

It seems plain that the resurrection of those "who are Christ's at His coming," includes both those who constitute the bride, who are raised at the Rapture when Christ comes into the air; and the Old Testament saints.[11] These are the friends of the Bridegroom,[12] who doubtless are raised in a different band from the church,[13] and also those who believe and suffer during the Tribulation.[14] They will be raised at the Revelation (when Christ comes to the earth), to take part with Him in the millennial kingdom.[15]

---

11. *Job 19:25-27.* For I know that my Redeemer liveth, and that he shall stand at the latter day upon the earth: and though after my skin worms destroy this body, yet in my flesh shall I see God: whom I shall see for myself, not another; though my reins by consumed within me.

Isaiah 26:19. Thy dead men shall live, together with my dead body shall they arise. Awake and sing, ye that dwell in dust: for thy dew is as the dew of herbs, and the earth shall cast out the dead.

Hosea 13:14. I will ransom them from the power of the grave; I will redeem them from death: O death, I will be thy plagues; O grave, I will be thy destruction: repentance shall be hid from mine eyes.

Ezekiel 37:12-14. Therefore prophesy and say unto them, Thus saith the LORD God; Behold, O my people I will open your graves, and cause you to come up out of your graves, and bring you into the land of Israel. And ye shall know that I am the LORD, when I have opened your graves, O my people, and brought you up out of your graves, and shall put my Spirit in you, and ye shall live; and I shall place you in your own land: then shall ye know that I the Lord have spoken it, and performed it, saith the LORD. See also *Hebrews 11:39-40.*

12. *John 3:28-29.* Ye yourselves bear me witness, that I said, I am not the Christ, but that I am sent before him. He that hath the bride is the bridegroom: but the friend of the bridegroom, which standeth and heareth him, rejoiceth greatly because of the bridegroom's voice: this my joy therefore is fulfilled.

13. *Revelation 6:9-11.* And when he had opened the fifth seal, I saw under the altar the souls of them that were slain for the word of God, and for the testimony which they held: and they cried with a loud voice, saying, How long, O Lord, holy and true, dost thou not judge and avenge our blood on them that dwell on the earth? And white robes were given unto every one of them; and it was said unto them, that they should rest yet for a little season, until their fellow servants also and their brethren, that should be killed as they were, should be fulfilled.

14. *Revelation 13:15.* And he had power to give life unto the image of the beast, that the image of the beast should both speak, and cause that as many as would not worship the image of the beast should be killed.

15. *Revelation 20:4-6.* And I saw thrones, and they sat upon them, and judgment was given unto them: and I saw the souls of them that were beheaded for

This latter we represent by "Resurrection" and "Tribulation" on the diagram, page 73.

The great harvest of the first Resurrection, or the Resurrection of Life includes:

Christ . . . .*The Firstfruits*

Those that are Christ's at His coming	{	At the Rapture	The church and Old Testament saints	}	The ingathering
		At the Revelation	The Tribulation saints	}	The gleaning

The second Resurrection, or Resurrection of Judgment,[16] occurs after the Millennium, and includes the remaining dead.[17]

Judgment

We often hear postmillennialists use the expression "General Judgment," thereby conveying the idea of some future day in which all mankind will simultaneously appear before God to be judged.

The expression is not in the Scriptures. Premillennialists believe that the judgment is general *only* in the sense

---

the witness of Jesus, and for the word of God, and which had not worshiped the beast, neither his image, neither had received his mark upon their foreheads, or in their hands: and they lived and reigned with Christ a thousand years. But the rest of the dead lived not again until the thousand years were finished. This is the first resurrection. Blessed and holy is he that hath part in the first resurrection: on such the second death hath no power, but they shall be priests of God and of Christ, and shall reign with him a thousand years. See also *Romans 11:15*.

16. *John 5:29*. And shall come forth; they that have done good, unto the resurrection of life; and they that have done evil, unto the resurrection of damnation [judgment].

17. *Revelation 20:12-14*. And I saw the dead, small and great, stand before God: and the books were opened; and another book was opened, which is the book of life: and the dead were judged out of those things which were written in the books, according to their works. And the sea gave up the dead which were in it; and death and hell delivered up the dead which were in them: and they were judged every man according to their works. And death and hell were cast into the lake of fire. This is the second death.

that all are judged—but *not all at the same time*. The judgment of believers as sinners, is past being accomplished in Christ on the cross. "He that heareth my word, and believeth on Him that sent me, *hath* everlasting life, and shall not come into condemnation [Greek, *judgment*]; but is passed from death unto life" (John 5:24). (See also John 3:17-19 (R. V.), *judged* instead of *condemned*).[18]

There is a judgment day coming, not a day of 24 hours, but a long series of years. "Day" is used to designate such a period in 2 Corinthians 6:2; Ephesians 6:13, and Hebrews 3:8.[19] The "hour" in John 5:25 has been many centuries long. So "the hour" in John 5:28 may be centuries of years.

This "day of judgment"* is also called "The day of the LORD,"*** "The last day,"**** and "The great day."***** It is ushered in with plagues[20] and closes in fire,[21] between

---

* Matthew 10:15; 11:22; 11:24; 12:36; Mark 6:11; 2 Peter 2:9; 3:7; 1 John 4:17.

** Isaiah 2:12; 13:6, 9; 34:8; Lamentations 2:22; Ezekiel 13:5; Joel 1:15; 2:1; 3:14; Amos 5:18; Obadiah 15; Zephaniah 1:7, 8, 18; 2:2, 3; Zechariah 14:1; 1 Corinthians 5:5; 2 Corinthians 1:14; 1 Thessalonians 5:2; 2 Peter 3:10.

*** John 6:39, 40, 44, 54; 11:24; 2 Timothy 3:1.

**** Jeremiah 30:7; Hosea 1:11; Joel 2:11, 31; Zephaniah 1:14; Malachi 4:5; Acts 2:20; Jude 6; Revelation 6:17; 16:14.

---

18. *John 3:17-18*. For God sent not the Son into the world to judge the world; but that the world should be saved through him. He that believeth on him is not judged: he that believeth not hath been judged already, because he hath not believed on the name of the only begotten Son of God.

19. *2 Corinthians 6:2*. (For he saith, I have heard thee in a time accepted, and in the day of salvation have I succoured thee: behold, now is the accepted time; behold, now *is* the day of salvation.)

Ephesians 6:13. Wherefore take unto you the whole armour of God, that ye may be able to withstand in the evil day, and having done all, to stand.

Hebrews 3:8. Harden not your hearts, as in the provocation, in the day of temptation in the wilderness.

20. *2 Thessalonians 1:6-10*. Seeing it is a righteous thing with God to recompense tribulation to them that trouble you; and to you who are troubled rest with us, when the Lord Jesus shall be revealed from heaven with his mighty angels, in flaming fire taking vengeance on them that know not God, and that obey not the gospel of our Lord Jesus Christ: who shall be punished with everlasting destruction from the presence of the Lord, and from the glory of his power; when he shall come to be glorified in his saints, and to be admired in all them that believe (because our testimony among you was believed) in that day. See also *Revelation 19:11-21*.

21. *Revelation 20:10, 15*. And the devil that deceived them was cast into the

which lies a long season of the "sure mercies of David,"[22] or the Millennium.[23]

Four Judgments

In this day there will be four visible judgments, in the following order:

1. The judgment of the saints for their works[24]

This is not on the earth. (Compare 1 Thessalonians 4:13-18, with 2 Thessalonians 1:6-10; Revelation 19:11-16.) These glorified saints receive their judgment undeniably before that of the ungodly (see Matthew 25:14–30). The judgment of the servants occurs before the judgment of the nations (Matthew 25:31-46; see also 1 Peter 4:17-18).[25]

---

lake of fire and brimstone, where the beast and the false prophet are, and shall be tormented day and night for ever and ever. And whosoever was not found written in the book of life was cast into the lake of fire.

22. *Isaiah 55:3.* Incline your ear, and come unto me: hear, and your soul shall live; and I will make an everlasting covenant with you, even the sure mercies of David.

Acts 13:34. And as concerning that he raised him up from the dead, now no more to return to corruption, he said on this wise, I will give you the sure mercies of David.

23. *Revelation 20:4-6.* And I saw thrones, and they sat upon them, and judgment was given unto them: and I saw the souls of them that were beheaded for the witness of Jesus, and for the word of God, and which had not worshiped the beast, neither his image, neither had received his mark upon their foreheads, or in their hands: and they lived and reigned with Christ a thousand years. But the rest of the dead lived not again until the thousand years were finished. This is the first resurrection. Blessed and holy is he that hath part in the first resurrection: on such the second death hath no power, but they shall be priests of God and of Christ, and shall reign with him a thousand years.

24. *1 Corinthians 4:5.* Therefore judge nothing before the time, until the Lord come, who both will bring to light the hidden things of darkness, and will make manifest the counsels of the hearts: and then shall every man have praise of God.

1 Corinthians 3:13-15. Every man's work shall be made manifest: for the day shall declare it, because it shall be revealed by fire; and the fire shall try every man's work of what sort it is. If any man's work abide which he hath built thereupon, he shall receive a reward. If any man's work shall be burned, he shall suffer loss: but he himself shall be saved; yet so as by fire.

2 Corinthians 5:10. For we must all appear before the judgment seat of Christ; that every one may receive the things done in his body, according to that he hath done, whether it be good or bad. See also *Romans 14:10-12.*

25. *1 Peter 4:17.* For the time is come that judgment must begin at the house of God: and if it first begin at us, what shall the end be of them that obey not the gospel of God?

2. *The judgment of the living nations, who are upon the earth at the Revelation.*

Jesus is Judge of the *quick* (or *living*) and the *dead*.[26] The church, or saints, having been before caught up in the Rapture, come with Christ to execute judgment[27] upon the world, or living nations.[28] This is the judgment of those who are living on the earth when Christ comes at the Revelation. He separates the sheep from the goats, gathering out all things that offends (Matthew 13:41-42), and sets up His kingdom (v. 43). The third party—His brethren—are the Israelites,[29] who are never to be reckoned among the nations.[30]

Then follows the Millennium, which is one continuous day of judgment (Acts 17:31), when the righteous Judge will be on earth (2 Timothy 4:8), and when justice becomes the measuring line and righteousness the plumb line (Isaiah 28:17).

3. *The judgment of the dead at the Great White Throne.*[31]

---

26. *Acts 10:42.* And he commanded us to preach unto the people, and to testify that it is he which was ordained of God to be the Judge of quick and dead. See also *1 Timothy 4:1*; *1 Peter 4*:5.

27. *1 Corinthians 6:2.* Do ye not know that the saints shall judge the world? and if the world shall be judged by you, are ye unworthy to judge the smallest matters? See also *Jude 14-15*.

28. *Matthew 13:40-43.* As therefore the tares are gathered and burned in the fire; so shall it be in the end of this world. The Son of man shall send forth his angels, and they shall gather out of his kingdom all things that offend, and them which do iniquity; and shall cast them into a furnace of fire: there shall be wailing and gnashing of teeth. Then shall the righteous shine forth as the sun in the kingdom of their Father. Who hath ears to hear, let him hear.

29. *Psalm 122:8.* For my brethren and companions' sakes, I will now say, Peace be within thee.

30. *Numbers 23:7-9.* And he took up his parable and said, Balak the king of Moab hath brought me from Aram, out of the mountains of the east, saying, Come, curse me Jacob, and come, defy Israel. How shall I curse, whom God hath not cursed? or how shall I defy, whom the LORD hath not defied? For from the top of the rocks I see him, and from the hills I behold him: lo, the people shall dwell alone, and shall not be reckoned among the nations.

31. *Revelation 20:12-15.* And I saw the dead, small and great, stand before God: and the books were opened; and another book was opened, which is the book of life: and the dead were judged out of those things which were written in the books, according to their works. And the sea gave up the dead which were in it; and death and hell delivered up the dead which were in them: and they were judged every man according to their works. And death and hell were cast into the lake of fire. This is the second death. And whosoever was not found written in the book of life was cast into the lake of fire.

4. The judgment of angels,[32] into fire "prepared for the devil and his angels."

The ungodly go there first (compare Revelation 19:20 with Revelation 20:7-10; 2 Peter 2:4; Jude 6).[33] Such events requiring intervals of time preclude the idea expressed in the term "general judgment."

The "Day of the Lord" has two aspects: judgment on God's enemies, and deliverance and blessing on God's people.[34]

So we have the judgment:

* of believers, as to their character, on the Cross.
* of believers, as to their works, at the judgment seat of Christ.
* of the living nations at the Revelation.
* of the ungodly at the Great White Throne.

---

2 Peter 2:9. The Lord knoweth how to deliver the godly out of temptation, and to reserve the unjust unto the day of judgment to be punished. See also *Matthew 10:15; 11:21-24; 12:41-42; Romans 2:15-16*.

32. *2 Peter 2:4*. For if God spared not the angels that sinned, but cast them down to hell, and delivered them into chains of darkness, to be reserved unto judgment.

Jude 6. And the angels which kept not their first estate, but left their own habitation, he hath reserved in everlasting chains under darkness unto the judgment of the great day. See also *1 Corinthians 6:3; Revelation 20:10*.

33. *Revelation 19:20*. And the beast was taken, and with him the false prophet that wrought miracles before them that had received the mark of the beast, and them that worshiped his image. These both were cast alive into a lake of fire burning with brimstone.

Revelation 20:7-10. And when the thousand years are expired, Satan shall be loosed out of his prison, and shall go out to deceive the nations which are in the four quarters of the earth, Gog and Magog, to gather them together to battle: the number of whom is as the sand of the sea. And they went up on the breadth of the earth, and compassed the camp of the saints about, and the beloved city: and fire came down from God out of heaven, and devoured them. And the devil that deceived them was cast into the lake of fire and brimstone, where the beast and the false prophet are, and shall be tormented day and night for ever and ever. See also *2 Peter 2:4; Jude 6*.

34. *Isaiah 2:2-3, 17*. And it shall come to pass in the last days, that the mountains of the Lord's house shall be established in the top of the mountains, and shall be exalted above the hills; and all nations shall flow unto it. And many people shall go and say, Come ye, and let us go up to the mountain of the Lord, to the house of the God of Jacob; and we will walk in his paths: for out of Zion shall go forth the law, and the word of the Lord from Jerusalem. And the loftiness of man shall be bowed down, and the haughtiness of men shall be made low: and the Lord alone shall be exalted in that day. See also *Isaiah 4:1-6; Joel 2:21-27, 31; 3:12-17; Daniel 7:9-14; Zechariah 14:1-21; Zephaniah 3:8-9; Malachi 4:1-3*.

12

THE ANTICHRIST

The name *Antichrist* introduces to us one of the most solemn and foreboding subjects in the Word of God. An antichrist—one absolutely opposed to Jesus Christ—we are told, will come.[1] The spirit of antichrist is already in the world, denying the coming of Jesus Christ in the flesh, either in the past[2] or in the future.[3]

This spirit of antichrist, now possessed by many, will culminate in one person, *Antichrist,* who will deny both the Father and the Son.[4] That he is a single individual is clearly taught in 2 Thessalonians 2, where he is called "the man of sin," "the son of perdition, that Wicked," or properly, "the lawless one."

As Christ is the express image of God,[5] so it appears that Antichrist is the culminating manifestation of Satan, "the prince of this world."[6] His coming is "after the working [energy, or inward working] of Satan, with all power and

---

1. *1 John 2:18.* Little children, it is the last time: and as ye have heard that antichrist shall come, even now are there many antichrists; whereby we know that it is the last time.

2. *1 John 4:3.* And every spirit that confesseth not that Jesus Christ is come in the flesh is not of God: and this is that spirit of antichrist, whereof ye have heard that it should come; and even now already is it in the world.

3. *2 John 7.* For many deceivers are entered into the world, who confess not that Jesus Christ is come in the flesh. This is a deceiver and an antichrist.

4. *1 John 2:22.* Who is a liar but he that denieth that Jesus is the Christ? He is antichrist, that denieth the Father and the Son.

5. *Hebrews 1:3.* Who being the brightness of his glory, and the express image of his person, and upholding all things by the word of his power, when he had by himself purged our sins, sat down on the right hand of the Majesty on high.

6. *John 14:30.* Hereafter I will not talk much with you: for the prince of this world cometh, and hath nothing in me.

signs and lying wonders and deceivableness of unrighteousness." He will be a "strong [or inward working] delusion," to those who do not believe the truth.[7]

This mystery of lawlessness (so the Greek) already was at work in the days of the apostle, but there has been a hindering power. This is the Holy Spirit in His present manifestation, or office as the reprover of the world and gatherer of the church. When He, the restraining one, is taken out of the way (or out of the midst), at the rapture of the church, then the mystery will be unveiled, and the lawless one be revealed (2 Thessalonians 2:7, 8).

Antichrist will be received, even by the Jews,[8] who, having returned to their own land and rebuilt their temple, will make a treaty with him, called by the prophet "a covenant with death and an agreement with hell."[9] And Antichrist will exalt himself "above all that is called God, or that is worshiped; so that he as God sitteth in the temple of God [the rebuilt temple at Jerusalem] and

---

7. *2 Thessalonians 2:3-12.* Let no man deceive you by any means: for that day shall not come, except there come a falling away first, and that man of sin be revealed, the son of perdition; who opposeth and exalteth himself above all that is called God, or that is worshiped; so that he as God sitteth in the temple of God, showing himself that he is God. And now ye know what withholdeth that he might be revealed in his time. For the mystery of iniquity doth already work: only he who now letteth will let, until he be taken out of the way. And then shall be revealed the lawless one, whom the Lord Jesus shall slay with the breath of his mouth, and bring to nought by the manifestation of his coming; even him, whose coming is after the working of Satan with all power and signs and lying wonders. And with all deceivableness of unrighteousness in them that perish; because they received not the love of the truth, that they might be saved. And for this cause God shall send them strong delusion, that they should believe a lie: that they all might be damned who believed not the truth, but had pleasure in unrighteousness.

8. *John 5:43.* I am come in my Father's name, and ye receive me not: if another shall come in his own name, him ye will receive.

9. *Isaiah 28:14-18.* Wherefore hear the word of the LORD, ye scornful men, that rule this people which is in Jerusalem. Because ye have said, We have made a covenant with death, and with hell are we at agreement; when the overflowing scourge shall pass through, it shall not come unto us: for we have made lies our refuge, and under falsehood have we hid ourselves. Therefore thus saith the LORD God, Behold, I lay in Zion for a foundation a stone, a tried stone, a precious corner stone, a sure foundation: he that believeth shall not make haste. Judgment also will I lay to the line, and righteousness to the plummet: and the hail shall sweep away the refuge of lies, and the waters shall overflow the hiding place. And your covenant with death shall be disannulled, and your agreement with hell shall not stand; when the overflowing scourged shall pass through, then ye shall be trodden down by it.

showeth himself that he is God" (2 Thessalonians 2:4). No doubt he is the king described in Daniel 11:36,[10] who will do according to his own will and magnify himself above every god. Again, he is seen as the beast described in Revelation 13:11-18[11] whose number is the number of a man, 666. He performs great wonders and deceives those who live on the earth by means of his miracles, and has the power to kill those who will not worship the image of the beast. And again he is seen in Lucifer, or the day star, of Isaiah 14,[12] of whom the king of Babylon was a type. He weakens the nations, exalts his "throne above the stars of God," and sits "upon the mount of the congregation."

Such, in brief, is the awful picture Scripture gives us of this great opponent of Christ. Many think that he has already been manifested in Antiochus Epiphanes, or the popes of Rome, or Mohammed and his successors—all of

---

10. *Daniel 11:36*. And the king shall do according to his will; and he shall exalt himself, and magnify himself above every god, and shall speak marvellous things against the God of gods, and shall prosper till the indignation be accomplished: for that that is determined shall be done.

11. *Revelation 13:11-18*. And I beheld another beast coming up out of the earth; and he had two horns like a lamb, and he spake as a dragon. And he exerciseth all the power of the first beast before him, and causeth the earth and them which dwell therein to worship the first beast, whose deadly wound was healed. And he doeth great wonders, so that he maketh fire come down from heaven on the earth in the sight of men, and deceiveth them that dwell on the earth by the means of those miracles which he had power to do in the sight of the beast; saying to them that dwell on the earth, that they should make an image to the beast, which had the wound by a sword, and did live. And he had power to give life unto the image of the beast, that the image of the beast should both speak, and cause that as many as would not worship the image of the beast should be killed. And he causeth all, both small and great, rich and poor, free and bond, to receive a mark in their right hand, or in their foreheads: and that no man might buy or sell, save he that had the mark, or the name of the beast, or the number of his name. Here is wisdom. Let him that hath understanding count the number of the beast: for it is the number of a man; and his number is Six hundred three-score and six.

12. *Isaiah 14:12-16*. How are thou fallen from heaven, O Lucifer, son of the morning! how art thou cut down to the ground, which didst weaken the nations! For thou hast said in thine heart, I will ascend into heaven, I will exalt my throne above the stars of God: I will sit also upon the mount of the congregation, in the sides of the north: I will ascend above the heights of the clouds; I will be like the Most High. Yet thou shalt be brought down to hell, to the sides of the pit. They that see thee shall narrowly look upon thee, and consider thee, saying, Is this the man that made the earth to tremble, that did shake kingdoms?

which we regard as erroneous. The popes have received
their exaltation and power, as the pretended vicars of
Christ, and not as His opponent. It is a great mistake,
therefore, to call them the Antichrist, or the opposing
one. Antiochus was doubtless a type of antichrist. And in
his opposition to the worship of God, in his sacrifice of
the hated swine in the temple and his merciless treatment
of the Jews, he has given us a miniature picture of what
the final Antichrist will do. But he passed away long
before Paul and John wrote of the Antichrist to come.
Likewise Mohammed may be in some sense a type, but
that is all.

No, Antichrist is still in the future, and he will not be
manifested until the true church has been taken away at
the Rapture, as described in 1 Thessalonians 4.[13] For
Paul says,[14] "We beseech you, brethren, by the coming of
our Lord Jesus Christ, and our gathering together unto
Him,"—this is by the very fact of the Rapture, of which
he had previously written them.[13] This must first occur
before the apostasy comes in fullness, and the man of
sin is revealed. This is confirmed by verse 7 of 2
Thessalonians 2.

The Holy Spirit, while he is gathering the bride,[15]
reproves the world of sin, righteousness and judgment.[16]

---

13. *1 Thessalonians 4:16-18.* For the Lord himself shall descend from heaven
with a shout, with the voice of the archangel, and with the trump of God: and
the dead in Christ shall rise first: then we which are alive and remain shall be
caught up together with them in the clouds, to meet the Lord in the air; and so
shall we ever be with the Lord. Wherefore comfort one another with these
words.

14. *2 Thessalonians 2:1, 2, 7.* Now we beseech you, brethren, by the coming of
our Lord Jesus Christ, and by our gathering together unto him. That we be
not soon shaken in mind, or be troubled, neither by spirit, nor by word, nor by
letter as from us, as that the day of Christ is at hand. For the mystery of
lawlessness doth already work: only there is one that restraineth now, until
he be taken out of the way.

15. *1 Corinthians 12:12-13.* For as the body is one, and hath many members,
and all the members of that one body, being many, are one body: so also is
Christ. For by one Spirit are we all baptized into one body, whether we be
Jews or Gentiles, whether we be bond or free; and have been all made to drink
into one Spirit.

Ephesians 4:30. And grieve not the Holy Spirit of God, whereby ye are
sealed unto the day of redemption.

16. *John 16:8.* And when he is come, he will reprove the world of sin, and of
righteousness, and of judgment.

When He is taken out of the way, He will catch up the bride to meet the Lord in the air, leaving the apostate church, adulterous Israel and the ungodly world to believe a lie,[17] and then the lawless one will be revealed. Praise God that the church is to be kept from this awful hour of temptation![18] She will be with her Lord,[19] while the world is ruled by Antichrist.

But, though Antichrist greatly exalts himself and rules over the world with such power, yet he will come to his end, and no one will help him.[20] The Lord will destroy him "with the brightness of His coming;" literally, "He will paralyze [him] with the forthshining of His arrival"[21] (see Rotherham's translation*), when He comes with His saints to execute judgment on the ungodly.[22]

Yes, Antichrist will "be brought down to hell [sheol], to the sides of the pit." Those who see him stare at him and consider him, saying, "Is *this* the man that made the earth to tremble, that did shake kingdoms; that made

---

* Joseph B. Rotherham, *The Emphasized Bible* (Kregel Publications), p. 212.

17. *2 Thessalonians 2:11*. And for this cause God shall send them strong delusion, that they should believe a lie.

18. *Luke 21:36*. Watch ye therefore, and pray always, that ye may be accounted worthy to escape all these things that shall come to pass, and to stand before the Son of man.

Revelation 3:10. Because thou hast kept the word of my patience, I also will keep thee from the hour of temptation, which shall come upon all the world, to try them that dwell upon the earth.

19. *1 Thessalonians 4:17-18*. Then we which are alive and remain shall be caught up together with them in the clouds, to meet the Lord in the air; and so shall we ever be with the Lord. Wherefore comfort one another with these words.

1 Thessalonians 5:9-10. For God hath not appointed us to wrath, but to obtain salvation by our Lord Jesus Christ, who died for us, that, whether we wake or sleep, we should live together with him.

20. *Daniel 11:45*. And he shall plant the tabernacles of his palace between the seas in the glorious holy mountain; yet he shall come to his end, and none shall help him.

21. *2 Thessalonians 2:8*. And then shall be revealed the lawless one, whom the Lord Jesus shall slay with the breath of his mouth, and bring to nought by the manifestation of his coming.

22. *Jude 14-15*. And to these also Enoch, the seventh from Adam, prophesied, saying, Behold, the Lord came with ten thousand of his holy ones, to execute judgment upon all, and to convict all the ungodly of all their works of ungodliness which they have ungodly wrought, and of all the hard things which ungodly sinners have spoken against him.

the world as a wilderness and destroyed the cities thereof?" (Isaiah 14:15-17).

I would call special attention to the fact that Antichrist denies the Father and the Son,[23] and that the Greek words in 2 Thessalonians 2:7-8 should be rendered "the mystery of lawlessness"—"the lawless one." This, I think, gives an alarming significance to the atheistic and lawless trio of socialism, nihilism and anarchy, so rapidly spreading in our day, and which seeks to wipe out all law relating to marriage, property, etc.

It may be that these are the immediate precursors of Antichrist. At any rate, he is surely coming, and sad indeed is the thought of a godless world, rushing on to such a culmination of evil.

---

23. *1 John 2:22*. Who is a liar but he that denieth Jesus is the Christ? He is antichrist, that denieth the Father and the Son.

13

THE PRINCIPAL EVENT

I believe that the preceeding outline of the order of events will commend itself to every careful student of the Word. However, I persistently urge but *ONE POINT,* and that is the *premillennial coming of Christ* and *rapture of the saints.* This I believe to be the great hope for the church, and the principle event for which believers wait.[1]

Much has been revealed in regard to the Tribulation, the kingdom, etc., which follow the Rapture; but it is, as it were, only an outline. And let us not be discouraged if we cannot fully understand it. Do not forget that THE KING is coming. And when He comes it will be time to make known, in detail, the manner of the kingdom.[2]

Postmillennial Questionings

Postmillennialists apparently forget this altogether, and because they can't fully understand those things in regard to the Lord's coming which we now see through a glass dimly, they reject what is plainly revealed. If, even in the present dispensation, we can't explain the doctrines of "free will" and "God's sovereignty," to our mutual

---

1. *1 Thessalonians 1:9-10.* For they themselves show of us what manner of entering in we had unto you, and how ye turned to God from idols to serve the living and true God; and to wait for his Son from heaven, whom he raised from the dead, even Jesus, which delivered us from the wrath to come.

2. *1 Samuel 10:24-25.* And Samuel said to all the people, See ye him whom the LORD hath chosen, that there is none like him among all the people? And all the people shouted, and said, God save the king. Then Samuel told the people the manner of the kingdom, and wrote it in a book, and laid it up before the LORD. And Samuel sent all the people away, every man to his house.

understanding, how much less can we comprehend the glory which will be revealed in us in the coming kingdom. Let us not be disturbed, then, by the questions which they ask, such as:

- How will men be saved during the Millennium?
- What will be the means of grace?
- What can take the place of the preaching of the gospel? and of the sacraments of the church?

The Jews could not have answered similar questions before the first coming of Christ. It was not revealed until He came.

Jesus is coming *again*, and it is just as consistent that we will receive an addition to the revealed Word of God when He comes, as it was when He came before. Christ will speak again, who spoke as no other man before.[3] Even the dead will hear His voice,[4] and the gracious words which will come out of His mouth[5] will be a continual revelation.[6] It will all be clear when Jesus comes, for we will be like Him and see Him as He is,[7] eye to eye,[8] face to face.[9]

Postmillennialists seem to think that all must be accomplished under the church, and with present instrumentalities. Premillennialists look for the main accomplishment under Christ Himself, who will cut short

---

3. *John 7:46.* The officers answered, Never man spake like this man.

4. *John 5:28.* Marvel not at this: for the hour is coming, in the which all that are in the graves shall hear his voice.

5. *Luke 4:22.* And all bare him witness, and wondered at the gracious words which proceeded out of his mouth. And they said, Is not this Joseph's son?

6. *Matthew 11:27.* All things are delivered unto me of my Father: and no man knoweth the Son, but the Father; neither knoweth any man the Father, save the Son, and he to whomsoever the Son will reveal him.

7. *1 John 3:2.* Beloved, now are we the sons of God, and it doth not yet appear what we shall be: but we know that, when he shall appear, we shall be like him; for we shall see him as he is.

8. *Isaiah 52:8.* Thy watchmen shall lift up the voice; with the voice together shall they sing: for they shall see eye to eye, when the Lord shall bring again Zion.

9. *1 Corinthians 13:12.* For now we see through a glass, darkly; but then face to face: now I know in part; but then shall I know even as also I am known.

the work in righteousness,[10] and with different instrumentalities.[11]

Postmillennialism exalts the church. Premillennialism exalts Jesus and fills the heart of the believer with a *living, personal, coming* Savior.

Postmillennialists, though *acknowledging* that the second coming of Christ is the very *pole star* of the church, have little heart in it, and are disposed to say very little about it. This is natural and perfectly consistent for those who believe the event is at least a thousand years away. They very seldom preach or talk about it.

Preach the Word

What a contrast to Paul, who charged Timothy to "proclaim the word" (2 Timothy 4:2);* and, when writing to Titus of the blessed hope and glorious appearing of Jesus, he said: "These things speak" (2:15).

And again, when writing to the Thessalonians of the descent of the Lord and the rapture of the church, he said: "Wherefore comfort [or exhort] one another with these words" (4:18; see also 2 Timothy 3:16; Hebrews 10:25; 2 Peter 1:19).[12]

I ask my postmillennial brethren, Why do you not give the church these comforting words—this "meat in due

---

* "I adjure [thee] before God and Christ Jesus—Who is about to be judging living and dead,—both as to his forthshining and his kingdom Proclaim the word." Joseph Bryant Rotherham, *The Emphasized Bible* (Grand Rapids: Kregel Publications), p. 219.

---

10. *Romans 9:28.* For he will finish the work, and cut it short in righteousness: because a short work will the Lord make upon the earth.

11. *Isaiah 4:4.* When the LORD shall have washed away the filth of the daughters of Zion, and shall have purged the blood of Jerusalem from the midst thereof by the spirit of judgment, and by the spirit of burning. See also *Zechariah 14*.

12. *2 Timothy 3:16.* All Scripture is given by inspiration of God, and is profitable for doctrine, for reproof, for correction, for instruction in righteousness.

Hebrews 10:25. Not forsaking the assembling of ourselves together, as the manner of some is; but exhorting one another: and so much the more, as ye see the day approaching.

2 Peter 1:19. We have also a more sure word of prophecy; whereunto ye do well that ye take heed, as unto a light that shineth in a dark place, until the day dawn, and the daystar arise in your hearts.

season?" "Blessed is that servant whom His Lord when He cometh shall find so doing" (Luke 12:43). Brethren, postmillennialism is hiding this *star of hope* from the church, and incurring thereby a responsibility that God alone can estimate. The church is languishing because of this neglected truth.

Solemn Warning

We beg of you to heed the following solemn words from Dr. Hugh McNeill: "My reverend brethren, watch, preach the coming of Jesus. I charge you, in the name of our common Master,—PREACH THE COMING OF JESUS; solemnly and affectionately, in the name of God, I charge you,—PREACH THE COMING OF JESUS. WATCH ye, therefore, lest, coming suddenly, He find the porter sleeping."

Premillennialism has a vital life in it, and gives the disciple a real love and desire for the Word of God, which opens up to him like a new book. Even Dr. Brown recognizes this, and he says: "Premillennialists have done the church a real service by calling attention to the place which the second advent holds in the Word of God and the scheme of divine truth."*

I have heard many say, "Why, the Bible is another book to me since I accepted this truth." And though one is almost lost in the unfolding majesty and infinity of God's plans revealed therein, yet we find it such a storehouse of truth and comfort that continual study always produces richer food.

It is the *most practical doctrine* in the Christian faith, for "every man that hath this hope in Him [Christ] purifieth himself even as He [Christ] is pure" (1 John 3:3). And do we not want *practical holiness*? Again, this doctrine when received into the heart is a mighty power to separate one from the love of the world. And were it thoroughly believed and preached in the church, she would readily give of her substance so liberally that we would not be begging for money to sustain our missions.

---

* David Brown, *The Second Advent*, page 13.

It was this doctrine that inspired the sainted Philip Bliss, and gave his songs such favor. How all of us love to sing "When Jesus Comes," or "Hold the Fort for I Am Coming." The church and the people want this truth, and God wants them to have it, I am assured, by the manifest interest and attention with which He blesses its presentation.

14

SOME OBJECTIONS CONSIDERED

No. 1 **It Discourages Missions**

It is objected that the doctrine of the premillennial coming of Christ discourages missions. This is not true. The missionary spirit among the evangelists of today is a sufficient answer to this. And let us name, among the missionaries who held this faith, Ben Ezra, Joseph Wolf, James McGregor Bertram, L.D. Mansfield, Gonsalves, Dr. Kelley and Hewitson.

"This was the hope that inspired Reginald Heber, the great missionary bishop of the English Church, who gave us that glorious missionary hymn, 'From Greenland's Icy Mountains,' and who spent his strength and rested from his labors 'on India's coral strand!'

"This was the hope that energized Karl F. A. Gutzlaff, the opener of China, and Bettleheim, the opener of Japan; that inspired the noble Alexander Duff, who, under its influence, woke moderate Scotland from its lethargy, and was the pioneer of his indomitable race in India. This was the hope that inspired and cheered and everjoyed Robert McCheyne and our own Poor, and Lowrie, and Rankin, and Lowenthal, and a host of others."

Mr. Lord affirms that among missionaries of all denominations, there is as great proportion of premillennialists, as there is among the ministry at home. They earnestly labor, as did the apostle, to save some from the wrath to come.[1]

No. 2 It Discourages Work

It is objected that it discourages work. This is very inconsistent and untrue, for the very essence of the doctrine is to WATCH, WORK and WAIT, and to work *now* for the night comes when no one can work.[2]

No. 3 So Many Unsaved Friends

Some object that they have so many unsaved friends, they cannot wish Jesus to come. Work then, for we read "all that my Father giveth me shall come to me" (John 6:37-39), and whosoever will may come.[3] Knowing the terror (fear) of the Lord, let us persuade men (2 Corinthians 5:11).

The Antedeluvians would not heed the preaching of Noah, and even Lot's relatives (his sons-in-law) would not go with him out of Sodom. So there will be those who will not accept Christ. But of all who believe in Him[4] not one will be lost.[5] The Israelites were often led to

---

1. *Romans 11:14.* If by any means I may provoke to emulation them which are my flesh, and might save some of them.

1 Corinthians 9:22. To the weak became I as weak, that I might gain the weak: I am made all things to all men, that I might by all means save some.

1 Thessalonians 1:9-10. For they themselves show of us what manner of entering in we had unto you, and how ye turned to God from idols to serve the living and true God; and to wait for his son from heaven, whom he raised from the dead, even Jesus, which delivered us from the wrath to come.

James 5:20. Let him know, that he which converteth the sinner from the error of his ways shall save a soul from dead, and shall hide a multitude of sins.

2. *John 9:4.* I must work the works of him that sent me, while it is day: the night cometh, when no man can work. See also page 145.

3. *Revelation 22:17.* And the Spirit and the bride say, Come. And let him that heareth say, Come. And let him that is athirst come. And whosoever will, let him take the water of life freely.

4. *John 1:12.* But as many as received him, to them gave he power to become the sons of god, even to them that believe on his name.

5. *John 10:27-28.* My sheep hear my voice, and I know them, and they follow me: and I give unto them eternal life; and they shall never perish, neither shall any man pluck them out of my hand.

Matthew 7:13. Enter ye in at the strait gate: for wide is the gate, and broad is the way, that leadeth to destruction, and many there be which go in thereat.

repentance, in the midst of adversity and calamity, and so if our friends will not be persuaded to accept Christ now, it is perhaps possible that they may do so under the visible judgments of God during the Tribulation.

But whether they will or not, let us remember, that the great mass of humanity is engulfed in the whirlpool of sin, which is sweeping its millions down to graves of destruction (Matthew 7:13). Compared to them the true believers are but a handful in number. In the Millennium all this will be changed, "for the earth shall be full of the knowledge of the Lord as the waters cover the sea" (Isaiah 11:9), and all men will bow to the righteous scepter of King Immanuel.[6]

We would not sacrifice the hundreds of lives on a passenger train to save the life of even a friend who willfully exposed himself to danger on the tracks; and are not all men our brothers? And will we not yearn to save them from the tide of spiritual death? Oh! then, let us cry with the Holy Spirit: "Even so come, Lord Jesus" (Revelation 22:20). For when Christ comes the work will be cut short in righteousness.[7]

No. 4 "My Kingdom Is Not of This World"

It is objected that Jesus said: "My kingdom is not of this world" (John 18:36). True! not of the spirit of the world (1 John 2:15-17), just as believers are not of the world (John 15:19). The correct rendering of the passage is, "My kingdom is not [εκ] *out of* this world." That is, it

---

6. *Isaiah 45:22-23*. Look unto me, and be ye saved, all the ends of the earth: for I am God, and there is none else. I have sworn by myself, the word is gone out of my mouth in righteousness, and shall not return, that unto me every knee shall bow, every tongue shall swear.

Philippians 2:10-11. That at the name of Jesus every knee should bow, of things in heaven, and things in earth, and things under the earth; and that every tongue should confess that Jesus Christ is Lord, to the glory of God the Father.

Luke 1:32-33. He shall be great, and shall be called the Son of the Highest; and the Lord God shall give unto him the throne of his father David: and he shall reign over the house of Jacob for ever; and of his kingdom there shall be no end. See also *Romans 14:11*; *Micah 4:1-7*.

7. *Romans 9:28*. For he will finish the work, and cut it short in righteousness: because a short work will the Lord make upon the earth.

does not emanate from this world. He is not (εκ) out of this world.[8] Both Christ and His kingdom are from above.[9] But it will be set up on this earth, in accordance with the prayer which He taught us: "Thy kingdom come. Thy will be done, as in heaven, so in earth" (Luke 11:2).[10] Earthly kingdoms are corrupted by the deception of Satan. But in the millennial kingdom he will not deceive them, for he will be bound.[11]

There is nothing essentially sinful in matter. Adam was sinless before his fall and he had a material body. Christ has a material body and is without sin. The earth was cursed because of sin and the spirit of the world clings to sin.[12] But when the curse is removed,[13] all things that offend are gathered out of the kingdom,[14] then will

---

8. *John 8:23*. And he said unto them, Ye are from beneath; I am from above: ye are of this world; I am not of this world.

9. *Colossians 3:1-4*. If ye then be risen with Christ, seek those things which are above, where Christ sitteth on the right hand of God. Set your affection on things above, not on things on the earth. For ye are dead, and your life is hid with Christ in God. When Christ, who is our life, shall appear, then shall ye also appear with him in glory.

Galatians 4:26. But Jerusalem which is above is free, which is the mother of us all.

10. *Daniel 2:44*. And in the days of these kings shall the God of heaven set up a kingdom, which shall never be destroyed: and the kingdom shall not be left to other people, but it shall break in pieces and consume all these kingdoms, and it shall stand for ever.

Daniel 7:18. But the saints of the Most High shall take the kingdom, and possess the kingdom for ever, even for ever and ever.

Jeremiah 23:5-6. Behold, the days come, saith the LORD, that I will raise unto David a righteous Branch, and a King shall reign and prosper, and shall execute judgment and justice in the earth. In his days Judah shall be saved, and Israel shall dwell safely: and this is his name whereby he shall be called, THE LORD OUR RIGHTEOUSNESS.

11. *Revelation 20:1-3*. And I saw an angel come down from heaven, having the key of the bottomless pit and a great chain in his hand. And he laid hold on the dragon, that old serpent, which is the Devil, and Satan, and bound him a thousand years, and cast him into the bottomless pit, and shut him up, and set a seal upon him, that he should deceive the nations no more, till the thousand years should be fulfilled: and after that he must be loosed a little season.

12. *Romans 1:32*. Who, knowing the judgment of God, that they which commit such things are worthy of death, not only do the same, but have pleasure in them that do them.

13. *Revelation 22:3*. And there shall be no more curse: but the throne of God and of the Lamb shall be in it; and his servants shall serve him.

14. *Matthew 13:41*. The Son of man shall send forth his angels, and they shall gather out of his kingdom all things that offend, and them which do iniquity.

all creation will have that for which it groans,[15] and the righteous will shine forth as the sun in the kingdom of their Father.[16]

No. 5 "The Kingdom of God Is Within You"

It is objected, that the kingdom of God is not material and visible, but that it is spiritual and invisible. In support of this the following words of Jesus in Luke 17:20-21 are cited: "When He was demanded of the Pharisees, when the kingdom of God should come, He answered them and said: The kingdom of God cometh not with observation; neither shall they say, lo, here! or lo, there! for behold, the kingdom of God is within you."

"Observation" should be translated "careful watching" (see Dr. Adam Clarke), or "narrow watching" (see Rotherham). The marginal, and better reading for "within you" is "among you" (see Rotherham, Wilson, Prof. Whitting, and others). He did not say that the kingdom of God was within, or in the hearts of those wicked Pharisees, but that it was among them, that is, within the Jewish nation. As Bengel states it, "within is here used, not in any respect of the heart of individual Pharisees, . . . but in respect to the whole Jewish people. The King, Messiah, and therefore the kingdom is here: ye see and ye hear."*

The sense, then, is as follows: The kingdom of God does not come with "careful watching;" that is, not in

---

* John Bengel, *Bengel's New Testament Commentary* (Grand Rapids: Kregel Publications). Vol. 1, p. 490.

---

15. *Romans 8:19-23.* For the earnest expectation of the creature waiteth for the manifestation of the sons of God. For the creature was made subject to vanity, not willingly, but by reason of him who hath subjected the same in hope; because the creature itself also shall be delivered from the bondage of corruption into the glorious liberty of the children of God. For we know that the whole creation groaneth and travaileth in pain together until now. And not only they, but ourselves also, which have the firstfruits of the Spirit, even we ourselves groan within ourselves, waiting the adoption, to wit, the redemption of our body.

16. *Matthew 13:42-43.* And shall cast them into a furnace of fire: there shall be wailing and gnashing of teeth. Then shall the righteous shine forth as the sun in the kingdom of their Father. Who hath ears to hear, let him hear.

such a way as to be discerned only by sagacious critics. Neither is it to be seen only by those who are scrupulously watching for it. They will not say, "Look here or there," for the kingdom of God is among you; that is, it was then visibly present among them in the person of Jesus the King. And so it will be visibly present when He comes again.[17]

It did not, and will not, need scrupulous watching to discern it. Had they received Him with faith, instead of slyly watching Him with deceitful spies,[18] they might have realized that their King was then visibly present, and ready to usher in the universal manifestation of the kingdom, which had been seen by the favored disciples of the Mount.[19] How gladly He would have then fully manifested Himself as King, and established His kingdom among them, is shown by His words of tender yearning in Matthew 23:37-39:

> "O Jerusalem, Jerusalem, thou that killest the prophets, and stonest them which are sent unto thee, how often would I have gathered thy children together, even as a hen gathereth her chickens under her wings, and ye would not! Behold, your house is left unto you desolate. For I say unto you, Ye shall not see me henceforth, till ye shall say, Blessed is He that cometh in the name of the Lord."

He came in His Father's name; but the Israelites to whom He spoke would not receive Him.[20] "He came unto

---

17. *Revelation 6:16–17*. And said to the mountains and rocks, Fall on us, and hide us from the face of him that sitteth on the throne, and from the wrath of the lamb. For the great day of his wrath is come; and who shall be able to stand?

18. *Luke 20:20*. And they watched him, and sent forth spies, which should feign themselves just men, that they might take hold of his words, that so they might deliver him unto the power and authority of the governor.

19. *Matthew 17:9*. And as they came down from the mountain, Jesus charged them, saying, Tell the vision to no man, until the Son of man be risen again from the dead.

2 Peter 1:16-18. For we have not followed cunningly devised fables, when we made known unto you the power and coming of our Lord Jesus Christ, but were eyewitnesses of his majesty. For he received from God the Father honor and glory, when there came such a voice to him from the excellent glory. This is my beloved Son, in whom I am well pleased. And this voice which came from heaven we heard, when we were with him in the holy mount.

20. *John 5:43*. I am come in my Father's name, and ye receive me not: if another shall come in his own name, him ye will receive.

His own and His own received Him not" (John 1:11).

Preferring a robber, they rejected and crucified their King and so the kingdom waits until they will accept Him,[21] when the kingdom of the world will become the kingdom of our Lord's and of His Christ's and He will reign for the *ages of ages* (see Greek).[22]

Oh! Blessed "KING OF KINGS!" *come*, and may *"Thy kingdom come."*

> The King there in His beauty,
> Without a veil is seen;
> It were a well-spent journey,
> Though sev'n deaths lay between.
> The Lamb, with His fair army,
> Doth on Mount Zion stand,
> And glory, glory dwelleth
> In Immanuel's land.

No. 6 "The Kingdom of God Is Not Meat and Drink"

It is objected that Paul said, "The kingdom of God is not meat and drink; but righteousness, and peace, and joy in the Holy Spirit" (Romans 14:17). Indeed it is not "meat and drink," or eating and drinking, or simply

---

21. *Zechariah 12:10.* And I will pour upon the house of David, and upon the inhabitants of Jerusalem, the spirit of grace and of supplications; and they shall look upon me whom they have pierced, and they shall mourn for him, as one mourneth for his only son, and shall be in bitterness for him, as one that is in bitterness for his firstborn.

Zechariah 13:6. And one shall say unto him, What are these wounds in thine hands? Then he shall answer, Those with which I was wounded in the house of my friends.

Matthew 23:39. For I say unto you, Ye shall not see me henceforth, till ye shall say, Blessed is he that cometh in the name of the Lord.

Romans 11:25-28. For I would not, brethren, that ye should be ignorant of this mystery, lest ye should be wise in your own conceits, that blindness in part is happened to Israel, until the fulness of the Gentiles be come in. And so all Israel shall be saved: as it is written, There shall come out of Sion the Deliverer, and shall turn away ungodliness from Jacob: for this is my covenant unto them, when I shall take away their sins. As concerning the gospel, they are enemies for your sakes: but as touching the election, they are beloved for the fathers' sakes.

22. *Revelation 11:15.* And the seventh angel sounded; and there followed great voices in heaven, and they said, The kingdom of the world is become the kingdom of our Lord, and of his Christ: and he shall reign for ever and ever [Greek: *unto the ages of the ages*].

outward observances. Neither was the kingdom of Israel meat and drink, nor the Roman Empire. But the subjects of each did eat and drink, and Paul simply taught that they should do so circumspectly and with charity. So will the subjects of the kingdom of God eat and drink. "Blessed is he that shall eat bread in the kingdom of God" (Luke 14:15). "Blessed are they which are called unto the marriage supper of the Lamb" (Revelation 19:9; see the Feast of Isaiah 25:6-8).[23]

Jesus himself said, "I will not drink henceforth of this fruit of the vine, until that day when I drink it new with you in my Father's kingdom" (Matthew 26:29). And again: "I appoint unto you a kingdom, as my Father hath appointed unto me; that ye may eat and drink at my table in my kingdom" (Luke 22:29-30). This is the strongest proof that the kingdom will be literal and material, though it will be freed from the curse of sin.[24]

No. 7 "Flesh and Blood"

It is objected that flesh and blood cannot inherit the kingdom of God.[25] Certainly we do not *inherit* it through the flesh—the unregenerate man. But through the Spirit we are born again,[26] recreated in Christ Jesus,[27] and made

---

23. *Isaiah 25:6-8*. And in this mountain shall the LORD of hosts make unto all people a feast of fat things, a feast of wines on the lees, of fat things full of marrow, of wines on the lees well refined. And he will destroy in this mountain the face of the covering cast over all people, and the veil that is spread over all nations. He will swallow up death in victory; and the LORD God will wipe away tears from off all faces; and the rebuke of his people shall he take away from off all the earth: for the LORD hath spoken it.

24. *Matthew 13:41-43*. The Son of man shall send forth his angels, and they shall gather out of his kingdom all things that offend, and them which do iniquity; and shall cast them into a furnace of fire: there shall be wailing and gnashing of teeth. Then shall the righteous shine forth as the sun in the kingdom of their Father. Who hath ears to hear, let him hear.

25. *1 Corinthians 15:50*. Now this I say, brethren, that flesh and blood cannot inherit the kingdom of God.

26. *John 3:3-5*. Jesus answered and said unto him, Verily, verily, I say unto thee, Except a man be born again, he cannot see the kingdom of God. Nicodemus saith unto him, How can a man be born when he is old? Can he enter the second time into his mother's womb, and be born? Jesus answered, Verily, verily, I saw unto thee, Except a man be born of water and of the Spirit, he cannot enter into the kingdom of God.

27. *Ephesians 2:10*. For we are his workmanship, created in Christ Jesus unto good works, which God hath before ordained that we should walk in them.

"joint heirs" with Him.[28] The flesh counts for nothing. The Spirit gives life.[29]

Paul in 1 Corinthians 15 is treating the subject of the resurrection which he proves to be so important that without it, we could not inherit, or become possessed of the kingdom of God. "Flesh and blood," he says, cannot inherit it, and therefore he shows that at the resurrection, our bodies of corruptible flesh and blood, which have died, will be raised in incorruption and immortality. And the bodies of those who are living at that time will be changed and "fashioned like unto His glorious body."[30] Now, in our flesh and blood, we bear the image of Adam, the first man, "which is of the earth, earthy." But at the resurrection we will be changed so as to "bear the image of the heavenly," "the second man," "the Lord from heaven."[31]

And He who raised up Christ from the dead, and who hath given us the Spirit of sonship hereby we become heirs of God and joint heirs with Christ, will, by His Spirit that dwells in us, also makes alive our mortal bodies.[32] Then, and then only, can we inherit,[33] or come

---

28. *Romans 8:15-17.* For ye have not received the spirit of bondage again to fear; but ye have received the Spirit of adoption, whereby we cry, Abba, Father. The Spirit itself beareth witness with our spirit, that we are the children of God: and if children, then heirs; heirs of God, and joint heirs with Christ; if so be that we suffer with him, that we may be also glorified together.

29. *John 6:63.* It is the Spirit that quickeneth; the flesh profiteth nothing: the words that I speak unto you, they are spirit, and they are life.

30. *Philippians 3:20-21.* For our conversation is in heaven; from whence also we look for the Savior, the Lord Jesus Christ: who shall change our vile body, that it may be fashioned like unto his glorious body, according to the working whereby he is able even to subdue all things unto himself.

31. *1 Corinthians 15:45-49.* And so it is written, The first man Adam was made a living soul; the last Adam was made a quickening spirit. Howbeit that was not first which is spiritual, but that which is natural; and afterward that which is spiritual. The first man is of the earth, earthy: the second man is the Lord from heaven. As is the earthy, such are they also that are earthy: and as is the heavenly, such are they also that are heavenly. And as we have borne the image of the earthy, we shall also bear the image of the heavenly.

32. *Romans 8:11.* But if the Spirit of him that raised up Jesus from the dead dwell in you, he that raiseth up Christ from the dead shall also quicken your mortal bodies by his Spirit that dwelleth in you.

33. *1 Corinthians 15:50.* Now this I say, brethren, that flesh and blood cannot inherit the kingdom of God; neither doth corruption inherit incorruption.

into possession of the kingdom[34] which God has promised to give to us.[35] Hence, we see the vital importance of the resurrection, without which we could not inherit the kingdom of God* (1 Corinthians 15:50).

The evident purpose of this objection is to support the assertion made by postmillenialists that the kingdom is only spiritual and that there is nothing literal or material in it. But Paul says nothing of the kind and his whole argument is entirely to the contrary. For he asserts that our σῶμα (sōma—body) which is sown in corruption, dishonor and weakness, will be raised in incorruption, glory and power; or if living, will be changed in the twinkling of an eye.[36] In these glorified bodies we shall inherit the kingdom prepared for us from the foundation of the world.[37] For Christ the rightful heir of all things[38] will be there and we will be there to reign with Him.[39]

---

* Here, let it be noticed, is another evidence that the kingdom is yet future.

---

34. *Daniel 7:22*. Until the Ancient of days come, and judgment was given to the saints of the Most High; and the time came that the saints possessed the kingdom.

35. *Luke 12:32*. Fear not, little flock; for it is your Father's good pleasure to give you the kingdom.

36. *1 Corinthians 15:42-45, 51-53*. So also is the resurrection of the dead. It is sown in corruption, it is raised in incorruption: it is sown in dishonor, it is raised in glory: it is sown in weakness, it is raised in power: it is sown a natural body, it is raised a spiritual body. There is a natural body, and there is a spiritual body. Behold, I show you a mystery; we shall not all sleep, but we shall all be changed, in a moment, in the twinkling of an eye, at the last trump: for the trumpet shall sound, and the dead shall be raised incorruptible, and we shall be changed. For this corruptible must put on incorruption, and this mortal must put on immortality.

37. *Matthew 25:34*. Then shall the King say unto them on his right hand, Come, ye blessed of my Father, inherit the kingdom prepared for you from the foundation of the world.

38. *Matthew 21:38*. But when the husbandmen saw the son, they said among themselves, This is the heir; come, let us kill him, and let us seize on his inheritance.
Hebrews 1:2. [God] hath at the end of these days spoken unto us in his Son, whom he appointed heir of all things, through whom also he made the worlds [Greek *ages*. Compare 1 Timothy 1:17]. See also *1 Timothy 6:15*.

39. *2 Timothy 2:12*. If we suffer, we shall also reign with him: if we deny him, he also will deny us. See also *Romans 8:17; John 17:24*.

Christ will have His glorified body, His body that was raised[40] and ascended[41] and entered into heaven.[42] It is His glorified body that Stephen saw there,[43] and which Paul saw (Acts 9:5), and also John (Revelation 1:13).

It is a body which bears the scars of the cross;[44] a Lamb as it had been slain. Yes, He will return in the flesh (Acts 1:11). The true reading of 2 John 7 is, "who confess not Jesus Christ coming* in the flesh" (see also Isaiah 63:1-6 and Revelation 19:11-16). And "we know that when He shall appear, we shall be like Him" (1 John 3:2). Therefore it is clear that we, in these same bodies which are changed into the image of Christ's glorious body, will inherit the kingdom of God.

No. 8 The Work of the Holy Spirit a Failure

It is objected that this doctrine disparages the work of the Holy Spirit. Not so! For what is the work of the Holy Spirit? He is gathering the bride. He teaches, guides, and comforts her[45] until she is presented to Christ.[46] At the

---

* Greek: ἐρχόμενον, *coming*; see page 202.

40. *Luke 24:39*. Behold my hands and my feet, that it is I myself: handle me, and see; for a spirit hath not flesh and bones as ye see me have.

41. *Acts 1:9*. And when he had spoken these things, while they beheld, he was taken up; and a cloud received him out of their sight.

42. *Hebrews 9:24*. For Christ is not entered into the holy places made with hands, which are the figures of the true; but into heaven itself, now to appear in the presence of God for us. See also *Hebrews 4:14*.

43. *Acts 7:55*. But he, being full of the Holy Spirit, looked up steadfastly into heaven, and saw the glory of God, and Jesus standing on the right hand of God.

44. *Revelation 5:6*. And I beheld, and, lo, in the midst of the throne and of the four beasts, and in the midst of the elders, stood a Lamb as it had been slain, having seven horns and seven eyes, which are the seven Spirits of God sent forth into all the earth.

45. *John 14:17, 26*. Even the Spirit of truth; whom the world cannot receive, because it seeth him not, neither knoweth him: but ye know him; for he dwelleth with you, and shall be in you. But the Comforter, which is the Holy Spirit, whom the Father will send in my name, he shall teach you all things, and bring all things to your remembrance, whatsoever I have said unto you.

John 16:13-15. Howbeit when he, the Spirit of truth, is come, he will guide you into all truth: for he shall not speak of himself; but whatsoever he shall hear, that shall he speak: and he will show you things to come. He shall glorify me: for he shall receive of mine, and shall show it unto you. All things that the Father hath are mine: therefore said I, that he shall take of mine, and shall show it unto you.

46. *Ephesians 5:25-27*. Husbands, love your wives, even as Christ also loved

same time the Holy Spirit reproves that world of sin, and of righteousness, and judgment (John 16:8).

The Holy Spirit may be grieved,[47] resisted,[48] and quenched[49] now, but He will not always strive with man.[50] His present work will be finished, and the King of kings and Lord of lords will come forth with the armies of heaven to subdue His enemies (Revelation 19) and finish the work.[51]

It was the Spirit of God, who "moved upon the face of the waters" in the beginning (Genesis 1:2), and we believe He had a part in all the work of creation (Genesis 1:26). He contended with sinners before the flood (Genesis 6:3). The Holy Spirit spoke by the prophets (Acts 1:16; 2 Peter 1:21). He was specially granted to Joseph and others (Genesis 41:38; Exodus 31:3; Numbers 11:17; 24:2; 27:18; 2 Kings 2:9, etc). In short, He has been engaged in all the work of creation and redemption. We do not believe that His work is a failure because of the flood, nor because the Jews have rejected Christ, and as natural branches have been broken off (Romans 11:20). Neither do we believe His work will be a failure, though the preaching of the

the church, and gave himself for it; that he might sanctify and cleanse it with the washing of water by the word. That he might present it to himself a glorious church, not having spot, or wrinkle, or any such thing; but that it should be holy and without blemish.

47. *Ephesians 4:30*. And grieve not the Holy Spirit of God, whereby ye are sealed unto the day of redemption.

48. *Acts 7:51*. Ye stiffnecked and uncircumcised in heart and ears, ye do always resist the Holy Spirit: as your fathers did, so do ye.

49. *1 Thessalonians 5:19*. Quench not the Spirit.

50. *Genesis 6:3*. And the LORD said, My Spirit shall not always strive with man, for that he also is flesh: yet his days shall be an hundred and twenty years.

51. *Revelation 19:11-16*. And I saw heaven opened, and behold a white horse; and he that sat upon him was called Faithful and True, and in righteousness he doth judge and make war. His eyes were as a flame of fire, and on his head he had a name written, that no man knew, but he himself. And he was clothed with a vesture dipped in blood: and his name is called The Word of God. And the armies which were in heaven followed him upon white horses, clothed in fine linen, white and clean. And out of his mouth goeth a sharp sword, that with it he should smite the nations, and he shall rule them with a rod of iron: and he treadeth the winepress of the fierceness and wrath of Almighty God. And he hath on his vesture and on his thigh a name written, KING OF KINGS, AND LORD OF LORDS.

Romans 9:28. For he will finish the work, and cut it short in righteousness: because a short work will the Lord make upon the earth.

gospel in the present dispensation will only result in the salvation of "some."[52] I feel sure that He will have a part in the glory and triumph of the millennial dispensation, for even the Israelites then will have a new Spirit within them.[53] And the nations are to be ruled in peace and righteousness by Him on whom the Spirit of the Lord does rest.[54]

Let us then have no fear of jealousy on the part of the Spirit, because of the triumphs of Christ. Rather let us understand that He desires to hasten the presentation of the bride—which is being sealed by Him (Ephesians 4:20) to her Lord—who has the Spirit without measure.[55] His purpose is that these both, united into one,[56] may be the one perfect man,[57] the holy temple,[58] built for the dwelling of God in Spirit.[59] And who can estimate what will be

52. *Luke 13:23-25*. Then said one unto him, Lord, are there few that be saved? And he said unto them, strive to enter in at the straight gate: for many, I say unto you, will seek to enter in, and shall not be able. When once the master of the house is risen up, and hath shut to the door, and ye begin to stand without, and to knock at the door, saying, Lord, Lord, open unto us; and he shall answer and say unto you, I know you not whence ye are.

1 Corinthians 9:22. To the weak became I as weak, that I might gain the weak: I am made all things to all men, that I might by all means save some.

53. *Ezekiel 11:19*. And I will give them one heart, and I will put a new spirit within you; and I will take the stony heart out of their flesh, and will give them an heart of flesh.

54. *Isaiah 11:2-4*. And the Spirit of the LORD shall rest upon him, the spirit of wisdom and understanding, the spirit of counsel and might, the spirit of knowledge and of the fear of the LORD; and shall make him of quick understanding in the fear of the LORD: and he shall not judge after the sight of his eyes, neither reprove after the hearing of his ears: but with righteousness shall he judge the poor, and reprove with equity for the meek of the earth: and he shall smite the earth with the rod of his mouth, and with the breath of his lips shall he slay the wicked. See also *Isaiah 61:1-3*. See pages 57-58.

55. *John 3:34*. For he whom God hath sent speaketh the words of God: for God giveth not the Spirit by measure unto him.

56. *Ephesians 5:30-32*. Because we are members of his body. For this cause shall a man leave his father and mother, and shall cleave to his wife; and the two shall become one flesh. This mystery is great: but I speak in regard of Christ and of the church.

57. *Ephesians 4:13*. Till we all come in the unity of the faith, and of the knowledge of the Son of God, unto a perfect man, unto the measure of the stature of the fulness of Christ.

58. *1 Corinthians 3:16*. Know ye not that ye are the temple of God, and that the Spirit of God dwelleth in you? See also *6:19* and *2 Corinthians 6:16*.

59. *Ephesians 2:20-22*. Being built upon the foundation of the apostles and prophets, Christ Jesus himself being the chief corner stone; in whom each several building, fitly framed together, groweth into a holy temple in the Lord; in whom ye also are builded together for a habitation of God in the Spirit.

accomplished by the Spirit through this holy, living Temple, in which He will dwell. No wonder that He yearns to hasten its completion (see the type of His haste in Genesis 24:56).[60] But this completion will not take place until the Lord comes, when the Head will forever be untied to the body (1 Thessalonians 4:18). Therefore, in this we may realize, to some extent, the meaning of that yearning cry of the Spirit, *"Even so come, Lord Jesus"* (Revelation 22:20).

No. 9 The Gospel a Failure

It is said that the second coming of Christ makes the gospel a failure. But this is not so. Man is a failure. The gospel is the power of God unto salvation to every one who believes (Romans 1:16). It is not the incompetency of the gospel, but the willful unbelief of sinners that prevents the conversion of the world. Jesus said: "Him that cometh unto me I will in no wise cast out" (John 6:37). But He also said, "Ye will not come unto me that ye might have life" (John 5:40).

While we are to preach the gospel everywhere, we are not to expect that all will receive it. For, when He said unto them, "Go ye into all the world, and preach the gospel to every creature," Christ also added, "He that believeth and is baptized shall be saved; but he that believeth not shall be damned" (Mark 16:15-16). But "what if some did not believe? Shall their unbelief make the *truth* of God of none effect? God forbid" (Romans 3:3). Salvation will be revealed in the last time.[61]

Jesus will see of the suffering of His soul and be satisfied (Isaiah 53:11).

---

60. *Genesis 24:56-58.* And he said unto them, Hinder me not, seeing the LORD hath prospered my way; send me away that I may go to my master. And they said, We will call the damsel, and enquire at her mouth. And they called Rebekah, and said unto her, Wilt thou go with this man? and she said, I will go.

61. *1 Peter 1:5.* Who are kept by the power of God through faith unto salvation ready to be revealed in the last time.

Colossians 1:23. If ye continue in the faith grounded and settled, and be not moved away from the hope of the gospel, which ye have heard, and which was preached to every creature which is under heaven.

> "After this I beheld, and lo, a great multitude, which no man could number, of all nations, and kindreds, and people, and tongues, stood before the throne and before the Lamb, clothed with white robes and palms in their hands, and cried with a loud voice, saying: Salvation to our God which sitteth upon the throne, and unto the Lamb" (Revelation 7:9-10).

Alleluia; Amen; Alleluia!

No. 10 The Gospel Not Preached in All the World

It is objected that the gospel has not yet been preached in all the world, as Christ asserted it should be in Matthew 24:14, and therefore we can't yet look for Christ, or the end to come. Let us carefully examine this passage:

> "This gospel of the kingdom shall be preached in all the world, for a witness unto all nations; and then shall the end come."

1. The end is unquestionably the end of the age (τοῦ αἰῶνος—*tou aiōnos*) of which the disciples asked in verse 3.
2. The word (οἰκουμένη—*oikoumenē*) means habitable, that is, the inhabited earth.
3. The gospel of the kingdom is the good news, or glad tidings of the kingdom come.

These glad tidings, it is asserted, will be proclaimed in all the inhabited earth for a witness unto all nations and then (τότε—*tote*) the end of this age (or dispensation) will come. It will be noticed that the time during which the preaching continues is determined entirely by the qualifying clause "for a witness unto all nations." When the witness is complete, then will the end come.

When the Witness Is Complete

Now, no finite mind can determine when the witness is complete. If we could, the evidence is to the effect that it has passed already. For when the gospel was preached on the day of Pentecost, there were present "devout men out of every nation under heaven" (Acts 2:5). Afterward the disciples were scattered abroad and went about preaching the Word (Acts 8:4). "And they went forth and preached everywhere" (Mark 16:20).* Paul says, in Romans 10:18, "Their sound went into all the earth, and their words unto the ends of the world"** ("world" here being from the same word οἰκουμένη–*oikoumenē* that is used in Matthew 24:14). And again Paul says in Colossians 1:23*** that the gospel had already been "preached to every creature which is under heaven."

These inspired statements as to the universal preaching of the gospel ought to be conclusive. Mighty as it makes the work of the early disciples, I do not see how we can refuse to accept it. (See Adam Clarke on Matthew 24:14 as to the special point of the universality of this preaching, also the authorities previously cited.) Surely we must give no broader meaning to the word οἰκουμένη (*oikoumenē*) used by the Holy Spirit in Matthew 24:14 than in Romans 10:18, or than to the equally strong words used in Colossians 1:6 and 23.[62] If we limit the one, we can, with equal propriety, limit the other. Because we have so full an account of Paul's work, we tend to depreciate what was accomplished by the other apostles and disciples. Peter was in Babylon (1 Peter 5:13), and tradition gives us account of the preaching of the gospel in Parthia, India, Ethiopia, Scythia, Spain and Britain.

So then we may rest confidently on the plain statement of Colossians 1:23, as being such fulfillment of Matthew 24:14; that the Church from that day to the present has not had, neither can have, in this text any sign or prophesied event standing between believers and the Lord's coming. If we take it upon ourselves to judge that the witness is not complete, or more presumptuously that

---

* See Bengel's *Commentary on the New Testament* (Kregel Publications), vol. 1, p. 374.
** See Jamieson, Faussett and Brown, *Commentary on the Whole Bible*; also Alford.
*** See both of the above works.

---

62. *Colossians 1:6, 23.* Which is come unto you, as it is in all the world; and bringeth forth fruit, as it doth also in you, since the day ye heard of it, and knew the grace of God in truth. (Verse 23) See page 132.

it can't be complete for centuries to come, then we are foolishly assuming a prerogative that belongs to God only.

Only God Knows

Surely only God can judge when the witness to all nations is complete, and here lies the essence of this entire question. If the church is the agent that is to proclaim the gospel until the witness is complete, no mortal can judge but what the witness will be completed this moment. But we have no evidence that the church is the only agent, and it is quite probable that she is not, for we read of another agent in Revelation 14:6.[63]

Therefore the witness may not be completed until after the church is taken away, and this other heavenly messenger proclaims the everlasting gospel to those who dwell on the earth, even unto every nation and tribe and tongue and people (Revelation 14:6; see Greek). In this case it is not the church that will complete the witness and it evidently can be no sign to her.

We conclude then that like the "day and hour,"[64] it is known to God only, and the church can have no definite sign in it. Therefore nothing is left for us to do but faithfully continue proclaiming the glad tidings of the coming kingdom while we watch momentarily for the Bridegroom.

No. 11 Some Here Live to See the Kingdom

It is objected that we are taught in Matthew 16:28; Mark 9:1, and Luke 9:27[65] that the coming of Christ and

---

63. *Revelation 14:6.* And I saw another angel fly in the midst of heaven, having the everlasting gospel to preach unto them that dwell on the earth, and to every nation, and kindred, and tongue, and people.

64. *Matthew 24:36.* But of that day and hour knoweth no man, no, not the angels of heaven, but my Father only.

65. *Matthew 16:28.* Verily I say unto you, There be some standing here, which shall not taste death, till they see the Son of man coming in his kingdom.

Mark 9:1. And he said unto them, Verily I say unto you, That there be some of them that stand here, which shall not taste of death, till they have seen the kingdom of God come with power.

Luke 9:27. But I tell you of a truth, there be some standing here, which shall not taste of death, till they see the kingdom of God.

of the kingdom would occur during the lifetime of some of
the multitude (Mark 8:34)[66] to whom Jesus spoke. Therefore it is said that His coming and kingdom can only be
interpreted *spiritually,* that is, the establishment of the
power of the gospel by the outpouring of the Holy Spirit
on the day of Pentecost; or as some hold, *figuratively,* that
is, *the destruction of Jerusalem* and the Jewish polity by
the Romans, and the establishment of the Church. They
say, Christ came, by His Spirit, on the day of Pentecost
and manifested His power through the disciples in the
preaching of the gospel, performing of miracles, etc.; or,
He came through the Roman army, destroyed Jerusalem
and overthrew the Jewish polity, and that His kingdom
is the church over which He now reigns, or (as some say)
in which or through which He now reigns over the nations
of the earth.

My answer is that the Holy Spirit is a distinct person,
not to be confused with the person of Christ. The Savior
expressly said: "I will pray the Father and He shall give
you another comforter" (John 14:16), and if it is another,
it can't be Himself. He, the Holy Spirit, came according
to the promises,[67] and it is entirely inconsistent to confuse
this event with Christ's return, which itself is in
accordance with other promises—that He would Himself
come again. They are two events, as distinct as the births
of Moses and John.

It is true that Christ is spiritually with, or in, believers,[68] and it is just as true that He always has been, and

---

66. *Mark 8:34.* And when he had called the people unto him with his disciples
also, he said unto them, Whosoever will come after me, let him deny himself,
and take up his cross, and follow me.

67. *John 14:16, 26.* And I will pray the Father, and he shall give you another
Comforter, that he may abide with you for ever. But the Comforter, which is
the Holy Spirit, whom the Father will send in my name, he shall teach you all
things, and bring all things to your remembrance, whatsoever I have said
unto you. See also *15:26* and *16:7.*

68. *John 14:23.* Jesus answered and said unto him, If a man love me, he will
keep my words: and my Father will love him, and we will come unto him, and
make our abode with him.

John 17:23. I in them, and thou in me, that they may be made perfect in
one; and that the world may know that thou hast sent me, and hast loved
them, as thou hast loved me.

that in this sense He has never left them, for He said: "Lo! I am with you alway" (Matthew 28:20). Notice the language: "I *am* with you alway." He was with them during those days of prayer previous to the day of Pentecost, and He has been with His people all the time. But suddenly the Comforter (*Paraklētos*) came—another person and for a special and glorious purpose. It is, therefore conclusive, that this coming of the Holy Spirit is a manifestation of the Divine presence, entirely different from the spiritual presence of Christ, which latter, according to His own language, has never been withdrawn from His people. He never went away spiritually, but He did go bodily and visibly, and in the same way He will return.[69]

After the day of Pentecost, the disciples continued to talk of the coming of Christ, which they surely would not have done if His promise to return was fulfilled on that day. And after the destruction of Jerusalem (about A.D. 71), John wrote the book of Revelation (about A.D. 96), in which he repeatedly speaks of the coming of Christ as being yet future, clearly showing that it could not have been fulfilled in the destruction of Jerusalem.

Again, as we have before shown, the church is not the kingdom, but the body of Christ,[70] and His bride (Ephesians 5). She is not to be reigned over,[71] but to suffer and reign with Christ.[72] She is "to be counted worthy of the

---

Galatians 4:19. My little children, of whom I travail in birth again until Christ be formed in you.

69. *Acts 1:11.* Which also said, Ye men of Galilee, why stand ye gazing up into heaven? This same Jesus, which is taken up from you into heaven, shall so come in like manner as ye have seen him go into heaven.

70. *Ephesians 1:22-23.* And hath put all things under his feet, and gave him to be the head over all things to the church, which is his body, the fulness of him that filleth all in all.

71. *John 15:15.* Henceforth I call you not servants; for the servant knoweth not what his lord doeth: but I have called you friends; for all things that I have heard of my Father I have made known unto you.

72. *Romans 8:17.* And if children, then heirs; heirs of God, and joint heirs with Christ; if so be that we suffer with him, that we may be also glorified together.

2 Timothy 2:12. If we suffer, we shall also reign with him: if we deny him, he also will deny us.

kingdom of God for which she suffers,"[73] and therefore Paul exhorts the disciples (members of the church) "that they must through much tribulation enter into the kingdom of God" (Acts 14:22). And Peter stirs us up, exhorting us to add the Christian graces and be all the more eager to make our calling and election sure, and we will receive a rich welcome "into the everlasting kingdom of our Lord and Savior, Jesus Christ" (2 Peter 1:5-11).

Surely this language plainly distinguishes between the church and the kingdom, and as plainly asserts that the kingdom is yet future. So we see that both the spiritual and figurative interpretations of the coming of Christ are without foundation.

Another theory has been advanced, that is, that the coming of Christ in His kingdom (Matthew 16:28) was fulfilled in what they term the spiritual coming on the day of Pentecost. They say that His coming in the clouds of heaven, in the glory of His Father, with the holy angels, etc., is His real, personal, visible coming at the end of the gospel age (which they also hold to be the end of time and of the world).

This seems to me to be founded upon a mere distinction of terms, where there is no difference in fact. For is it not at Christ's coming in His kingdom that He will be manifested in His glory?[74] History proves—and all our ideas of the glory of kings coincide with the fact—that such glory is identical with the majesty and manifestation of their kingdoms.

It is in Christ's kingdom that He will rule all nations with a rod of iron,[75] and it is in His kingdom that He is to be manifested as "the blessed and only Potentate, the

---

73. *2 Thessalonians 1:5*. Which is a manifest token of the righteous judgment of God, that ye may be counted worthy of the kingdom of God, for which ye also suffer.

74. *2 Thessalonians 1:10*. When he shall come to be glorified in his saints, and to be admired in all them that believe (because our testimony among you was believed) in that day.

75. *Psalm 2:8-9*. Ask of me, and I shall give thee the heathen for thine inheritance, and the uttermost parts of the earth for thy possession; thou shalt break them with a rod of iron; thou shalt dash them in pieces like a potter's vessel. See also *Revelation 12:5* and *19:15*.

King of kings, and Lord of lords."[76] Therefore His coming in His kingdom and His coming in His glory are synonymous, and both are yet future.

Some of Them Did See the Kingdom

Then what do the passages mean? Matthew 16:28 says, "Verily I say unto you, there be some standing here which shall not taste death, till they see the Son of Man coming in His kingdom;" or as in Mark 9:1, "till they have seen the kingdom of God come with power;" or as in Luke 9:27, "till they see the kingdom of God."

First, I answer that the limiting clause, "shall not taste of death" may have the deep meaning, in which sense the true believers, who were standing there, will never experience it.[77] This is certainly the meaning the same language has in Hebrews 2:9,[78] and if we understand it this way in these passages, then we have all eternity for the fulfillment. However, I only suggest this. I do not rely on it, for I believe the word "till" more than intimates that the "some" would taste of death, and that therefore natural death or separation of soul and body was meant.

Peter Saw It

But now let us mark well what the "some" standing there were to see, and then let us go up the Mount of Transfiguration and look through the favored eyes of Peter, James and John at the scene which is recorded immediately after the passage we are considering. Behold His face shining as the sun and His clothes white and

---

76. *1 Timothy 6:14-15*. That thou keep this commandment without spot, unrebukable, until the appearing of our Lord Jesus Christ: which in his times he shall show, who is the blessed and only Potentate, the King of kings, and Lord of lords.

Revelation 19:16. And he hath on his vesture and on his thigh a name written, KING OF KINGS, AND LORD OF LORDS.

77. *John 8:51-52*. Verily, verily, I say unto you, if a man keep my saying, he shall never see death. Then said the Jews unto him, Now we know that thou hast a devil. Abraham is dead, and the prophets; and thou sayest, If a man keep my saying, he shall never taste of death.

78. *Hebrews 2:9*. But we see Jesus, who was made a little lower than the angels for the suffering of death, crowned with glory and honor; that He by the grace of God should taste death for every man.

glistening as the snow, or as the light. See Moses and Elias as they appear in *glory* with Him, and listen to the sharing of this exalted trio. Then bow in silent awe, as the cloud of surpassing glory overshadows them, and reverently listen to the voice of God, the Father, saying, "This is my beloved Son in whom I am well pleased, hear ye Him" (Matthew 17:5). No wonder that even the favored and beloved disciples trembled with fear beneath this supernatural majesty and effulgent glory. Surely this was I Am[79] spanning the centuries and giving these apostles a view of His coming and kingdom.

So they understood it and Peter especially confirms it when he says:

> "For we have not followed cunningly devised fables, when we made known unto you the power and *coming* of our Lord Jesus Christ, but were eye witnesses of His majesty. For He received from God the Father honor and glory, when there came such a voice to Him from the excellent glory. This is my beloved Son, in whom I am well pleased. And this voice which came from heaven we heard, when we were with Him in the holy mount" (2 Peter 1:16-18).

We cannot tell how much of the future they saw in that enraptured hour, but doubtless they had a specific vision of the coming of our Lord Jesus Christ in His kingdom and glory.

John Saw It

We have only to turn to Revelation, where we find that He "which is and which was, and which is to come" permitted John to *see* (Revelation 1:2, 11, etc.) it most definitely. His enraptured vision swept the centuries. Time, to him, was annihilated and he gazed upon the literal facts. He actually saw them. Thirty-six times he says, "I saw;" seven times "I beheld;" and five times "I looked," besides many similar expressions. And he saw the very things mentioned in the passages:

---

79. *John 8:58.* Jesus said unto them, Verily, verily, I say unto you, Before Abraham was, I am.

> "And I *saw* heaven opened, and behold a white horse; and He that sat upon him was called Faithful and True, and in righteousness He doth judge and make war. His eyes were as a flame of fire and on His head were many crowns . . . and He was clothed with a vesture dipped in blood: and His name is called the Word of God. And the armies which were in heaven followed Him upon white horses, clothed in fine linen, white and clean. . . . And He hath on His vesture and on His thigh a name written, KING OF KINGS AND LORD OF LORDS (Revelation 19:11-16).

He saw the beast and kings of the earth gathered and taken and thrown into the lake of fire. He saw Satan bound, and he saw Christ and His saints reigning for a thousand years. He saw it all in perfect fulfillment of the statements in the passages we are considering (Revelation 19:20).

Paul Saw It

Paul also saw Christ in His glory and doubtless he saw all that John did, and probably more, for he saw things that it was impossible for a man to speak (2 Corinthians 12:4). Surely these are an absolute and literal fulfillment of what Jesus promised "some" would see, and satisfactorily explain the passages in question.

"Ye Shall Not Have Gone Over the Cities of Israel"

Another passage is cited in support of the above theories, that is, the *spiritual* coming on the day of Pentecost or the figurative coming in the destruction of Jerusalem, etc., and that is Matthew 10:23: "Verily I say unto you, Ye shall not have gone over [or finish] the cities of Israel, till the Son of man be come."

In regard to this I answer that this was spoken to the twelve disciples, when Jesus sent them forth two by two with a message especially for and exclusively to Israel. We find from Mark 6:30 and Luke 9:10[80] that they

---

80. *Mark 6:30*. And the apostles gathered themselves together unto Jesus, and told him all things, both what they had done, and what they had taught.

Luke 9:10. And the apostles, when they were returned, told him all that they have done. And he took them, and went aside privately into a desert place belonging to the city called Bethsaida.

returned to the Master, of course, without finishing the cities. And there is no evidence that they ever, in the same way, revisited them preaching the message "the kingdom of heaven is at hand."[81] Indeed they could not, for Israel had rejected their King, and the kingdom had become like a nobleman who went into a distant country to receive for himself a kingdom and then return.[82]

But from the force of the word "till" I believe that the message will be renewed (perhaps by the two witnesses after the church is taken away) to the unbelieving Israelites, who will still return to their land and restore Judaism.[83] And before they will have gone over the rebuilt cities, the Son of man will appear again.

No. 12 Gloomy View of the Future

It is objected that this doctrine presents a gloomy view of the future; that "it is the philosophy of despair;" that it stands opposed to the popular idea: that the world is growing better. And "if it is true," it is sarcastically said, "we might as well fold our hands and wait for Christ to come." I honestly think that many who raise these objections have altogether misunderstood the spirit and work of premillennialists.

We Do Not Despair

We neither despair, nor fold our hands to sleep. On the contrary, we are filled with a living hope (1 Peter 1:3), the most "blessed hope" (Titus 2:13). At the same time

---

81. *Matthew 10:7*. And as ye go, preach saying, The kingdom of heaven is at hand.

82. *Luke 19:11-12*. And as they heard these things, he added and spake a parable, because he was nigh to Jerusalem, and because they thought that the kingdom of God should immediately appear. He said therefore, A certain nobleman went into a far country to receive for himself a kingdom, and to return.

83. *Isaiah 40:9-11*. O thou that tellest good tidings to Zion, get thee upon a high mountain; O thou that tellest good tidings to Jerusalem, lift up thy voice with strength; lift it up, be not afraid; say unto the cities of Judah, Behold your God; behold the LORD Jehovah will come as a mighty one, and his arm will rule for him: Behold his reward is with him, and his recompense before him. He will feed his flock like a shepherd, he will gather the lambs in his arms, and carry them to his bosom, and will gently lead those that have their young.

we strive to save some from this worldly, sinful, and adulterous generation, which is in danger of being cursed and whose end is to be burned.[84]

We would not deceive them with the hallucination that they are "growing better," for, as the apostle has said, "we know that we are of God and the whole world lieth in wickedness" (Greek—*in the wicked one*; 1 John 5:19). Therefore we would tell them in the plain words of Scripture, that they are on the broad road that leads to destruction (Matthew 7:13), and that they must repent or perish (Luke 13:3). And further, this same world, once overflowed by the flood, is now "stored with fire* against the day of judgment and perdition of ungodly men" (2 Peter 3:5-7).

We rejoice over every one of those who, by believing the gospel—the good news of the coming kingdom,[85] are saved from this awful fate and made "joint heirs with Christ" (Romans 8:16-17) "to an inheritance . . . reserved in heaven for us;" and "who are kept by the power of God through faith unto salvation, ready to be revealed in the last time;" and who "hope to the end for the grace that is to be brought unto" us "at the revelation of Jesus Christ" (1 Peter 1:4-5, 13).

Surely this positive conviction of coming doom is a stronger incentive to action than can be the quieting fallacy that things are moving on prosperously and that *even the world is getting better*. And this is clearly proved by the zeal and faithful work of the ministers, evangelists

---

* See the Greek.

84. *Galatians 1:4.* Who gave himself for our sins, that he might deliver us from this present evil world [age], according to the will of God and our Father.

Hebrews 6:8. But that which beareth thorns and briers is rejected, and is nigh unto cursing; whose end is to be burned.

Malachi 4:1. For, behold, the day cometh that shall burn as an oven; and all the proud, yea, and all that do wickedly, shall be stubble: and the day that cometh shall burn them up, saith the LORD of hosts, that it shall leave them neither root nor branch.

85. *Acts 14:21-22.* And when they had preached the gospel to that city, and had taught many, they returned again to Lystra, and to Iconium, and Antioch, confirming the souls of the disciples, and exhorting them to continue in the faith, and that we must through much tribulation enter into the kingdom of God.

and laymen who hold and proclaim this doctrine of the premillennial coming of Christ.

It is true that they do not expect the conversion of the world in this present evil age* (Galatians 1:4), but they do believe that a millennial age of peace is coming, and they do strive "in the midst of a crooked and perverse generation," to "shine as lights in the world holding forth the word of life" (Philippians 2:15-16). They do desire to snatch some from the fire (Malachi 4:1; 1 Corinthians 3:13-15; Jude 23), and to increase the godly company who will be ready to welcome the Bridegroom.[86]

Why, then, should they be so bitterly opposed for proclaiming this Scripture doctrine? Are they not all members of the body of Christ?[87] And, as such, do they not deserve the warmest sympathy and prayers of the church? Will they be condemned because, like the early church, they are holding the traditions (or teachings handed down) of the apostles,[88] and looking for Jesus?[89] God forbid! But let us remember that we are brethren, strangers and pilgrims (Hebrews 11:13), whose citizenship is in heaven (Philippians 3:20). And let us speak the truth in love, be built up in love (Ephesians 4:15-16), and walk in love (Ephesians 5:2), "redeeming the time, because the days are evil."[90]

---

* See the Greek.

---

86. *Matthew 25:10-13*. And while they went to buy, the bridegroom came; and they that were ready went in with him to the marriage: and the door was shut. Afterward came also the other virgins, saying, Lord, Lord, open to us. But he answered and said, Verily I say unto you, I know you not. Watch therefore; for ye know neither the day nor the hour wherein the Son of man cometh.

87. *1 Corinthians 12:25-26*. That there should be no schism in the body; but that the members should have the same care one for another. And whether one member suffer, all the members suffer with it; or one member be honored, all the members rejoice with it.

88. *2 Thessalonians 2:5, 15*. Remember ye not, that, when I was yet with you I told you these things? Therefore, brethren, stand fast, and hold the traditions which ye have been taught, whether by word, or our epistle.

89. *Philippians 3:20*. For our conversation is in heaven; from whence also we look for the Savior, the Lord Jesus Christ.

  Hebrews 9:28. So Christ was once offered to bear the sins of many; and unto them that look for him shall he appear the second time without sin unto salvation. See also *Titus 2:13*.

90. *Ephesians 5:15-16*. See then that ye walk circumspectly, not as fools, but as wise, redeeming the time, because the days are evil.

The Days Are Evil

Yes, *the days are evil,* and we freely admit that this doctrine does present a gloomy future in the present evil age for this world of sinners, who are full of unbelief and radically opposed to Christ, His people and His salvation.[91] They are rejecting God's gracious appeals for reconciliation,[92] and rushing madly on toward the day of wrath (Revelation 6:15-17).

But there is no gloom in the future for those "who have fled for refuge to lay hold on the hope set before us,"[93] and "who have received the Spirit of adoption;" who become "children" and "heirs of God and joint heirs with Christ. . . . For I reckon that the sufferings of this present time are not worthy to be compared with the glory that shall be revealed in us" (Romans 8:15-18).

There seems to be a prevailing disposition to balance up the good and the bad in the world by a process of general average, in which the triumphs of art and science, the progress in inventions, discoveries, etc., are counted as moral goodness, and it is concluded that the

---

91. *2 Corinthians 6:14-18.* Be ye not unequally yoked together with unbelievers; for what fellowship hath righteousness with unrighteousness? And what communion hath light with darkness? And what concord hath Christ and Belial? Or what part hath he that believeth with an infidel? And what agreement hath the temple of God with idols? For ye are the temple of the living God; as God hath said, I will dwell in them, and walk in them; and I will be their God, and they shall be my people. Wherefore come out from among them, and be ye separate, saith the Lord, and touch not the unclean thing; and I will receive you, and will be a Father unto you, and ye shall be my sons.

Ephesians 5:11-12. And have no fellowship with the unfruitful works of darkness, but rather reprove them. For it is a shame even to speak of those things which are done of them in secret.

1 John 2:15. Love not the world, neither the things that are in the world. If any man love the world, the love of the Father is not in him. See also *John 14:18-22; 16:33; 17:14; James 4:14; 1 John 5:19.*

92. *2 Corinthians 5:20-21.* Now then we are ambassadors for Christ, as though God did beseech you by us: we pray you in Christ's stead, be ye reconciled to God. For he hath made him to be sin for us, who knew no sin; that we might be made the righteousness of God in him.

93. *Hebrews 6:18-20.* That by two immutable things, in which it was impossible for God to lie, we might have a strong consolation, who have fled for refuge to lay hold upon the hope set before us: which hope we have as an anchor of the soul, both sure and steadfast, and which entereth into that within the vail; whither the forerunner is for us entered, even Jesus, made a high priest for ever after the order of Melchisedec.

world, on the average, is growing better. But this is utterly fallacious and, I fear, a grand deception of Satan.

The Church and the World

First, there is no such thing as averaging together the true church and the world. There is no possible relationship. The one is "from beneath," the other "from above." The one "is of this world," the other "not of this world" (John 8:23). They must not be yoked together, for there is no fellowship, communion, accord, part, or agreement between them. They are and always must be separate.* The true church is in the world, but not of it.[94] There are three parties in the world: the Jew, the Gentile and the church of God.[95] As the Jews were a separate, called-out and peculiar people,[96] not to be reckoned among the nations,[97] so is this true church a separate and peculiar people,[98] called to cleansing and holiness,[99] sealed by the

---

* See footnote 91, page 145.

---

94. *John 17:11, 15-16.* And now I am no more in the world, but these are in the world, and I come to thee. Holy Father, keep through thine own name those whom thou hast given me, that they may be one, as we are. I pray not that thou shouldest take them out of the world, but that thou shouldest keep them from the evil. They are not of the world, even as I am not of the world.

95. *1 Corinthians 10:32.* Give none offence, neither to the Jews, nor to the Gentiles, nor to the church of God.

96. *Exodus 19:5, 6.* Now therefore, if ye will obey my voice indeed, and keep my covenant, then ye shall be a peculiar treasure unto me above all people: for all the earth is mine. And ye shall be unto me a kingdom of priests, and an holy nation. These are the words which thou shalt speak unto the children of Israel.

Exodus 33:16. For wherein shall it be known here that I and thy people have found grace in thy sight? Is it not in that thou goest with us? so shall we be separated, I and thy people, from all the people that are upon the face of the earth. See also *Deuteronomy 7:6; Psalm 135:4.*

97. *Numbers 23:9.* For from the top of the rocks I see him, and from the hills I behold him: lo, the people shall dwell alone, and shall not be reckoned among the nations.

98. *Titus 2:14.* Who gave himself for us, that he might redeem us from all iniquity, and purify unto himself a peculiar people, zealous of good works.

1 Peter 2:9. But ye are a chosen generation, a royal priesthood, a holy nation, a peculiar people; that ye should show forth the praises of him who hath called you out of darkness into his marvellous light.

99. *2 Corinthians 7:1.* Having therefore these promises, dearly beloved, let us cleanse ourselves from all filthiness of the flesh and spirit, perfecting holiness in the fear of God. See also *Ephesians 5:25-27.*

Spirit of God to the day of redemption (Ephesians 4:30). They are no longer darkness, but "children of light," and exhorted to "have no fellowship with the unfruitful works of darkness" (Ephesians 5:8-11). They are of God, while the whole world lies in the wicked one.[100] There is an irrepressible conflict between them—no possible harmony exists. On the contrary, their principles and tendencies are absolutely opposite. It is therefore entirely inconsistent that they should be spoken of as forming one general mass.

Art, Science, and Invention

Second, the triumphs of art and science, the progress in inventions, discoveries, etc., by no means argue an increase in godliness. Many of the acknowledged leaders today in science and philosophy—yes, even those who rank the very highest among them—are positive infidels. And very many more, who disclaim absolute infidelity, deny the divinity of Jesus Christ.

It is strange, indeed, that the Christian optimists, in their noisy trumpetings of the strides of science, should lose sight of this momentous fact. And history bears a similar testimony. The power, splendor and wisdom of David and Solomon were followed by the idolatry and innocent blood of Ahab and Manasseh, resulting in the overthrow of Jerusalem and the Babylonian captivity.

The temple, built by Herod, was one of the grandest works of art. If fairly flashed with splendor, and the temple service was conducted on a magnificent scale. The Jews of his time enjoyed great privileges in literature and learning, and yet they crucified the Lord Jesus.

The Greeks rose to a pinnacle of triumph in literature, poetry and art, and yet they failed by wisdom to find out God. To them he was the unknown God.[101] See how plainly this is brought out in 1 Corinthians 1, 2, and 3:

---

100. *1 John 5:19*. We know that we are of God, and the whole world lieth in the evil one.

101. *Acts 17:23*. For as I passed by, and beheld your devotions, I found an altar with this inscription, TO THE UNKNOWN GOD. Whom therefore ye ignorantly worship, him declare I unto you.

"For after that, in the wisdom of God, the world by wisdom knew not God, it pleased God by the foolishness of preaching to save them that believe" (1:21). The trouble is not with the heads, but with the hearts of people. No matter how great the education a person must have a new heart, and this is obtained not by learning, but by the operation of the Spirit of God. It was not many wise men after the flesh who received the grace of God in Corinth, but the simple and the despised. "I thank Thee, O Father, Lord of heaven and earth," said Jesus, "that thou hast hid these things from the wise and prudent [discerning ones] and hast revealed them unto babes" (Luke 10:21).

The world, then, by "wisdom" or "philosophy" (Colossians 2:8), or "science falsely so called" (1 Timothy 6:20), can never find out God. Indeed, we have a clear evidence of this in the rationalism, infidelity and atheism of our day. No matter how refined and polished their dress is or the delicacy with which they may be presented, still they are only the poisonous deceptions of the one who can appear as "an angel of light."[102] The truth is that Satan is the arch enemy of God, and the world, in this present evil age (Galatians 1:4), is in his power (1 John 5:19). He harrases the people of God with his schemes, and deploys against them "principalities . . . powers . . . and the rulers of the darkness of this world" (Ephesians 6:11-13). Therefore, the Christian must "love not the world, neither the things that are in the world. If any man love the world, the love of the Father is not in him. For all that is in the world, that lust of the flesh, and the lust of the eyes, and the pride of life, is not of the Father, but is of the world" (1 John 2:15-16).

The World Is Not Growing Better

Surely, then, this wicked world, which is so radically

---

102. *2 Corinthians 11:13-15.* For such are false apostles, deceitful workers, transforming themselves into the apostles of Christ. And no marvel; for Satan himself is transformed into an angel of light. Therefore it is no great thing if his ministers also be transformed as the ministers of righteousness; whose end shall be according to their works.

opposed to God and is under the present control of His arch enemy, is not growing better. On the contrary, judgment, fire and damnation are before it.[103] Perilous times are coming.[104] Evil men and seducers will go from bad to worse, deceiving and being deceived (2 Timothy 3:13). The tares, which naturally grow much faster than the wheat, will continue up to the harvest (Matthew 13:40). "The mystery of iniquity" which already worked in the days of the apostles, will culminate in "the man of sin," the personal antichrist. Even the mass of Jews will receive him,[105] and he will be so great and rule with such universal authority that he is to be destroyed only by the personal appearing of the Lord Himself.[106]

There is no hope, then, for the world, except in the coming of Christ the King. And, praise be to God for the promises, the Lord will come at the end of this age. The Antichrist will be destroyed.[106] All things that offend will be gathered out,[107] and the millennial kingdom of righteousness will be established on the earth. So, while there is a gloomy prospect for the world during this evil age, there is a bright and glorious prospect during the coming millennial age.

---

103. *2 Peter 2-3*. And many shall follow their pernicious ways; by reason of whom the way of truth shall be evil spoken of. And through covetousness shall they with feigned words make merchandise of you: whose judgment now of a long time lingereth not, and their damnation slumbereth not.

    2 Peter 3:7. But the heavens and the earth, which are now, by the same word are kept in store, reserved unto fire against the day of judgment and perdition of ungodly men. See also *Jude 7*; *Mark 9:43-48*.

104. *1 Timothy 4:1*. Now the Spirit speaketh expressly, that in the latter times some shall depart from the faith, giving heed to seducing spirits, and doctrines of devils.

    2 Timothy 3:1. This know also, that in the last days perilous times shall come.

105. *John 5:43*. I am come in my Father's name, and ye receive me not: if another shall come in his own name, him ye will receive. See also *Isaiah 28:15-22*.

106. *2 Thessalonians 2:8-9*. And then shall that Wicked be revealed, whom the Lord shall consume with the spirit of his mouth, and shall destroy with the brightness of his coming: even him, whose coming is after the working of Satan with all power and signs and lying wonders. See also *Revelation 19:20*.

107. *Matthew 13:41-43*. The Son of man shall send forth his angels, and they shall gather out of his kingdom all things that offend, and them which do iniquity; and shall cast them into a furnace of fire: there shall be wailing and gnashing of teeth. Then shall the righteous shine forth as the sun in the kingdom of their Father. Who hath ears to hear, let him hear.

Civilization and Benevolent Institutions

But perhaps it is still insisted that the world has made great progress in civilization and refinement, in benevolence, in personal liberty, international fraternity, Christian work, etc. In proof of this, the abrogation of slavery is cited; also the cessation of the inquisition and martyrdom, the establishment of charitable institutions, the great postal and commercial means of communication, built on great technological advances; the right of trial by jury, international arbitration, missionary triumphs, etc.

Well, first of all I would answer that *civilization and refinement are not the source of holiness.* They may elevate the head, while the heart is untouched. The gilded palace of sin is as certainly the gateway to hell as the darkest den of vice. The cultured and scientific atheist is as surely in the service of Satan as the thief or the murderer. Jesus Himself classed them all together when He said, "He that is not with me is against me" (Matthew 12:30). So it does not matter how much more like an angel of light the serpent may appear, or how civilized and refined the world may be. Satan is still the devil, and the world is still the world.

His manifestations and methods may be changed, but the spirit of darkness is the same. And accordingly we see that while slavery is disappearing, communism, socialism and nihilism are lifting their godless, headless forms. And darker are their forebodings than were even the days of the inquisition and martyrdom. Oppressing monopolies, systematic embezzlement and fraud are parallel with charitable institutions. The postal system, so useful for news and correspondence, afford a most convenient avenue for disseminating the flood of obscene literature that is blasting away the morality of our youth. Trial by jury has too often proved a mere farce, by which the criminal escapes.

The nation which opened the way for the missionary also forced upon the teeming millions of China the awful curse of opium. While missionary efforts have been greatly blessed abroad (and praise God that they have), infallibility, ritualism, skepticism and desecration of the Lord's day have more than equally triumphed at home. And let it not be forgotten that the monstrous assumption of infallibility has triumphed in what was once an apostolic church of Christ.

The recent past has had its full share of war and carnage. Numerous, dark, and fearful have been the fields of blood up to this very day. In short, Satan is on the alert and fully up to the times, multiplying his deceptions on either hand, as he will continue to do until he is chained by the angel at the beginning of the Millennium.[108]

Is the Church Progressing?

Lastly, it is argued that, as Christians are the light of the world and the salt of the earth,[109] the greatly increased number of professed Christians must certainly have augmented the light and the salt, and consequently have made the world better.

Jesus was indeed the Light of the world, but He shone in the darkness and the darkness did not comprehend it. Men were loving and clinging to the darkness; because their deeds were evil, they would not see the light, and were not made better by it.[110] So true Christians, reflecting the light from heaven, only intensify the darkness around them. The darkness is still darkness and can't be

---

108. *Revelation 20:1-3.* And I saw an angel come down from heaven, having the key of the bottomless pit and a great chain in his hand. And he laid hold on the dragon, that old serpent, which is the Devil, and Satan, and bound him a thousand years. And cast him into the bottomless pit, and shut him up, and set a seal upon him, that he should deceive the nations no more, till the thousand years should be fulfilled; and after that he must be loosed a little season.

109. *Matthew 5:13.* Ye are the salt of the earth: but if the salt have lost his savor, wherewith shall it be salted? It is thenceforth good for nothing, but to be cast out, and to be trodden under foot of men.

Philippians 2:15. That ye may be blameless and harmless, the sons of God, without rebuke, in the midst of a crooked and perverse nation, among whom ye shine as lights in the world.

110. *John 1:4-5.* In him was life; and the life was the light of men. And the light shineth in darkness; and the darkness comprehended it not.

John 3:19-21. And this is the condemnation, that light is come into the world, and men loved darkness rather than light, because their deeds were evil. For everyone that doeth evil hateth the light, neither cometh to the light, lest his deeds should be reproved. But he that doeth truth cometh to the light, that his deeds may be made manifest, that they are wrought in God.

improved. Sinners must forsake it and come to the light, or they can never be saved.

Losing the Saltiness

Let us notice carefully that Jesus speaks of *the salt losing its saltiness* and becoming good for nothing, and He also intimates that *the light can be hidden* under a bowl. And therefore He exhorts, "Have salt in yourselves" (Mark 9:50). Evidently the Jews lost their saltiness (Matthew 5:13) and "were broken off."[111] This leads to the serious question, Is the professing church progressing or declining in faith and spiritual life? The kingdom in mystery,[112] or the state of Christendom until Christ comes again, is explained to us by the parables of Matthew 13.

The Parables

The parable of the sower shows the varied and imperfect reception of the Word. The parable of the Tares shows the early and continued effects of Satan's presence among the saints. The parable of the mustard-seed shows outward growth sheltering evil. The parable of the leaven shows the gradual and utter corruption of truth. The parable of the treasure hidden in the field shows what Israel is to be in the world. The parable of the pearl of great price shows what the church is to Christ. And the parable of the fishing net shows the cleansing of the kingdom at His second coming.

The Leaven

There is probably only a little opposition to this interpretation of the parables, except that of the leaven, which has quite extensively been interpreted to teach exactly the opposite; that is, that the power and influence of the gospel or Christian life is to permeate the masses

---

111. *Romans 11:20-21*. Well; because of unbelief they were broken off, and thou standest by faith. Be not highminded, but fear: for if God spared not the natural branches, take heed lest he also spare not thee.

112. *Matthew 13:10-11*. And the disciples came, and said unto him, Why speakest thou unto them in parables? He answered and said unto them, Because it is given unto you to know the mysteries of the kingdom of heaven, but to them it is not given.

of the world until the whole is leavened into holiness. The inconsistency of this is seen when we consider that precisely the contrary is taught by the parable of the sower and the tares, each of which undisputedly shows that evil is to continue and grow up to the end of the age. This is surely the most sufficient and scriptural reason for assigning the same typical meaning to the leaven, both in this and the correlative passage.[113] We also see this usage in the numerous other passages where the same word is used, that is, the corrupting influence of evil and the symbol of death (see carefully Matthew 16:6-12.)[114]

In this passage we are most emphatically taught not only that the world is growing no better, but that the professing church itself will lose its saltiness, becoming nominal and lukewarm, fit only to be spued out of the Master's mouth.[115] The entire teaching of the Word of God, I believe, agrees with this.

---

113. *Luke 13:20-21.* And again he said, Whereunto shall I liken the kingdom of God? It is like leaven, which a woman took and hid in three measures of meal, till the whole was leavened.

114. *Matthew 16:6-8, 11-12.* Then Jesus said unto them, Take heed and beware of the leaven of the Pharisees and of the Sadducees. And they reasoned among themselves, saying, It is because we have taken no bread. Which when Jesus perceived, he said unto them, O ye of little faith, why reason ye among yourselves, because ye have brought no bread? How is it that ye do not understand that I spake it not to you concerning bread, that ye should beware of the leaven of the Pharisees and of the Sadducees? Then understood they how that he bade them not beware of the leaven of bread, but of the doctrine of the Pharisees and of the Sadducees.

Mark 8:15. And he charged them, saying, Take heed, beware of the leaven of the Pharisees, and of the leaven of Herod.

Luke 12:1. In the meantime, when there were gathered together an innumerable multitude of people, insomuch that they trode one upon another, he began to say unto his disciples first of all, Beware ye of the leaven of the Pharisees, which is hypocrisy.

1 Corinthians 5:6-8. Your glorying is not good. Know ye not that a little leaven leaveneth the whole lump? Purge out therefore the old leaven, that ye may be a new lump, as ye are unleavened. For even Christ our passover is sacrificed for us: therefore let us keep the feast, not with old leaven, neither with the leaven of malice and wickedness; but with the unleavened bread of sincerity and truth.

Galatians 5:7-9. Ye did run well; who did hinder you that ye should not obey the truth? This persuasion cometh not of him that calleth you. A little leaven leaveneth the whole lump.

115. *Revelation 3:16.* So then because thou art lukewarm, and neither cold nor hot, I will spew thee out of my mouth.

All we have to do is take an unprejudiced survey of the church even now to see the truth of it. The loss of spiritual power in the different branches of the great nominal church has not resulted from the throwing out of truth, but from the imbibing and internal workings of false doctrine, which, like leaven, has fermented the mass. Little by little the ordinary bishop of Rome has developed into an infallible pope. Image worship, the confessional, world conformity and postmillennialism have all worked out their enormous growth like the little leaven in the meal.

How do the great papal and Greek churches, in their stateliness, formality, popularity and spiritual weakness of today, compare with the despised Nazarene and His followers,[116] or with the persecuted, consecrated and godly congregations (*ekklēsias*) of the first two centuries? And are not the present evangelical denominations, by worldly conformity and increeping doubts regarding the inspiration of the Word of God, etc., dangerously going in the same direction? How very few of the members in them are today crying out for separation and holiness. Surely, no one can fail to see the corrupting influences of the leaven permeating them.

I realize this is an awful fact. It is not even pleasant to state it. But, while Noah's preaching was not pleasant to those that heard it, still it was true and the flood did come. Likewise the prophesying of Jeremiah was exceedingly unpleasant, but it was true and was followed by the terrible fate of the city and the Babylonian captivity. The preaching of Jesus was at times of fearful severity,[117] but was it not true? So would we humbly yet

---

116. *1 John 4:17.* Herein is our love made perfect, that we may have boldness in the day of judgment: because as he is, so are we in this world.

117. *Matthew 11:20-24.* Then began he to upbraid the cities wherein most of his mighty works were done, because they repented not: woe unto thee, Chorazin! woe unto thee, Bethsaida! for if the mighty works, which were done in you, had been done in Tyre and Sidon, they would have repented long ago in sackcloth and ashes. But I say unto you, It shall be more tolerable for Tyre and Sidon at the day of judgment, than for you. And thou, Capernaum, which are exalted unto heaven, shalt be brought down to hell: for if the mighty works, which have been done in thee, had been done in Sodom, it would have

faithfully proclaim the Word of God. We would "cry aloud and spare not,"[118] fully believing that, upon an apostate church,[119] rebellious and murderous Israel,[120] and a sinful world, the day of darkness is coming.[121]

The Faithful Remnant

But even in the darkness, which is so gloomy for the ungodly, there is hope—bright, glorious hope for the

---

remained until this day. But I say unto you, That it shall be more tolerable for the land of Sodom in the day of judgment, than for thee.

Matthew 18:7-9. Woe unto the world because of offences! for it must needs be that offences come; but woe to that man by whom the offences cometh! Wherefore if thy hand or thy foot offend thee, cut them off, and cast them from thee: it is better for thee to enter into life halt or maimed, rather than having two hands or two feet to be cast into everlasting fire. And if thine eye offend thee, pluck it out, and cast if from thee: it is better for thee to enter into life with one eye.

Matthew 23:13-15, 27, 31-33. But woe unto you, scribes and Pharisees, hypocrites! for ye shut up the kingdom of heaven against men: for ye neither go in yourselves, neither suffer ye them that are entering to go in. Woe unto you, scribes and Pharisees, hypocrites! for ye devour your widows' houses, and for a pretence make long prayer: therefore ye shall receive the greater damnation. Woe unto you, scribes and Pharisees, hypocrites! for ye compass sea and land to make one proselyte; and when he is made, ye make him twofold more the child of hell than yourselves. Woe unto you, scribes and Pharisees, hypocrites! for ye are like unto whited sepulchres, which indeed appear beautiful outward, but are within full of dead men's bones, and of all uncleanness. Wherefore ye be witnesses unto yourselves, that ye are the children of them which killed the prophets. Fill ye up then the measure of your fathers. Ye serpents, ye generation of vipers, how can ye escape the damnation of hell?

118. *Isaiah 58:1*. Cry aloud, spare not, lift up thy voice like a trumpet, and show my people their transgression, and the house of Jacob their sins.

119. *2 Timothy 4:2-5*. Preach the word; be instant in season, out of season; reprove, rebuke, exhort with all longsuffering and doctrine. For the time will come when they will not endure sound doctrine; but after their own lusts shall they heap to themselves teachers, having itching ears; and they shall turn away their ears from the truth, and shall be turned unto fables. See also *2 Timothy 3:5-9, Revelation 17*.

120. *Matthew 27:25*. Then answered all the people, and said, His blood be on us, and our children.

121. *Joel 1:15*. Alas for the day! for the day of the Lord is at hand, and as a destruction from the Almighty shall it come.

Amos 5:18-20. Woe unto you that desire the day of the Lord! to what end is it for you? the day of the Lord is darkness, and not light. As if a man did flee from a lion, and a bear met him; or went into the house, and leaned his hand on the wall, and a serpent bit him. Shall not the day of the Lord be darkness, and not light? even very dark, and no brightness in it?

2 Peter 2:17. These are wells without water, clouds that are carried with a tempest; to whom the midst of darkness is reserved for ever. See also *Zephaniah 1:14-18*; *Malachi 4:1*; *Jude 5-13*.

faithful.[122] For God has always had, and ever will have, a faithful remnant.[123] There were those in blind, unbelieving Israel, who waited for and accepted the Messiah (Luke 2, etc). So there will be those in the church who will wait for (1 Thessalonians 1:10) and welcome the coming Bridegroom (Matthew 25:10). And there will be a remnant in Israel, who, passing through the darkness and fire (Zechariah 13:9), will yet accept their King (Zechariah 12:10; Romans 9:27; 11:25-26). And there will even be a remnant (residue or remainder) among the Gentiles (ungodly world) who will seek after the Lord.[124]

Glory to God! The darkness will one day flee away before the Sun of righteousness, arising with healing in His wings,[125] when He comes to sit in the throne of His glory.[126] The mountain of the Lord's house will be established and all nations will flow to it (Isaiah 2:1-6; Micah 4:1-5; please read it) during that bright millennial day of peace and glory.[127] This day will follow "this present evil

---

122. *1 Thessalonians 5:4-8.* But ye, brethren, are not in darkness that that day should overtake you as a thief. Ye are all the children of light, and the children of the day: we are not of the night, nor of darkness. Therefore let us not sleep, as do others; but let us watch and be sober. For they that sleep sleep in the night; and they that be drunken are drunken in the night. But let us, who are of the day, be sober, putting on the breastplate of faith and love; and for an helmet, the hope of salvation.

1 Peter 1:13. Wherefore gird up the loins of your mind, be sober, and hope to the end for the grace that is to be brought unto you at the revelation of Jesus Christ.

123. *1 Kings 19:18.* Yet I have left me seven thousand in Israel, all the knees which have not bowed unto Baal, and every mouth which hath not kissed him.

Romans 11:5. Even so then at this present time also there is a remnant according to the election of grace.

124. *Acts 15:16-17.* After this I will return, and will build again the tabernacle of David, which is fallen down; and I will build again the ruins thereof, and I will set it up: that the residue of men might seek after the Lord, and all the Gentiles, upon whom my name is called, saith the Lord, who doeth all these things.

125. *Malachi 4:2-3.* But unto you that fear my name shall the Sun of righteousness arise with healing in his wings; and ye shall go forth, and grow up as calves of the stall. And ye shall tread down the wicked; for they shall be ashes under the soles of your feet in the day that I shall do this, saith the LORD of hosts.

126. *Matthew 19:28.* And Jesus said unto them, Verily I say unto you, That ye which have followed me, in the regeneration when the Son of man shall sit in the throne of his glory, ye also shall sit upon twelve thrones, judging the twelve tribes of Israel.

127. *Acts 17:31.* Because he hath appointed a day, in the which he will judge

age" (Galatians 1:4) and in which even the creature "will be delivered from the bondage of corruption into the glorious liberty of the children of God" (Romans 8:21). "They shall not hurt nor destroy in all my holy mountain: for the earth shall be full of the knowledge of the Lord, as the waters cover the sea" (Isaiah 11:9).

> A better day is coming, a morning promised long,
> When girded Right, with holy Might, will overthrow the wrong;
> When God the Lord will listen to every plaintive sigh,
> And stretch His hand o'er every land, with justice by and by.
>
> The boast of haughty error no more will fill the air,
> But age and youth will love the truth and spread it everywhere;
> No more from want and sorrow will come the hopeless cry;
> And strife will cease, and perfect peace will flourish by and by.
>
> Oh! for that holy dawning we watch, and wait, and pray,
> Till o'er the height the morning light shall drive the gloom away;
> And when the heavenly glory shall flood the earth and sky,
> We'll bless the Lord for all His Word, and praise Him by and by.

No. 13 Cruel to the Unsaved

It is objected that it would be cruel for Christ to come in judgment upon the world while there are so many millions unsaved. I answer, Is not this declaration a presumptuous criticism of God's motives? Was the flood an expression of cruelty, or rather was it not a manifestation of God's love and mercy toward those who would live after, in that He swept away the great overflow of wickedness? Surely it was done in mercy. And now let us remember that *this world dies every 33 years.* The

---

the world in righteousness by that man whom he hath ordained; whereof he hath given assurance unto all men, in that he hath raised him from the dead.

Romans 13:12. The night is far spent, the day is at hand: let us therefore cast off the works of darkness, and let us put on the armor of light.

Revelation 20:4-6. And I saw thrones, and they sat upon them, and judgment was given unto them: and I saw the souls of them that were beheaded for the witness of Jesus, and for the word of God, and which had not worshiped the beast, neither his image, neither had received his mark upon their foreheads, or in their hands: and they lived and reigned with Christ a thousand years. But the rest of the dead lived not again until the thousand years were finished. This is the first resurrection. Blessed and holy is he that hath part in the first resurrection; on such the second death hath no power, but they shall be priests of God and of Christ, and shall reign with him a thousand years.

average of human life is even a little less than this. The
world is in the power of the devil,[128] and he has the power
of death.[129] He has slain this world with the sword of
death many times over in the present dispensations.

Think of it! *Many, many worlds have gone down in the
whirlpool of death.* Each generation brings onto the scene
an entirely new world. And how few out of these are
converted. How few are reached by the gospel lifeboat,
and how few of those reached heed the message of
salvation. The great mass sweeps on, like a wrecked
vessel, in darkness and unbelief to the judgment.

The coming of Christ will inaugurate a far better state
of things. For when He comes, all things that offend will
be gathered out and the kingdom will be established in
righteousness.[130] And even though the subjects of the
kingdom (not the reigning ones)[131] may die during the
millennial age, they will die in a good old age. The one
even a hundred years old will be thought to be a child,[132]
and their death will be blessed.[133] And though the
Millennium is not the perfect state, judgment will speedily
follow the sinner of that day, or the nation which swerves
from serving God.[134]

---

128. *1 John 5:19.* We know that we are of God, and the whole world lieth in the
evil one.

129. *Hebrews 2:14-15.* Forasmuch then as the children are partakers of flesh
and blood, he also himself likewise took part of the same; that through death
he might destroy him that had the power of death, that is, the devil; and
deliver them, who through fear of death were all their lifetime subject to
bondage.

130. *Matthew 13:49-50.* So shall it be at the end of the world: the angels shall
come forth, and sever the wicked from among the just, and shall cast them into
the furnace of fire: there shall be wailing and gnashing of teeth. See also verses
31-43.

131. *Luke 20:35-36.* But they which shall be accounted worthy to obtain that
world, and the resurrection from the dead, neither marry, nor are given in
marriage: neither can they die any more: for they are equal unto the angels;
and are the children of God, being the children of the resurrection. See also
Revelation 20:4-6.

132. *Isaiah 65:20.* There shall be no more thence an infant of days, nor an old
man that hath not filled his days: for the child shall die an hundred years old;
but the sinner, being an hundred years old, shall be accursed.

133. *Revelation 14:13.* And I heard a voice from heaven saying unto me, Write,
Blessed are the dead which die in the Lord from henceforth: Yea saith the
Spirit, that they may rest from their labors.

134. *Zechariah 14:16-19.* And it shall come to pass, that every one that is left of

Surely, then, Christ's speedy coming can't be seen as an unmerciful event. The amazing thing is rather the long-suffering of God, which now[135] (as before the flood[136]) waits in such patient pleading. But He will fulfill His promise, and the Coming One* will come[137] and cut short the work in righteousness (Romans 9:28).

Then let us not look upon Christ's coming as cruel or unmerciful. He has said, *"surely I come quickly,"* and let us have the mind of the Holy Spirit, who replied, *"even so come, Lord Jesus"* (Revelation 22:20).

Then welcome, thrice welcome, ye token of God.
What else but His coming can comfort afford?
What presence but His set this prisoned earth free?
O Star of the Morning, our hope is in Thee!

No. 14 This Generation

Jesus said: "This generation shall not pass away till all be fulfilled" (Luke 21:32; see also Matthew 24:34; Mark 13:30.) Some have construed "generation" to mean a time of 30 or 40 years; and, as Jerusalem was destroyed within 40 years after Christ spoke, they refer all He said to that event.

Israel the Generation That Does Not Pass Away

We believe "generation" as is here used means the whole

---

* So the Greek.

---

all the nations which came against Jerusalem shall even go up from year to year to worship the King, the Lord or hosts, and to keep the feast of taber-nacles. And it shall be, that whoso will not come up of all the families of the earth unto Jerusalem to worship the King, the Lord of hosts, even upon them shall be no rain. And if the family of Egypt go not up, and come not, that have no rain, there shall be the plague wherewith the Lord will smite the heathen that come not up to keep the feast of tabernacles. This shall be the punish-ment of Egypt, and the punishment of all nations that come not up to keep the feast of tabernacles. See also *Isaiah 65:20*.

135. *2 Peter 3:9*. The Lord is not slack concerning his promise, as some men count slackness; but is longsuffering to usward, not willing that any should perish, but that all should come to repentance.

136. *1 Peter 3:20*. Which sometime were disobedient, when once the longsuffer-ing of God waited in the days of Noah, while the ark was a preparing, wherein few, that is, eight souls were saved by water.

137. *Hebrews 10:36-37*. For ye have need of patience, that, after ye have done the will of God, ye might receive the promise. For yet a little while, and he that shall come will come, and will not tarry.

existence of the Israelite race. Compare the following passages where the same Greek word is used.[138] In Psalm 22:30 we read: "A seed shall serve Him; it shall be accounted to the Lord for a generation." And in Psalm 24:6: "This is the generation of them that seek Him." In Proverbs 30:11-14 the generation of the righteous and the generation of the wicked are clearly distinguished. Therefore we conclude that the generation of the Israelites were not only to see the destruction of Jerusalem, but the *coming* of Christ (at the revelation) and the end of the age (Matthew 24:3).

Their wonderful preservation as a distinct people, through all the persecutions, vicissitudes and wanderings of the past 18 centuries down to the present moment, is a standing miracle, attesting the truth of God's Word, and assuring us of His purposes in their future history. Frederick the Great said to his chaplain: "Doctor, if your religion is a true one, it ought to be capable of very brief and simple proof. Will you give me an evidence of its truth in *one word*?" The good man answered, "Israel."

Other nations come and go, but Israel remains. She does not pass away. God says of her, "For a small moment have I forsaken thee; but with great mercies will I gather thee. In a little wrath I hid my face from thee for a moment; but with everlasting kindness will I have mercy on thee, saith the LORD, thy Redeemer" (Isaiah 54:7-8).

---

138. *Matthew 11:16.* But whereunto shall I liken this generation? It is like unto children sitting in the markets, and calling unto their fellows.

Matthew 16:4. A wicked and adulterous generation seeketh after a sign; and there shall no sign be given unto it, but the sign of the prophet Jonas. And he left them, and departed.

Luke 9:41. And Jesus answering said, O faithless and perverse generation, how long shall I be with you, and suffer you? Bring thy son hither.

Luke 11:49-51. Therefore also said the wisdom of God, I will send them prophets and apostles, and some of them they shall slay and persecute: that the blood of all the prophets, which was shed from the foundation of the world, may be required of this generation; from the blood of Abel unto the blood of Zacharias, which perished between the altar and the temple: verily I say unto you, It shall be required of this generation.

Philippians 2:15. That ye may become blameless and harmless, children of God without blemish in the midst of a crooked and perverse generation, among whom ye are seen as lights in the world. See also *Mark 8:38; Luke 7:31; 11:29–32; 16:8; 17:25; Acts 2:40.*

15

ISRAEL IS TO BE RESTORED

Perhaps you say, "I don't believe the Israelites are to be restored to Canaan, and Jerusalem rebuilt."

Have you read the declarations in God's Word about it? Surely nothing is more plainly stated in the Scriptures. I wish I had space to quote the passages, but we can only give you a portion of the references. I simply ask you to read them thoughtfully. Divest yourself of prejudice and preconceived notions, and let the Holy Spirit show you, from His Word, the glorious future of God's chosen people, "who are beloved" (Romans 11:28), and dear unto Him as "the apple of His eye" (Zechariah 2:8).

1. God calls Abraham (Genesis 12:1).[1]
2. God's promise to Abraham (Genesis 12:2–7; 13:14–17;[2] 15:18; 17:8).
   God's promise to Isaac (Genesis 26:1–5).
   God's promise to Jacob (Genesis 28:1–15; 35:10–12).

---

1. *Genesis 12:1-3, 6-7.* Now the LORD had said unto Abram, Get thee out of thy country, and from thy kindred, and from thy father's house, unto a land that I will show thee: and I will make of thee a great nation, and I will bless thee, and make thy name great; and thou shalt be a blessing: and I will bless them that bless thee, and curse him that curseth thee: and in thee shall all families of the earth be blessed. And Abram passed through the land unto the place of Sichem, unto the plain of Moreh. And the Canaanite was then in the land. And the LORD appeared unto Abram, and said, Unto thy seed will I give this land: and there builded he an altar unto the LORD, who appeared unto him.

2. *Genesis 13:14-17.* And the LORD said unto Abram, after that Lot was separated from him, Lift up now thine eyes, and look from the place where thou art northward, and southward, and eastward, and westward; for all the land which thou seest, to thee will I give it, and to thy seed for ever. And I will make thy seed as the dust of the earth: so that if a man can number the dust of the earth, then shall thy seed also be numbered. Arise, walk through the land, in the length of it, and in the breadth of it; for I will give it unto thee.

3. The land described (Exodus 23:31; Numbers 34; Deuteronomy 11:24; 34:1–4; Joshua 1:2–6).
4. The land partially possessed (1 Kings 4:21).
5. Punishment prophesied for disobedience (Leviticus 26:14–39; Deuteronomy 4:22; 28:15; 31:16).
6. Israel's sins (Judges 2:11–19; 1 Samuel 8:6; 2 Kings 21:11; 2 Kings 24:3; Jeremiah 15:4; and many others, especially Matthew 27:25).
7. The promises to be remembered and restoration assured:
    Leviticus 26:40–45, especially verses 42, 44, 45.[3]
    Deuteronomy 4:30–31.[4]
    Deuteronomy 30:1–10, especially verses 4, 5, 6.[5]
    2 Samuel 7:10–11.[6]
    Joel 2:18–32.
    Joel 3:1–21.
    Amos 9:11–15, especially verse 15.[7]
    Hosea 1:10–11.
    Hosea 2:14–23.
    Hosea 3:4–5.

---

3. *Leviticus 26:44-45*. And yet for all that, when they be in the land of their enemies, I will not cast them away, neither will I abhor them, to destroy them utterly, and to break my covenant with them: for I am the LORD their God. But I will for their sakes remember the covenant of their ancestors, whom I brought forth out of the land of Egypt in the sight of the heathen, that I might be their God: I am the LORD.

4. *Deuteronomy 4:30-31*. When thou art in tribulation, and all these things are come upon thee, even in the latter days, if thou turn to the LORD thy God, and shalt be obedient unto his voice; (for the LORD thy God is a merciful God;) he will not forsake thee, neither destroy thee, not forget the covenant of thy fathers which he sware unto them.

5. *Deuteronomy 30:1-6*. And it shall come to pass, when all these things are come upon thee, the blessing and the curse, which I have set before thee, and thou shalt call them to mind among all the nations whither the LORD thy God hath driven thee. And shalt return unto the LORD thy God, and shalt obey his voice, according to all that I command thee this day, thou and thy children, with all thine heart, and with all thy soul; that then the LORD thy God will turn thy captivity, and have compassion upon thee, and will return and gather thee from all the nations, whither the LORD thy God hath scattered thee. If any of thine be driven out unto the outmost parts of heaven, from thence will the LORD thy God gather thee, and from thence will he fetch thee: and the LORD thy God will bring thee into the land which thy fathers possessed, and thou shalt possess it; and he will do thee good, and multiply thee above thy fathers. And the LORD thy God will circumcise thine heart, and the heart of thy seed, to love the LORD thy God with all thine heart, and with all thy soul, that thou mayest live.

6. *2 Samuel 7:10*. Moreover I will appoint a place for my people Israel, and will plant them, that they may dwell in a place of their own, and move no more; neither shall the children of wickedness afflict them any more, as beforetime.

7. *Amos 9:11-15*. In that day will I raise up the tabernacle of David that is fallen, and close up the breaches thereof; and I will raise up his ruins, and I

Isaiah 2:2–5.

Isaiah 9:6–7.

Isaiah 10:20–23, especially verses 21, 22.

Isaiah 11:10–16, especially verse 11, second time.

Isaiah 19:23–25.

Isaiah 27:12–13[8]

Isaiah 33:20–24.

Isaiah 43:1–7, especially verses 5, 6, 7.

Isaiah 49:13–26, especially verses 22, 23.

Isaiah 60:1–22, especially verses 8, 9, 10, 15, 16, 18, 21.

Isaiah 61:1–11.

Isaiah 62:1–12.

Isaiah 65:8–10.

Isaiah 65:17–25.

Isaiah 66:19–24.

Jeremiah 3:12–19, especially verses 17, 18.

Jeremiah 11:4–5.

Jeremiah 16:14–16.[9]

Jeremiah 23:3–8, especially verses 3, 4, 6.

Jeremiah 29:10–14.

Jeremiah 30:1–24, especially verses 8, 9, 10, 11, 20.

Jeremiah 31:1–40, especially verses 8, 9, 10, 12, 28, 33, 38.

Jeremiah 32:36–44, especially verses 37, 39, 40, 41, 42.

Jeremiah 34:7–17, especially verses 7, 8, 14, 15, 16.

Jeremiah 44:28.

---

will build it as in the days of old: that they may possess the remnant of Edom, and of all the heathen, which are called by my name, saith the Lord that doeth this. Behold, the days come, saith the LORD, that the plowman shall overtake the reaper, and the treader of grapes him that soweth seed; and the mountains shall drop sweet wine, and all the hills shall melt. And I will bring again the captivity of my people of Israel, and they shall build the waste cities, and inhabit them; and they shall plant vineyards, and drink the wine thereof; they shall also make gardens, and eat the fruit of them. And I will plant them upon their land, and they shall no more be pulled up out of their land which I have given them, saith the LORD thy God.

8. *Isaiah 27:12-13*. And it shall come to pass in that day, that the LORD shall beat off from the channel of the river unto the stream of Egypt, and ye shall be gathered one by one, O ye children of Israel. And it shall come to pass in that day, that the great trumpet shall be blown, and they shall come which were ready to perish in the land of Assyria, and the outcasts in the land of Egypt, and shall worship the LORD in the holy mount at Jerusalem.

9. *Jeremiah 16:14-16*. Therefore, behold, the days come, saith the LORD, that it shall no more be said, The LORD liveth, that brought up the children of Israel from the land of the north, and from all the lands whither he had driven them: and I will bring them again into their land that I gave unto their fathers. Behold, I will send for many fishers, saith the LORD, and they shall fish them; and after will I send for many hunters, and they shall hunt them from every mountain, and from every hill, and out of the holes of the rocks.

Jeremiah 46:27–28.
Jeremiah 50:4–8.
Jeremiah 50:17–20.
Ezekiel 6:8–10, especially verse 9.
Ezekiel 20:36–44, especially verses 40, 41, 42, 43, 44.[10]
Ezekiel 28:24–26, especially verses 25, 26.
Ezekiel 34:11–31, especially verses 11, 12, 13, 14, 23, 24, 25, 28.
Ezekiel 36:1–38, especially verses 8, 10, 11, 12, 15, 21, 28, 31, 35, 37, 38.
Ezekiel 37:1–28, especially verses 11, 12, 14, 16–28.
Ezekiel 39:23–29, especially verses 25, 26, 27, 29.
Ezekiel 40—48, the New Temple.
Ezekiel 48, see the order in which the tribes will be settled.
Micah 4:1–7.
Micah 7:8–20, especially verses 12, 19, 20.[11]
Zephaniah 3:8–20, especially verses 11, 13, 19, 20.[12]
Zechariah 2:4–13.
Zechariah 3:1–10, especially verse 9.
Zechariah 8:1–23, especially verses 4, 5, 8, 12, 16, 17, 20 to 23.
Zechariah 10:5–12, all of them.[13]
Zechariah 12:1–14, especially verses 10, 11.

---

10. *Ezekiel 20:40-44.* For in mine holy mountain, in the mountain of the height of Israel, saith the LORD God, there shall all the house of Israel, all of them in the land, serve me: there will I accept them, and there will I require your offerings, and the firstfruits of your oblations, with all your holy things. I will accept you with your sweet savour, when I bring you out from the people, and gather you out of the countries wherein ye have been scattered; and I will be sanctified in you before the heathen. And ye shall know that I am the LORD, when I shall bring you into the land of Israel, into the country for the which I lifted up mine hand to give it to your fathers. And there shall ye remember your ways, and all your doings, wherein ye have been defiled; and ye shall loathe yourselves in your own sight for all your evils that ye have committed. And ye shall know that I am the LORD, when I have wrought with you for my name's sake, not according to your wicked ways, nor according to your corrupt doings, O ye house of Israel, saith the LORD God.

11. *Micah 7:18-20.* Who is a God like unto thee, that pardoneth iniquity, and passeth by the transgression of the remnant of his heritage? he retaineth not his anger for ever, because he delighteth in mercy. He will turn again, he will have compassion upon us; he will subdue our iniquities; and thou wilt cast all their sins into the depths of the sea. Thou wilt perform the truth to Jacob, and the mercy to Abraham, which thou hast sworn unto our fathers from the days of old.

12. *Zephaniah 3:19*-20. Behold, at that time I will undo all that afflict thee; and I will save her that halteth, and gather her that was driven out; and I will get them praise and fame in every land where they have been put to shame. At that time will I bring you again, even in the time that I gather you: for I will make you a name and a praise among all people of the earth, when I turn back your captivity before your eyes, saith the LORD.

13. *Zechariah 10:6-10.* And I will strengthen the house of Judah, and I will

Zechariah 13:1–9, especially verses 6, 8, 9.

Zechariah 14:1–21, especially verses 11, 16, 20, 21.

Malachi 3:10–12.[14]

Matthew 23:37–39, especially in verse 39, "till."

Luke 13:34–35, especially in verse 35, "until."

Luke 21:24, especially "until." "Jerusalem shall be trodden down of the Gentiles *until* the times of the Gentiles be fulfilled."

Romans 11:17–28, especially verses 17, 20, 24–28.[15]

Acts 15:13–16, very important, as it is the apostle's summary of the prophets.[16]

Psalm 51:18; 102:16.

---

save the house of Joseph, and I will bring them again to place them: for I have mercy upon them: and they shall be as though I had not cast them off: for I am the LORD their God, and will hear them. And they of Ephraim shall be like a mighty man, and their heart shall rejoice as through wine: yea, their children shall see it, and be glad; their heart shall rejoice in the LORD. I will hiss for them, and gather them; for I have redeemed them: and they shall increase as they have increased. And I will sow them among the people: and they shall remember me in far countries; and they shall live with their children, and turn again. I will bring them again also out of the land of Egypt, and gather them out of Assyria: and I will bring them into the land of Gilead and Lebanon; and place shall not be found for them.

14. *Malachi 3:11-12*. And I will rebuke the devourer for your sakes, and he shall not destroy the fruits of your ground; neither shall your vine cast her fruit before the time in the field, saith the LORD of hosts. And all nations shall call you blessed: for ye shall be a delightsome land, saith the LORD of hosts.

15. *Romans 11:11-13, 19-21, 25-27*. I say then, Have they stumbled that they should fall? God forbid: but rather through their fall salvation is come unto the Gentiles, for to provoke them to jealousy. Now if the fall of them be the riches of the world, and the diminishing of them the riches of the Gentiles; how much more their fulness? For I speak to you Gentiles, inasmuch as I am the apostle of the Gentiles, I magnify mine office: Thou wilt say then, The branches were broken off, that I might be graffed in. Well; because of unbelief they were broken off, and thou standest by faith. Be not highminded, but fear: for if God spared not the natural branches, take heed lest he also spare not thee. For I would not, brethren, that ye should be ignorant of this mystery, lest ye should be wise in your own conceits, that blindness in part is happened to Israel, until the fulness of the Gentiles be come in. And so all Israel shall be saved: as it is written, There shall come out of Sion the Deliverer, and shall turn away ungodliness from Jacob: for this is my covenant unto them, when I shall take away their sins.

16. *Acts 15:13-17*. And after they had held their peace, James answered, saying, Men and brethren, hearken unto me: Simeon hath declared how God at the first did visit the Gentiles, to take out of them a people for his name. And to this agree the words of the prophets; as it is written, after this I will return, and will build again the tabernacle of David, which is fallen down; and I will build again the ruins thereof, and I will set it up; that the residue of men might seek after the LORD, and all the Gentiles, upon whom my name is called, saith the LORD, who doeth all these things.

And now, if you have faithfully studied these pasages, or if you have even read them, do you understand why the great mass of Jews, at the present time, have an abiding faith that they are to be returned to Canaan? All the orthodox Jews tenaciously cling to this hope; and will we, who have accepted so much greater light, refuse this overwhelming testimony of the Word? God forbid! It may be that you say, "These prophesies were fulfilled in the return from Babylon."

Not so, that was the *first time*. But there is to be a second restoration.

The Second Restoration

"And it shall come to pass in that day, that the Lord shall set His hand *again* the *second time* to recover the remnant of His people, which shall be left, from Assyria, and from Egypt, and from Pathros, and from Cush, and from Elam, and from Shinar, and from Hamath, and from the islands of the sea" (Isaiah 11:11).

In the first restoration only those who *wanted to* came back from Babylon (Ezra 7:13), while many remained there, in Egypt and elsewhere. But in the future, or second restoration, not one will be left.

"If any of thine be driven out unto the outmost parts of heaven, from thence will the LORD thy God gather thee, and from thence will He fetch thee" (Deuteronomy 30:4).

"Fear not; for I am with thee: I will bring thy seed from the east, and gather thee from the west; I will say to the north, give up; and to the south, keep not back; bring my sons from far, and my daughters from the ends of the earth; *even every one* that is called by my name: for I have created him for my glory, I have formed him; yea, I have made him" (Isaiah 43:5–7).

"For thus saith the LORD God; Behold, I, even I, will both search my sheep and seek them out. As a shepherd seeketh out his flock in the day that he is among his sheep that are scattered, so will I seek out my sheep, and will deliver them out of all places where they have been scattered in the cloudy and dark day; and I will bring them out from the people, and gather them from the countries, and will bring them to their own land, and feed them upon the mountains of Israel" (Ezekiel 34:11–13).

"Then shall they know that I am the LORD their God, which caused them to be led into captivity, among the heathen; but I have gathered them unto their own land, and *have left none of them any more there*" (Ezekiel 39:28–29).

In the first restoration it was only Jews who returned. In the second, or future restoration, it will be both Judah (the two tribes) and Israel (the ten tribes).[*]

"In those days the house of Judah shall walk with the house of Israel, and they shall come together out of the land of the north to the land that I have given for an inheritance unto your fathers" (Jeremiah 3:18).

"And I will multiply men upon you, all the house of Israel, *even all of it*, and the cities shall be inhabited, and the wastes shall be builded" (Ezekiel 36:10).

Ezekiel was directed to take two sticks, representing Judah and Joseph, which should be joined and become one stick in his hand, and when the people enquired what it meant, he was directed to say unto them:

"Thus saith the LORD God; Behold, I will take the children of Israel from among the heathen, whither they be gone, and will gather them on every side, and bring them into their own land: and I will make them *one nation* in the land upon the mountains of Israel; and one king shall be king to them *all*; and they shall be *no more* two nations, neither shall they be divided into two kingdoms any more at all" (Ezekiel 37:15–22).

Permanent Restoration

At the first restoration they returned to be overthrown and driven out again. But in the second, they will return to remain, no more to go out. They will be exalted and dwell safely, and the Gentile nations will flow to them.

"I will plant them upon their land, and they *shall no*

---

[*] Except in this place, we use the word Israel in its broader sense, meaning the whole twelve tribes.

more be pulled up out of their land which I have given them, saith the LORD their God" (Amos 9:15).

"And they shall no more be a prey to the heathen, neither shall the beasts of the land devour them: but they shall *dwell safely*, and none shall make them afraid" (Ezekiel 34:28).

"And I will settle you after your old estates, and will do better unto you than at your beginnings:—yea, I will cause men to walk upon you, even my people Israel;—and thou shalt *no more henceforth bereave them of men*" (Ezekiel 36:11–12).

"Whereas thou hast been forsaken and hated, so that no man went through thee, I will make thee an eternal excellency, a joy of many generations. Thou shalt also suck the milk of the Gentiles, and shall suck the breast of kings; and thou shalt know that I the LORD am thy Savior and thy Redeemer, the mighty One of Jacob" (Isaiah 60:15–16).

All Nations Shall Flow Unto Israel

"As I *live*, saith the LORD, thou shalt surely clothe thee with them all, as with an ornament, and bind them on thee, as a bride doeth. . . I will lift up my hand to the Gentiles, and set up my standard to the people: and they shall bring thy sons in their arms, and thy daughters shall be carried upon their shoulders, and kings shall be thy nursing fathers, and their queens thy nursing mothers; they shall bow down to thee with their face toward the earth, and lick up the dust of thy feet" (Isaiah 49:18, 22, 23).

"But in the last days it shall come to pass, that the mountain of the house of the LORD shall be extablished in the top of the mountains and it shall be exalted above the hills; and people shall flow into it. And many nations shall come, and say, Come, and let us go up to the mountain of the LORD, and to the house of the God of Jacob; and he will teach us of his ways, and we will walk in his paths: for the law shall go forth of Zion, and the word of the LORD from Jerusalem" (Micah 4:1–2).

"Thus saith the LORD of hosts; It shall yet come to pass, that there shall come people, and the inhabitants of many cities. And the inhabitants of one city shall go to another, saying, Let us go speedily to pray before the

LORD, and to seek the LORD of hosts: I will also go. Yea, *many people* and *strong nations* shall come to seek the LORD of hosts in Jerusalem, and to pray before the LORD. Thus saith the LORD of hosts: In those days it shall come to pass, that ten men shall take hold out of all languages of the nations, even shall take hold of the skirt of him that is a Jew, saying, We will go with you: for we have heard that God is with you" (Zechariah 8:20–23).

"And it shall come to pass, *that every one that is left of all the nations* which came against Jerusalem, shall even go up from year to year to worship the King, the LORD of hosts, and to keep the feast of tabernacles" (Zechariah 14:16).

In the first restoration, because of their blindness and hard, stony hearts, they rejected and killed Jesus. But in the future restoration they will *repent* of all this, and have *clean hearts*, and *accept Christ*, who will be their King.

Look Upon Me

"And I will pour upon the house of David, and upon the inhabitants of Jerusalem, the spirit of grace and of supplications; and they shall look upon me whom they have *pierced, and they shall mourn for him, as one mourneth for his only son, and shall be in bitterness for him, as one that is in bitterness for his first-born.* In that day there shall be a great mourning in Jerusalem, as the mourning of Hadadrimmon in the valley of Megiddon. And the land shall mourn, every family apart; the family of the house of David apart, and their wives apart; the family of the house of Nathan apart, and their wives apart; the family of the house of Levi apart, and their wives apart; the family of Shimei apart, and their wives apart; all the families that remain, every family apart, and their wives apart" (Zechariah 12:10–14).

"They shall come with weeping, and with supplications will I lead them: I will cause them to walk by the rivers of waters in a straight way, wherin they shall not stumble: for I am a father to Israel, and Ephraim is my firstborn. Hear the word of the LORD, O ye nations, and declare it in the isles afar off, and say, He that scattereth Israel will gather him, and keep him, as a shepherd doth his flock. But this shall be the covenant that I will make with the house of Israel; after those days, saith the LORD, I will put my law in their *inward parts, and write it in their hearts*; and will be their God, and they shall be my people" (Jeremiah 31:9, 10, 33).

The Cleansing of Israel

"For I will take you from among the heathen, and gather you out of all countries, and will bring you into your own land. Then will I sprinkle clean water upon you, and you shall be clean: from all your filthiness, and from all your idols, will I cleanse you. A new heart also will I give you. And a new spirit will I put within you; and I will take away the stony heart out of your flesh, and I will give you a heart of flesh. And I will put my Spirit within you, and cause you to walk in my statutes, and ye shall keep my judgments, and do them. And ye shall dwell in the land that I gave to your fathers; and ye shall be my people, and I will be your God. I will also save you from all your uncleanness: and I will call for the corn, and will increase it, and lay no famine upon you" (Ezekiel 36:24–28).

"Neither shall they defile themselves any more with their idols nor with their detestable things, nor with any of their transgressions; but I will save them out of all their dwelling places, wherein they have sinned, and will cleanse them; so shall they be my people, and I will be their God. And David my servant shall be king over them; and they all shall have one shepherd: . . . and they shall dwell in the land that I have given unto Jacob my servant, wherein your fathers have dwelt; and they shall dwell therein, forever: and my servant David shall be their prince, forever, . . . my tabernacle shall also be with them: yea, I will be their God and they shall be my people" (Ezekiel 37:23–27).

"And I will gather the remnant of my flock out of all countries whither I have driven them, and will bring them again to their folds; and they shall be fruitful and increase. And I will set up shepherds over them which shall feed them: and they shall fear no more, nor be dismayed, neither shall they be lacking, saith the Lord. Behold, the days come, saith the LORD, that I will raise to David a righteous Branch and a King shall reign and prosper, and shall execute judgment and justice in the earth. In his days Judah shall be saved, and Israel shall dwell safely: and this is his name whereby he shall be called, 'the LORD our righteousness' [Jehovah, Tsidkenu]" (Jeremiah 23:3–6).

"And I will set up one shepherd over them, and he shall feed them, even my servant David: he shall feed them, and he shall be their shepherd. And I the LORD will be their God, and my servant David a prince among them; I the LORD have spoken it" (Ezekiel 34:23–24).

Nothing has ever yet been built like the temple which Ezekiel describes in chapters 40 to 48, and this includes a definite description of the location of each tribe, as they will be settled in this great future restoration (see Ezekiel 48).

Confusing Israel With the Church

It would seem that such overwhelming testimony would convince every fair-minded reader that there is a glorious future restoration in store for Israel. And yet, many say that we must interpret all this Scripture "spiritually," and they fritter away the point and the force of such explicit declarations, in attempting to apply them to the persecuted church.

This is a great error, and I believe it has arisen, principally, from a misunderstanding of Paul's arguments in his epistles. He does not confuse Israel with the church when he says, "They are not all Israel which are of Israel." Nor does he confuse the church with Israel when he makes us children of Abraham by faith; but he demonstrates that we all stand by faith alone.

In 1 Corinthians 10:32,[17] he makes a clear distinction between the Jews, the Gentiles, and the church of God.* There are special blessings for the church, and special blessings for Israel. He plainly shows that not all the natural seed are true Israelites. He only is a Jew who has circumcision of heart in the spirit.[18] And though

---

* The Jews who accept Christ in this dispensation become part of the church. See pages 89-90.

---

17. *1 Corinthians 10:32*. Give none offence, neither to the Jews, nor to the Gentiles, nor to the church of God.
18. *Romans 2:29*. But he is a Jew, which is one inwardly; and circumcision is that of the heart, in the spirit, and not in the letter; whose praise is not of men, but of God.

multitudes of Israelites have passed away in unbelief, still Paul distinctly declares that there is a remnant *which will be saved.*[19] He so loved them that he could sacrifice himself, and even be separated from Christ for their sakes.[20] He saw their future glory as the natural branches yet to be grafted into their own olive tree, which would be nothing less than life from the dead.[21]

Jesus said in Luke 21:24, "And they shall fall by the edge of the sword, and shall be led away captive into all nations; and Jerusalem shall be trodden down of the Gentiles, until the times of the Gentiles be fulfilled." And Paul understood this mystery, that when "the fullness of the Gentiles be come in," "there should come out of Zion the Deliverer, who should turn away ungodliness from Jacob" (Romans 11:25–26).

And this is fully confirmed by the following: In Amos 8 and 9 we read of the awful calamities which would come upon Israel. And not until they had been *sifted among all nations* would the Lord gather and plant them, and raise up the tabernacle of David that is fallen. When the apostles and elders were gathered in the first council at Jerusalem, they were considering this same question about Israelites and the church. The Holy Spirit directed the mind of James to this very prophecy in Amos, to show that during this sifting of Israel, God was to *take out* of the Gentiles a people to His name, and *after this* to build again the tabernacle of David (Acts 15:13–17). So we see that these restoration prophecies cannot be applied to the church, which is first to be *taken out* before Israel and Jerusalem are to be restored.

Again, one of the most specific prophecies of their restoration is addressed, not to the people, but to the

---

19. *Romans 9:27.* Esaias also crieth concerning Israel, Though the number of the children of Israel be as the sand of the sea, a remnant shall be saved.

   Romans 11:5. Even so then at this present time also there is a remnant according to the election of grace.

20. *Romans 9:3.* For I could wish that myself were accursed from Christ for my brethren, my kinsmen according to the flesh.

21. *Romans 11:15.* For if the casting away of them be the reconciling of the world, what shall the receiving of them be, but life from the dead?

mountains of Israel, which leaves no possible doubt as to the literal meaning intended.[22]

The Day of Jacob's Trouble

Surely Israel *will be restored* but there is an *awful time of trouble* awaiting her. Israel's sins are mountain high. The guilt of innocent blood is on the Israelite's—the precious blood of Jesus Christ (Matthew 27:25).

The faithful prophet saw it when he wrote:

> "And these are the words that the Lord spake concerning Israel and concerning Judah. For thus saith the LORD: We have heard a voice of trembling, of fear, and not of peace. Ask ye now, and see whether a man doth travail with child? wherefore do I see every man with his hands on his loins, as a woman in travail, and all faces are turned into paleness. Alas! for that day is great, so that none is like it: it is even the time of Jacob's trouble; but he shall be saved out of it" (Jeremiah 30:4–7).

> "Then shall ye remember your own evil ways, and your doings that were not good, and shall loathe yourselves in your own sight for your iniquities and for you abominations" (Ezekiel 36:31).

Yes, they will repent and loathe themselves. They "shall pass through the sea with affliction."[23] Many shall die, but the third part shall be saved.

> "And I will bring the *third part* through the fire, and will refine them as silver is refined, and will try them

---

22. *Ezekiel 36:1, 8-11.* Also, thou son of man, prophesy unto the mountains of Israel, and say, Ye mountains of Israel, hear the word of the LORD. But ye, O mountains of Israel, ye shall shoot forth your branches, and yield your fruit to my people of Israel; for they are at hand to come. For, behold, I am for you and I will turn unto you, and ye shall be tilled and sown: and I will multiply men upon you, all the house of Israel even all of it: and the cities shall be inhabited, and the wastes shall be builded: and I will multiply upon you man and beast; and they shall increase and bring fruit: and I will settle you after your old estates, and will do better unto you than at your beginings; and ye shall know that I am the LORD.

23. *Zechariah 10:11.* And he shall pass through the sea with affliction, and shall smite the waves in the sea, and all the deeps of the river shall dry up; and the pride of Assyria shall be brought down, and the sceptre of Egypt shall depart away.

Ezekiel 7:1-4, 8-9. Moreover the word of the LORD came unto me, saying, Also, thou son of man, thus saith the LORD God unto the land of Israel; an end, the end is come upon the four corners of the land. Now is the end come upon

as gold is tried; they shall call on my name and I will hear them; I will say, it is my people; and they shall say, the LORD is my God" (Zechariah 13:9).

All this is intimately connected with the coming of Christ, not at the Rapture, but at the Revelation (see diagram, page 74). For we read, "When the Lord shall build up Zion, *He shall appear in His glory*" (Psalm 102:16). It is when He appears with His saints (the church) in flaming fire to execute judgment (2 Thessalonians 1:7–10; Jude 14) on the nations and on Israel, who are the third party in Matthew 25:36, etc.,[24] and who are not to be reckoned among the nations (Numbers 23:9). It is when He sits as a refiner and purifier.

"Behold I will send my messenger, and he shall prepare the way before me; and the LORD whom ye seek, shall suddenly come to His temple, even the messenger of the covenant, whom ye delight in: behold, He shall come, saith the LORD of hosts. But who may abide the day of His coming? and who shall stand when He appeareth? for He is like a refiner's fire, and like fuller's soap. And he shall sit as a refiner and purifier of silver; and He shall purify the sons of Levi, and purge them as gold and silver, that they may offer unto the LORD an offering in righteousness. Then shall the offering of Judah and Jerusalem be pleasant unto the Lord, as in the days of old, and as in former years. And I will come near you to judgment; and I will be a swift witness against the sorcerers, and against the adulterers, and against false swearers, and against those that oppress the hireling in his wages, the widow, and the fatherless, and that turn aside the stranger from his right, and fear not me, saith the LORD of hosts" (Malachi 3:1–5).

---

thee, and I will send mine anger upon thee, and will judge thee according to thy ways, and will recompense upon thee all thine abominations. And mine eye shall not spare thee, neither will I have pity: but I will recompense thy ways upon thee, and thine abominations shall be in the midst of thee; and ye shall know that I am the LORD. Now will I shortly pour out my fury upon thee, and accomplish mine anger upon thee; and I will judge thee according to thy ways, and will recompense thee for all thine abominations. And mine eye shall not spare, neither will I have pity: I will recompense thee according to thy ways and thine abominations that are in the midst of thee: and ye shall know that I am the LORD that smiteth.

24. *Matthew 25:40.* And the King shall answer and say unto them. Verily I say unto you, Inasmuch as ye have done it unto one of the least of these my brethren, ye have done it unto me.

He will indeed refine Israel in "the furnace of affliction."[25] And they will arise and shine, for *their light will come.*[26]

> Arise and shine in youth immortal,
> Thy light is come, thy King appears!
> Beyond the centuries' swinging portal,
> Breaks a new dawn—THE THOUSAND YEARS!

I could fill a book with comments about how Israel will be restored, but all I have desired to do was to show that it is an incontrovertible fact of prophecy, and that it is intimately connected with our Lord's appearing. I trust I have satisfactorily accomplished this.

The detail of the manner of their restoration, and of their repentance and acceptance of Christ, is not so important to us. For those who are of the church are to be taken away first in the Rapture, and escape all these things through which Israel must pass.[27]

True, many have found the study of this detail a rich blessing, and I give the results one has reached on pages 193 to 201. And yet I believe that we cannot now discern the order of these things so clearly as Israel will in the great rush of events, after the church is taken away, and when the Book is more completely unsealed and opened (Daniel 12:4).

It is enough for us to know that it will be in the latter days (Isaiah 2:2) that Antichrist is to be revealed and

---

25. *Isaiah 48:10*. Behold, I have refined thee, but not with silver; I have chosen thee in the furnace of affliction.
    Psalm 66:10. For thou, O God, hast proved us: thou hast tried us, as silver is tried.
26. *Isaiah 60:1-4*. Arise, shine; for thy light is come, and the glory of the LORD is risen upon thee. For, behold, the darkness shall cover the earth, and gross darkness the people: but the LORD shall arise upon thee, and his glory shall be seen upon thee. And the Gentiles shall come to thy light, and kings to the brightness of thy rising. Lift up thine eyes round about, and see: all they gather themselves together, they come to thee: thy sons shall come from far and thy daughters shall be nursed at thy side.
27. *Luke 21:36*. Watch ye therefore, and pray always, that ye may be accounted worthy to escape all these things that shall come to pass, and to stand before the Son of man.

destroyed by Jesus the King of the Jews, who *is* coming (2 Thessalonians 2:8), and that Israel, His people, will soon come home (Ezekiel 36:8).

16

THE STUDY OF PROPHECY

It may be that you disapprove of the study of prophecy, because Jesus said: "But of that day and hour knoweth no man" (Matthew 24:36), and, "It is not for you to know the times or the seasons which the Father hath put in his own power" (Acts 1:7).

Don't assume that the study of prophecy consists merely in the setting of dates or forecasting future events. For wise reasons the Master has withheld from us "the day and the hour" when He will come, but He called the Pharisees hypocrites because they could not discern the signs of the times. He has commanded us to *watch*, and he has pronounced a blessing upon the study of prophecy.[1] Peter exhorts us to *pay attention to* the sure word of prophecy.[2] "All Scripture is given by inspiration of God, and is profitable for doctrine, for reproof, for correction, for instruction in righteousness" (2 Timothy 3:16).

The greater part of this Scripture consists of prophecy, and if Christians would give more attention to it, they would not find themselves distracted from present service,

---

1. *Revelation 1:3*. Blessed is he that readeth and they that hear the words of this prophecy, and keep those things which are written therein: for the time is at hand.
    Revelation 22:7. Behold, I come quickly: blessed is he that keepeth the sayings of the prophecy of this book.
    Luke 11:28. But he said, Yea, rather, blessed are they that hear the word of God, and keep it.
2. *2 Peter 1:19*. And we have the word of prophecy made more sure; whereunto ye do well that ye take heed, as unto a lamp shining in a dark place, until the day dawn, and the day-star arise in your hearts.

but they would find much light thrown on their present path, and much practical encouragement given to their ministry. Their faith would rest on a broader and deeper comprehension of God's character and ways, and their spiritual horizon would stand out in clearer outline than before.

But to perceive and understand all this requires much more than a surface study of Scripture, or the mere forecasting of future events. It must be read in its more profound teachings, in those wonderful depths of meaning that underlie its illustrations, its metaphors, its history, as well as sparkle up to the sunlight in its bright prophetic announcement of coming glory.

Such a study of God's word will be found of paramount importance to meet the skepticism of the day, for it furnishes us out of God's own armory, and trains us in His school of warfare. See how God uses prophetic truth to confound the philosophers and skeptics.[3] And He points to the prophecies fulfilled as an assurance of the accomplishment of the new things declared by Him. "Before they spring forth I tell you of them."[4] And He sets forth Israel as the *witnesses* before all nations of the Word He has declared and that He is God.[5]

---

3. *Isaiah 41:21-23*. Produce your cause, saith the LORD; bring forth your strong reasons, saith the King of Jacob. Let them bring them forth, and show us what shall happen: let them show the former things, what they be, that we may consider them, and know the latter end of them; or declare us things for to come. Show the things that are to come hereafter, that we may know that ye are gods; yea, do good, or do evil that we may be dismayed, and behold it together.

4. *Isaiah 42:8-9*. I am the LORD; that is my name: and my glory will I not give to another, neither my praise to graven images. Behold, the former things are come to pass, and new things do I declare: before they spring forth I tell you of them.

5. *Isaiah 43:9-12*. Let all the nations be gathered together, and let the people be assembled: who among them can declare this, and show us former things? let them bring forth their witnesses, that they may be justified: or let them hear, and say, It is truth. Ye are my witnesses, saith the LORD, and my servant whom I have chosen; that ye may know and believe me, and understand that I am he: before me there was no God formed, neither shall there be after me. I, even I, am the LORD; and besides me there is no Savior. I have declared, and have saved, and I have showed, when there was no strange god among you: therefore ye are my witnesses, saith the LORD, that I am God.

And such is Israel today. Prophecy is their history. Who but God could preserve them like He has? Who but God could foretell their history? This weapon alone out of God's armory can cut through all the sophistries and opposition of men. God forbid then that we despise prophecies (1 Thessalonians 5:20). "O earth, earth, earth, hear the Word of the LORD" (Jeremiah 22:29).

17

A PRACTICAL DOCTRINE

I have asserted that this truth of the coming of the Lord is eminently practical. In proof of this, I here append the following references, to show how Jesus and the apostles used the prophecies of His coming again as a motive to incite us:

1. To watchfulness, Matthew 24:42–44; 25:13; Mark 13:32–37; Luke 12:35–38; Revelation 16:15.
2. To self-control, 1 Thessalonians 5:2–6; 1 Peter 1:13; 4:7; 5:8.
3. To repentance, Acts 3:19–21; Revelation 3:3.
4. To faithfulness, Matthew 25:19–21; Luke 12:42–44; 19:12–13.
5. Not to be ashamed of Christ, Mark 8:38.
6. Against worldliness, Matthew 16:26–27.
7. To moderation or mildness, Philippians 4:5.
8. To patience, Hebrews 10:36–37; James 5:7–8.
9. To mortification of fleshly lusts, Colossians 3:3–5.
10. To sincerity, Philippians 1:9–10.
11. To practical sanctification of the entire being, 1 Thessalonians 5:23.
12. To ministerial faithfulness, 2 Timothy 4:1–2.
13. To induce obedience to the apostle's injunctions, 1 Timothy 6:13–14.
14. To pastoral diligence and purity, 1 Peter 5:2–4.
15. To purify ourselves, 1 John 3:2–3.
16. To abide in Christ, 1 John 2:28.
17. To endure manifold temptations and the severest trial of faith, 1 Peter 1:7.
18. To bear persecution for the sake of our Lord, 1 Peter 4:13.
19. To holy conversation and godliness, 2 Peter 3:11–13.
20. To brotherly love, 1 Thessalonians 3:12–13.
21. To keep in mind our heavenly citizenship, Philippians 3:20–21.
22. To love the second coming of Christ, 2 Timothy 4:7–8.
23. To look for Him, Hebrews 9:27–28.

24. To confidence that Christ will finish the work, Philippians 1:6.
25. To hold fast the hope firm unto the end, Revelation 2:25; 3:11.
26. To separation from worldly lusts and to live Godly, Titus 2:11–13.
27. To watchfulness because of its suddenness, Luke 17:24–30.
28. To guard against hasty judgment, 1 Corinthians 4:5.
29. To the hope of a rich reward, Matthew 19:27–28.
30. To assure the disciples of a time of rejoicing, 2 Corinthians 1:14; Philippians 2:16; 1 Thessalonians 2:19.
31. To comfort the apostles in view of Christ's departure from them, John 14:3; Acts 1:11.
32. Practical faith in the second coming is a crowning grace and assurance of blamelessness in the day of the Lord, 1 Corinthians 1:4–8.
33. It is the principal event for which the believer waits, 1 Thessalonians 1:9–10.
34. It is declared to be the time of reckoning with the servants, Matthew 25:19.
35. Of judgment for the living nations, Matthew 25:31–46.
36. Of the resurrection of the saints, 1 Corinthians 15:23.
37. Of the manifestation of the saints, 2 Corinthians 5:10; Colossians 3:4.
38. It is declared to be the source of consolation to those who sorrow over the dead who sleep in Jesus, 1 Thessalonians 4:14–18.
39. It is declared to be the time of tribulation to unbelievers, 2 Thessalonians 1:7–9.
40. It is proclaimed every time the Lord's Supper is celebrated, 1 Corinthians 11:26.

Such are some of the uses made of this doctrine in the New Testament. It is employed to arm the appeals, to point the arguments, and to enforce the exhortations. What is there more *practical* in any other doctrine? I wish I had space to give the passages referred to in full. But it will be a greater blessing to you, dear reader, if you go to the Word and search them out. We have made no distinction between those passages that refer to the Rapture and those which refer to the Revelation, both classes being equally used as a motive for the practical purposes mentioned.

The following outline and arrangement of Scripture has been taken principally from a little pamphlet published in London. It is a concise view of the premillennial coming, along with clear proof-texts which are conveniently arranged for reference and study. As the texts cited are necessarily brief, it will be found of great profit to read the context of each in the Word of God.

Combined with the diagrams on pages 73 and 229, I believe this outline will enable every prayerful reader to apprehend the order of events that pertain to the coming of Christ, both as the Bridegroom and as the King.

18

THE COMING OF THE LORD

The following outline portrays some subsequent events in their connection with the church's future, "howbeit, when He, the Spirit of truth is come . . . He will show you things to come" (John 16:13).

THE LORD'S PROMISE	"I go to prepare a place for you. And if I go and prepare a place for you, I will come again, and receive you unto myself." John 14:2, 3
	"I go away, and come again unto you." John 14:28
	"A little while, and ye shall not see me: and again a little while, and ye shall see me, because I go to the Father." John 16:16
	"I will see you again, and your heart shall rejoice." John 16:22
HIS FAITHFULNESS	"The Lord is not slack concerning His promise." 2 Peter 3:9
	"Let us hold fast the confession of our hope[1] without wavering; for He is faithful that promised; . . . and so much the more as ye see the day approaching." Hebrews 10:23, 25
	"For yet a little while, and He that shall come will come, and will not tarry." Hebrews 10:37
	"The coming of the Lord draweth nigh." James 5:8
	"Surely I come quickly: Amen." Revelation 22:20
THE HOPE OF THE CHURCH [2]	"Unto them that look for Him shall He appear the second time, without sin, unto salvation." Hebrews 9:28

1. So the Greek.
2. All believers of the present dispensation (1 Corinthians 12:12, 13, 27).

"Our conversation[3] is in heaven; from whence also we look for the Savior, the Lord Jesus Christ."
Philippians 3:20

"Waiting for the adoption, to-wit, the redemption of our body."
Romans 8:23

"Waiting for the coming of our Lord Jesus Christ."
1 Corinthians 1:7

"Looking for that blessed hope."   Titus 2:13

"The patient waiting for Christ."
2 Thessalonians 3:5

"To wait for His Son from heaven, whom He raised from the dead, even Jesus."
1 Thessalonians 1:10

THE RAPTURE

THE COMING OF THE LORD IN THE AIR AS THE BRIDEGROOM FOR HIS CHURCH [7]

"The Lord Himself[4] shall descend from heaven with a shout,[5] with the voice of the archangel and with the trump of God."[6]   1 Thessalonians 4:16

"At the last trump; for the trumpet shall sound."
1 Corinthians 15:52

"Them also which sleep in Jesus will God bring with him."[8]   1 Thessalonians 4:14

THE DEAD IN CHRIST RAISED

"The dead in Christ shall rise first."
1 Thessalonians 4:16

"In Christ shall all be made alive . . . They that are Christ's at His coming." 1 Corinthians 15:22, 23

"The dead shall be raised incorruptible."
1 Corinthians 15:52

"Raised in incorruption; . . . raised in glory; . . . raised in power; . . . raised a spiritual body."
1 Corinthians 15:42–44

---

3. Or "citizenship" (see John 17:16; Ephesians 2:19; Hebrews 11:10, 13, 16; 12:22).

4. "Watch, therefore; for ye know not what hour your Lord doth come" (Mark 13:32, 37; 1 Thessalonians 5:6).

5. That is, personally, yet seen by none but believers (see John 14:19; Acts 1:3, 4, 9; 9:7; 10:40, 41; 1 Corinthians 15:5–8).

6. Understood by those only to whom addressed (see John 12:28, 29; Acts 9:4, 7).

7. The trumpet sounded twice when the Lord descended upon Sinai (see Exodus 19:11, 17). And so when He descends to take the church unto Himself, at its first sounding the dead in Christ will be raised, and at its last sounding, the living saints will be changed.

8. The Old Testament saints also will doubtless at this time receive their glorified bodies (see Hebrews 11:39, 40).

LIVING BELIEVERS CHANGED

"We which are alive, and remain unto the coming of the Lord, shall not prevent[9] them which are asleep."   1 Thessalonians 4:15

"We shall not all sleep, but we shall all be changed, in a moment, in the twinkling of an eye . . . and we shall be changed."[10]
1 Corinthians 15:51, 52

"The Lord Jesus Christ . . . shall change our vile body,[11] that it may be fashioned like unto His glorious body."   Philippians 3:20, 21

"And as we have borne the image of the earthy, we shall also bear the image of the heavenly."
1 Corinthians 15:49.

"For this corruptible must put on incorruption, and this mortal must put on immortality."
1 Corinthians 15:53

BOTH CAUGHT UP INTO THE CLOUDS[12]

"Then we which are alive and remain, shall be caught up together, with them in the clouds, to meet the Lord in the air."   1 Thessalonians 4:17

"The coming of our Lord Jesus Christ, and . . . our gathering together unto Him."
2 Thessalonians 2:1

TO BE EVER WITH THE LORD

"So shall we ever be with the Lord."
1 Thessalonians 4:17

"That where I am, there ye may be also."
John 14:3

"Where I am, there shall also my servant be."
John 12:26

"With me where I am; that they may behold my glory."   John 17:24

"They shall never perish."   John 10:28

"Because I live, ye shall live also."   John 14:19

"That we should live together with Him."
1 Thessalonians 5:10

"An . . . eternal weight of glory."
2 Corinthians 4:17

"Eternal inheritance." Hebrews 9:15; 1 Peter 1:4

"He[13] shall go no more out."   Revelation 3:12

---

9. That is, "anticipate" or "go before."
10. "Then . . . death is swallowed up in victory" (1 Corinthians 15:54); and "Mortality swallowed up of life" (2 Corinthians 5:4).
11. The body of our "humble" or "low estate" (Luke 1:48; Acts 8:33; Philippians 2:8).
12. "The redemption of the purchased possession" (Romans 8:23; Ephesians 1:14).
13. The overcomer (Revelation 3:12; 1 John 5:4, 5).

THE JUDGMENT SEAT OF CHRIST[15]

"We[14] must all appear before the judgment seat of Christ; that every one may receive the things done, in his body, according to that he hath done, whether it be good or bad."   2 Corinthians 5:10

"We[14] shall all stand before the judgment seat of Christ; . . . every one of us shall give account of himself to God."   Romans 14:10-12.

"Behold, I come quickly; and my reward is with me, to give every man according as his work shall be."   Revelation 22:12.

MANIFESTATION OF WORKS

"Every man's work shall be made manifest: . . . and the fire shall try every man's work of what sort it is."   1 Corinthians 3:13

"Therefore judge nothing before the time, until the Lord come, who both will bring to the light the hidden things of darkness, and will make manifest the counsels of the hearts. . . ."   1 Corinthians 4:5

WHETHER GOOD

"If any man's work abide which he hath built thereupon,[16] he shall receive a reward."
            1 Corinthians 3:14

"Whatsoever good thing[17] any man doeth, the same shall he receive of the Lord."   Ephesians 6:8

OR BAD

"But he that doeth wrong shall receive for the wrong which he hath done."   Colossians 3:25

"If any man's work shall be burned, he shall suffer loss: but he himself shall be saved;[18] yet so as by fire. . . For the temple of God is holy which temple ye are."   1 Corinthians 3:15–17

REWARD

"Every man shall receive his own reward according to his own labor."   1 Corinthians 3:8

"The prize of the high calling."   Philippians 3:14

"The reward of the inheritance."   Colossians 3:24

"The kingdom."   James 2:5

"The crown of life."   James 1:12; Revelation 2:10

"A crown of Righteousness."   2 Timothy 4:8

"A crown of glory."   1 Peter 5:4

"An incorruptible" (crown).   1 Corinthians 9:25

"The things which God hath prepared."
            1 Corinthians 2:9

---

14. "The church, the saints" (2 Corinthians 1:1).
15. For Christians only, in reference to service (Romans 14:4, 10, 12).
16. The foundation, "which is Jesus Christ" (Isaiah 28:16; 1 Corinthians 3:11).
17. "Service as to the Lord" (Ephesians 6:7).
18. "No condemnation" (John 5:24; Romans 8:1).

"And then shall every man have praise of God."
1 Corinthians 4:5

THE MARRIAGE OF THE LAMB AND THE CHURCH

"The marriage of the Lamb is come, and his wife[19] hath made herself ready. And to her was granted that she should be arrayed in fine linen, clean and white; for the fine linen is the righteousness of saints."   Revelation 19:7, 8

"Christ also loved the church, and gave Himself for it, . . . that He might present it to Himself a glorious church, not having spot, or wrinkle, or any such thing; but that it should be holy and without blemish."   Ephesians 5:25–27

[The Tribulation is the time between the Rapture and the Revelation in which there will be a period of seven years.[20] At its commencement those Jews who will have returned to their land in unbelief, [21] and have rebuilt or are rebuilding their temple,[22] enter into a seven-years' covenant with Antichrist.[23] On the expiration of three and a half years he is revealed in his true character as the man of sin,[24] kills the two witnesses who had been prophesying during that time,[25] stops the daily sacrifice which had been resumed,[26] and has his own image set up in the holy place.[27] The Devil and his angels are cast out into the earth, showing great wrath, because their time is short.[28] Then follow, during the last three and a half years[29] the treading under foot of the holy city[30] and the time of the "great tribulation, such as was not since the beginning of the world, no, nor ever shall be,"[31] which, under Antichrist[32] and his Prophet,[33] shall come upon all the world.[34] The penalty of death will be suffered by all who refuse to worship the image of the Beast,[35] and unparalleled persecution will come to all who have not received his mark.[36] A third part of the Jews in the land

---

19. "Christ and the church" (Ephesians 5:32).
20. Daniel 9:27; Revelation 11:3, 7 with 13:5.
21. Isaiah 6:13; 17:10, 11; 18:4, 5; 66:3, 4.
22. Isaiah 66:1, 2; Revelation 11:1, 2.
23. Daniel 9:27; John 5:43.
24. Daniel 9:27; 2 Thessalonians 2:3; Revelation 11:7; 13:1.
25. Revelation 11:3–7.
26. Daniel 9:27; 11:31; 12:11.
27. Matthew 24:15; 2 Thessalonians 2:4; Revelation 13:14, 15.
28. Revelation 12:7–12.
29. Daniel 7:25; 9:27; Revelation 13:5.
30. Daniel 9:26; Luke 21:24; Revelation 11:2.
31. Jeremiah 30:7; Daniel 12:1; Matthew 24:21; Revelation 13:14, 17.
32. Daniel 7:21, 25; 2 Thessalonians 2:2; Revelation 13:1, 8.
33. Revelation 13:11, 17; 19:20.
34. Revelation 3:10.
35. Revelation 13:15; 20:4.
36. Revelation 13:16, 17.

are brought through this time of trouble,[37] and are gathered by the Lord into Jerusalem[38] to be purged of their dross.[39] The nations are assembled against the city, which is taken by them. Great suffering is inflicted on the inhabitants, half of whom are carried into captivity.[40] The remnant no more again stay upon him that smote them, but stay upon the Lord, the Holy One of Israel, in truth.[41] The kings of the earth are gathered to battle against Jehovah and against His Anointed.[42] Then the Lord will go forth[43] with His saints for the destruction of His enemies and the deliverance of his people.[44]]

THE REVELATION

THE COMING OF THE LORD

"This same Jesus, which is taken up from you into heaven, shall so come in like manner as ye have seen Him go into heaven."   Acts 1:11

"And His feet shall stand in that day upon the mount of Olives."   Zechariah 14:4

"Immediately after the tribulation of those days . . . they shall see the Son of man coming in the clouds of heaven, with power and great glory."
               Matthew 24:29, 30 (Mark 13:26; Luke 21:27)

AS KING TO THE EARTH

"Ye shall see the Son of man sitting on the right hand of power, and coming in the clouds of heaven."
               Mark 14:62 (Matthew 26:64)

"Behold, He cometh with clouds; and every eye shall see Him."   Revelation 1:7

"And they shall look upon me whom they have pierced."   Zechariah 12:10

"The Lord Jesus shall be revealed from heaven with His mighty angels."
               2 Thessalonians 1:7 (Matthew 25:31)

"And I saw heaven opened, and behold a white horse, and he that sat upon him was called Faithful and True."   Revelation 19:11.

"Behold, the LORD cometh out of His place to punish the inhabitants of the earth for their iniquity."   Isaiah 26:21 (Micah 1:3)

"The Redeemer shall come to Zion, and unto them that turn from transgressions in Jacob."
               Isaiah 59:20

---

37. Zechariah 13:8, 9.
38. Ezekiel 22:19.
39. Isaiah 1:21–25; 4:3; Ezekiel 22:17–22; Zephaniah 1:12, 13; Zechariah 13:9.
40. Zechariah 14:2.
41. Isaiah 4:3; 10:20, 21; 17:6–8; Jeremiah 2:27; Hosea 5:15; Zechariah 13:9.
42. Psalm 2:1–3; Revelation 16:14, 16; 17:14; 19:19.
43. Isaiah 13:3–6; 26:21; Zechariah 14:3.
44. Isaiah 50:2; 66:5, 6; Hosea 5:15; Zechariah 12:9, 10; Malachi 4:1–3; Luke 21:28.

"Sing and rejoice, O daughter of Zion; for lo, I come, and I will dwell in the midst of thee, saith the LORD."   Zechariah 2:10

"And the armies which were in heaven, followed him upon white horses, clothed in fine linen, white and clean."[45]   Revelation 19:14

TOGETHER WITH THE CHURCH

"They that are with Him are called, and chosen and faithful."[46]   Revelation 17:14

"The LORD my God shall come, and all the saints with thee."   Zechariah 14:5

"Behold the Lord cometh with ten thousand of His saints."   Jude 14

"The coming of our Lord Jesus Christ with all his saints."   1 Thessalonians 3:13

"When Christ, who is our life, shall appear, then shall ye[47] also appear with Him in glory."
                                                Colossians 3:4

"When He shall appear, we shall be like Him."
                                                  1 John 3:2

"The manifestation of the sons of God."
                                                Romans 8:19

———

[The power of Antichrist is broken and destroyed by the voice of the Lord;[48] he and the False Prophet are taken and cast alive into the lake of fire burning with brimstone.[49] And the ten allied kings and their armies are killed by the sword coming out of the mouth of the King of kings.[50] The Devil is bound for a thousand years in the bottomless pit,[51] during which time the martyrs under Antichrist, who will have been raised as the completion of the first resurrection, will reign over the earth with the Lord Jesus and their fellow-saints.[52]]

THE RESURRECTION OF LIFE[54]

"And I saw the souls of them that were beheaded for the witness of Jesus, and for the word of God,[53] and which had not worshiped the beast, neither his image, neither had received His mark upon their foreheads, or in their hands; and they lived and reigned with Christ a thousand years."
                                                Revelation 20:4

———

45. "The fine linen is the righteousness of saints" (Revelation 19:8).
46. "Called," those "whom he did foreknow" (Romans 8:29–30; Matthew 7:23; Revelation 1:6). "Chosen" (Ephesians 1:4). "Faithful" (Ephesians 1:1).
47. "The saints" (Colossians 1:2).
48. Isaiah 11:4; Daniel 7:11; 2 Thessalonians 2:8.
49. Isaiah 30:31, 33; Revelation 17:8; 19:20.
50. Psalm 2:4, 5; 110:5; Zechariah 12:9; Revelation 17:14; 19:21.
51. Revelation 20:2–3.
52. Revelation 20:4–6.
53. Under Antichrist (Revelation 6:9; 13:15).
54. For the rest of the dead, see Revelation 20:5.

"Shall come forth; they that have done good, unto the resurrection of life."   John 5:29

"Shall awake, . . . to everlasting life."
Daniel 12:2

"This is the first resurrection."[55]   Revelation 20:5

THE LORD REIGNS OVER THE EARTH

"And in the days of these kings[56] shall the God of heaven set up a kingdom which shall never be destroyed."   Daniel 2:44

"I will raise unto David a righteous Branch, and a king shall reign and prosper, and shall execute judgment and justice in the earth."   Jeremiah 23:5

"And the Lord God shall give unto him the throne of his father David."   Luke 1:32 (Isaiah 9:7)

"My king upon my holy hill of Zion."   Psalm 2:6

"The LORD of hosts shall reign in Mount Zion and in Jerusalem, and before his ancients, gloriously."   Isaiah 24:23 (Micah 4:7)

"The king of Israel, even the LORD is in the midst of thee."   Zephaniah 3:15

"He must reign till He hath put all enemies under his feet."[57]   1 Corinthians 15:25

"Yea, all kings shall fall down before Him; all nations shall serve Him."   Psalm 72:11

"The kingdoms of this world are become the kingdoms of our Lord and of His Christ."
Revelation 11:15

"He shall have dominion also from sea to sea and from the river unto the ends of the earth"
Psalm 72:8 (Zechariah 9:10)

"And the LORD shall be king over all the earth; in that day there shall be one LORD, and His name one."   Zechariah 14:9

"King of kings, and Lord of lords."
Revelation 19:16

WITH HIS BRIDE, THE CHURCH

"We shall also reign with Him."   2 Timothy 2:12

"Heirs of God, and joint-heirs with Christ; . . . glorified together."   Romans 8:17

"To him that overcometh will I grant to sit with me in my throne."   Revelation 3:21

---

55. Including, "Christ the firstfruits: afterward they that are Christ's at his coming." The ingathering, 1 Corinthians 15:23; and here the martyrs under Antichrist (the Gleanings) (Revelation 20:4).

56. Antichrist and the allied kings (Daniel 7:24; Revelation 17:12–13).

57. "Unto me every knee shall bow" (Isaiah 45:23; Philippians 2:9, 11).

"Thou . . . hast made us unto our God kings and priests; and we shall reign on[58] the earth"

Revelation 5:9, 10

"Kings and priests unto God and His Father."

Revelation 1:6

"The Father . . . who hath translated us into the kingdom of His dear Son." Colossians 1:12, 13

"And I saw thrones, and they[59] sat upon them, and judgment was given unto them."

Revelation 20:4

"The saints shall judge the world."

1 Corinthians 6:2

[The kingdom having been set up, and all that offends having been gathered out of the land,[60] the Lord Jesus judges first His own people, the Jews, as to their fidelity to Him,[61] and then the nations on earth as to their treatment of His people in their trouble.[62] The ten tribes of Israel, after purification,[63] are brought into the land[64] and together with the two tribes of Judah become one nation.[65] The Lord makes the new covenant with His people, Israel and Judah,[66] forgiving their iniquity, and remembering their sin no more;[67] while punishments are visited by Him upon His enemies,[68] including Gog and his armies,[69] who are overthrown and destroyed.[70] The Jewish people come into possession of the full extent of their land[71] according to promise,[72] including the Great Desert, which "blossoms as the rose."[73] The temple[74] and the city[75] are rebuilt after the divine plan; and the Levitical sacrifices and form of worship are with some modifications re-established.[76] Nothing will hurt or destroy in all the holy mountain.[77]

---

58. Or, "over."

59. The saints, "the armies which were in heaven" (Revelation 19:8, 14).

60. Isaiah 13:9; 33:14; Matthew 13:30, 41.

61. Matthew 25:14–30; Luke 19:12–27.

62. Joel 3:2, 12; Matthew 25:31–46; Acts 17:31.

63. Ezekiel 20:33–38; Amos 9:9, 10.

64. Isaiah 49:12–23; Ezekiel 20:40–42; 36:24; Amos 9:14, 15.

65. Isaiah 11:13; Ezekiel 37:16–24; Hosea 1:11.

66. Jeremiah 31:31–33; 32:40; 50:4, 5; Ezekiel 37:26; Romans 11:26, 27; Hebrews 8:11.

67. Isaiah 60:21; Jeremiah 31:34; 33:8; 50:20; Ezekiel 36:25–33; Micah 7:18, 19; Hebrews 8:12.

68. Isaiah 2:17–21; 26:9; 34:2; Ezekiel 28:26; Micah 5:15; Nahum 1:8.

69. Ezekiel 38:1–17.

70. Ezekiel 38:18—39:21.

71. Ezekiel 47:13—48:29.

72. Genesis 15:18; Deuteronomy 11:24; Joshua 1:4.

73. Isaiah 32:15; 35:1, 2; 51:3; Ezekiel 36:33–36.

74. Ezekiel 40:1—43:17.

75. Isaiah 60:10; Jeremiah 31:38, 40; Ezekiel 48:15–17, 30–35; Zechariah 14:10, 11.

76. Ezekiel 43:18—46:24; Malachi 3:3, 4.

77. Isaiah 11:6–9; 33:24; 35:9; 55:13; 65:25; Ezekiel 34:25; Hosea 2:18; Revelation 22:3.

The Lord sets His hand again the second time to recover the remnant of His people, both Israel and Judah, from the four corners of the earth.[78] Jerusalem is made a praise, the joy of the whole earth.[79] The Lord in her midst[80] is her glory and everlasting light; there will be no night there.[81] All nations go to worship the King and keep the Feast of Tabernacles.[82] The earth is full of the glory of the Lord.[83]|

THE HEAVENLY CITY, THE HOME OF THE BRIDE	"And there came unto me one of the seven angels . . . saying, Come hither, I will show thee the bride, the Lamb's wife. And he . . . showed me that great city, the holy Jerusalem, descending out of heaven from God." Revelation 21:9–10
	"The city of my God, which is New Jerusalem, which cometh down out of heaven, from my God." Revelation 3:12
ITS MAGNITUDE AND BEAUTY	"And had a wall great and high, and had twelve gates, and at the gates twelve angels, and names written thereon, which are the names of the twelve tribes of the children of Israel." Revelation 21:12
	"And the wall of the city had twelve foundations, and in them the names of the twelve apostles of the Lamb." Revelation 21:14
	"And the building of the wall of it was of jasper; and the city was pure gold, like unto clear glass." Revelation 21:18
	"And the foundations of the wall of the city were garnished with all manner of precious stones." Revelation 21:19
	"And the twelve gates were twelve pearls; every several gate was of one pearl, and the street of the city was pure gold, as it were transparent glass." Revelation 21:21
ITS GLORY AND PURITY	"And I saw no temple therein, for the Lord God Almighty and the Lamb are the temple of it. And the city had no need of the sun, neither of the moon to shine in it; for the glory of God did lighten it, and the Lamb is the light thereof." Revelation 21:22, 23
	"Having the glory of God; and her light was like unto a stone most precious, even like a jasper stone, clear as crystal." Revelation 21:11

78. Isaiah 11:11, 12; Jeremiah 50:4–5; Ezekiel 39:25, 28.
79. Psalm 48:2; Isaiah 1:26; 60:14; 62:7; 65:18; Jeremiah 31:23; Zechariah 8:3.
80. Ezekiel 48:35; Joel 3:17, 21; Zephaniah 3:15–17; Zechariah 2:10.
81. Isaiah 60:19, 20; Zechariah 2:5; Revelation 22:5.
82. Isaiah 2:1–3; Jeremiah 3:17; Micah 4:2; Zechariah 8:20–22, 14:16–19.
83. Numbers 14:21; Psalm 72:19; Isaiah 11:9; Habbakuk 2:14.

"And the nations of them which are saved shall walk in the light of it; and the kings of the earth do bring their glory and honor into it. And the gates of it shall not be shut at all by day; for there shall be no night there. And they shall bring the glory and honor of the nations into it."   Revelation 21:24–26

"And there shall in no wise enter into it any thing that defileth, neither whatsoever worketh abomination, or maketh a lie; but they which are written in the Lamb's book of Life."

Revelation 21:27

[On the expiration of the Millennium, or thousand years, Satan is loosed from his prison for a short time,[84] and he goes out to deceive the nations in the four quarters of the earth—Gog and Magog—and to gather them together to battle.[85] They surround the camp of the saints and the beloved city,[86] but fire from God out of heaven devours them.[87] And the Devil who deceived them is cast into the lake of fire and brimstone, where the Beast and the False Prophet are, and will be tormented day and night forever and ever.[88]]

THE JUDGE OF ALL THE EARTH

"And I saw a great white throne, and Him that sat on it."   Revelation 20:11

"The Lord Jesus Christ, who shall judge the quick and the dead."   2 Timothy 4:1

"He which was ordained of God to be the Judge of quick and dead.   Acts 10:42 (1 Peter 4:5)

"The Father . . . hath committed all judgment unto the Son."   John 5:22

"And I saw the dead[89] small and great stand before God"[90]   Revelation 20:12

THE RESURRECTION OF DAMNATION

"And the sea gave up the dead which were in it and death and hades[91] delivered up the dead which were in them."   Revelation 20:13

"Shall come forth . . . they that have done evil, unto the resurrection of damnation."   John 5:29

"Shall awake . . . to shame and everlasting contempt."   Daniel 12:2

---

84. Revelation 20:3–7.
85. Revelation 20:8.
86. Jerusalem, see Isaiah 4:3.
87. Revelation 20:9.
88. Revelation 20:10.
89. Those who had no part in the first resurrection, see Revelation 20:5, 6.
90. "The Son" (see John 5:22; Romans 2:16).
91. So the Greek.

**THE LAST
JUDGMENT**

"And the books were opened; and another book was opened, which is the book of life; and the dead were judged out of those things which were written in the books, according to their works."

Revelation 20:12

"And whosoever was not found written in the book of life was cast into the lake of fire."

Revelation 20:15

"The lake which burneth with fire and brimstone; which is the second death."   Revelation 21:8

**THE LAST
ENEMY**

"The last enemy that shall be destroyed is death."
1 Corinthians 15:26

"And death and hades[92] were cast into the lake of fire. This is the second death."   Revelation 20:14

**HEAVEN AND
EARTH PASS
AWAY**

"Heaven and earth shall pass away."

Mark 13:31

"The heavens shall pass away with a great noise, and the elements shall melt with fervent heat; the earth also, and the works that are therein, shall be burned up.[93] . . . The heavens, being on fire, shall be dissolved, and the elements shall melt with fervent heat."   2 Peter 3:10–12

"The heavens shall vanish away like smoke, and the earth shall wax old like a garment." Isaiah 51:6

"They shall perish . . . they all shall wax old as doth a garment; and as a vesture shalt thou fold them up, and they shall be changed."

Hebrews 1:11–12

"From whose face the earth and the heaven fled away;[94] and there was found no place for them."

Revelation 20:11.

"And he that sat upon the throne said, Behold, I make all things new."   Revelation 21:5

**NEW HEAVENS
AND
NEW EARTH**

"Behold, I create new heavens and a new earth"
Isaiah 65:17

"And I saw a new heaven and a new earth; for the first heaven and the first earth were passed away; and there was no more sea." Revelation 21:1

"New heavens and a new earth, wherein dwelleth all righteousness."   2 Peter 3:13

---

92. So the Greek.
93. Compare Genesis 6:11, 13; 9, 11, 16, with Isaiah 24:5; 2 Peter 3:7.
94. See also Psalm 68:8; Nahum 1:5; and Job 15:15; 25:5.

GOD ALL IN ALL

"Then cometh the end, when he shall have delivered up the kingdom to God, even the Father; when he shall have put down all rule and all authority and power." 1 Corinthians 15:24

"And when all things shall be subdued unto Him, then shall the Son also Himself be subject unto Him, that put all things under Him, that God may be all in all." 1 Corinthians 15:28

THE LAMB'S WIFE

"And I John saw the holy city, New Jerusalem, coming down from God out of heaven, prepared as a bride adorned for her husband."[95] Revelation 21:2.

GOD DWELLS WITH MEN

"Behold, the tabernacle of God is with men, and He will dwell with them, and they shall be His people, and God Himself shall be with them and be their God. And God shall wipe away all tears from their eyes; and there shall be no more death, neither sorrow nor crying, neither shall there be any more pain; for the former things are passed away."
Revelation 21:3–4

REFERENCES

For convenience we give the following references to some of the *principal* passages that refer to our Lord's return, in the consecutive order in which they occur in the Word, together with catch words to distinguish the same:

Deuteronomy 33:2—Mt. Sinai, Mt. Seir, Transfiguration and Second Coming.
Psalm 2—The Son's possession, etc.
Psalm 67:4—Judges and governs the nations.
Psalm 96:10–13—The Lord comes to judge.

---

95. *Ephesians 2:7.* "That in the ages to come he might show the exceeding riches of his grace in his kindness toward us through Christ Jesus."

1 Corinthians 2:9, 10. "Eye hath not seen, nor ear heard, neither have entered into the heart of man the things which God hath prepared for them that love him. But God hath revealed them unto us by his Spirit; for the Spirit searcheth all things, yea, the deep things of God."

2 Corinthians 5:5. "Now he that hath wrought us for this selfsame thing is God, who also hath given unto us the earnest of the Spirit."

Ephesians 3:21. "Unto him be glory in the church by Christ Jesus throughout all ages, world without end. Amen."

2 Peter 3:14. "Wherefore, beloved, seeing that ye look for such things, be diligent that ye may be found of him in peace, without spot, and blameless."

Psalm 98:9—The Lord comes to judge.
Psalm 102:16—Builds up Zion and appears in glory.
Daniel 7:13—Son of man comes to possess the kingdom.
Hosea 6:3—He comes as the latter and former rain.
Zechariah 12:10—Israel *sees* and accepts Christ.
Zechariah 14:4—He stands on the Mount of Olives.
Zechariah 14:5—Comes with the saints.
Matthew 16:26–27—Will come in glory of His Father.
Matthew 19:28—Sits on throne of His glory.
Matthew 24—The three questions answered.
Matthew 25:1–12—The Bridegroom.
Matthew 25:13–30—Judgment of servants.
Matthew 25:31–46—Judgment of nations.
Matthew 26:64—Coming in the clouds of heaven.
Mark 8:38—Of Him, Son, be ashamed when He comes.
Mark 13—The three questions answered.
Mark 14:62—Coming in the clouds of heaven.
Luke 9:26—Of Him, Son be ashamed when He comes.
Luke 12:35–48—Loins girded; lights burning.
Luke 17:20–37—Noah, Lot, etc.
Luke 18:8—Little faith on earth.
Luke 19:11–28—Gone to receive kingdom and return. The ten talents.
Luke 21—The three questions answered.
John 1:51—Heaven opens; angels descending.
John 14:3—The promise: Come and receive you.
John 14:18—I will come to you.
John 14:28—Go away and come again.
John 21:22—If he remains alive until I return.
Acts 1:10–11—The same Jesus comes again.
Acts 3:19–21—The times of refreshing.
1 Corinthians 1:4–8—Waiting for the coming.
1 Corinthians 4:5—Judge nothing until the Lord comes.
1 Corinthians 11:26—Communion, until He comes.
1 Corinthians 15:23—Order of Resurrection; Christ's at His coming.
1 Corinthians 16:22—Anathema Maran–atha.
2 Corinthians 1:14—Rejoicing in the day of Lord.
Philippians 1:6–10—Until the day of Christ.
Philippians 2:16—Rejoicing in the day of Christ.
Philippians 3:11.—Resurrection from among the dead.
Philippians 3:20–21—Citizenship; looking for the Savior.
Philippians 4:5—The Lord is at hand.
Colossians 3:3–5—Appearing with Him.
1 Thessalonians 1:9—Wait for His Son from heaven.
1 Thessalonians 2:19—Hope, joy, crown at His coming.
1 Thessalonians 3:13—Unblamable, at the coming.

1 Thessalonians 4:13–18—The Rapture.

1 Thessalonians 5:1–10—Times and seasons; night and day.

1 Thessalonians 5:23—Blameless unto the coming.

2 Thessalonians 1:7–10—Revealed in flaming fire.

2 Thessalonians 2:1–8—The wicked one destroyed with the brightness of His coming.

1 Timothy 6:13–15—Keep the commandment until the appearing.

2 Timothy 4:1—Judge, at appearing and kingdom.

2 Timothy 4:8—Crown for all that love His appearing.

Titus 2:11–15—The blessed hope and glorious appearing.

Hebrews 9:24–28—The three appearings.

Hebrews 10:22–24—Faith, hope, love.

Hebrews 10:25—Day approaching.

Hebrews 10:35–37—Patience, a little while.

James 5:7–8—Be patient until the coming; early and latter rain.

1 Peter 1:7—Trial of faith.

1 Peter 1:13—Hope to the end.

1 Peter 4:13—When His glory will be revealed.

1 Peter 5:1–4—When the Chief Shepherd will appear.

2 Peter 3.—Scoffers—The day of the Lord.

1 John 2:28—When He will appear we may have confidence.

1 John 3:2–3—Now sons be like Him; has this hope—purifies himself.

2 John 7—Coming in the flesh.

Jude 14–15—The Lord comes with saints to execute judgment.

Revelation 1:7—Behold he comes with clouds.

Revelation 2:25—Hold fast until I come.

Revelation 3:3—If not watch, come as a thief.

Revelation 3:10–11—Keep from the hour of temptation; Behold I come quickly.

Revelation 14:14–16—The earth reaped.

Revelation 16:15—Behold, I come as a thief; blessed is he that *watches*.

Revelation 22:20—Even so come, Lord Jesus.

19

ANATHEMA OR COMFORT

There are several passages which convey a very serious ramification in connection with this subject, but especially two, as follows: One occurs in the salutation of Paul in 1 Corinthians 16:22. Before he pronounces the blessing, he excludes those who do not love Jesus in the following words: "If any man love not the Lord Jesus Christ, let him be Anathema Maranatha."

"Anathema Maranatha!"

Anathema means accursed, condemned, devoted to destruction. Maranatha means "the Lord comes." Let him be accursed—the Lord comes.

It is easy now, while the long suffering of God waits[1] for men to reject, despise and hate the Lord Jesus. But JESUS IS COMING, and woe be unto those who now reject Him, "when once the Master of the house is risen up and hath shut to the door."[2] Paul understood this, and

---

1. *1 Peter 3:19-20*. By which also he went and preached unto the spirits in prison; which sometime were disobedient, when once the long-suffering of God waited in the days of Noah, while the ark was a preparing, wherein few, that is, eight souls were saved by water.

2 Peter 3:9. The Lord is not slack concerning his promise, as some men count slackness; but is longsuffering to us-ward, not willing that any should perish, but that all should come to repentance.

2. *Luke 13:25*. When once the master of the house is risen up, and hath shut to the door, and ye begin to stand without, and to knock at the door, saying, Lord, Lord, open unto us; and he shall answer and say unto you, I know you not whence ye are.

Mark 13:35-37. Watch ye therefore: for ye know not when the master of the house cometh, at even, or at midnight, or at the cockcrowing, or in the morning: lest coming suddenly he find you sleeping. And what I say unto you I say unto all, Watch.

therefore he says, "I am made all things to all men, that I might by all means save some" (1 Corinthians 9:22), "from the wrath to come" (1 Thessalonians 1:10). Oh! that men would "seek the Lord while He may be found,"[3] and "flee from the wrath to come."[4]

The other passage is 2 John 7: "For many deceivers have entered into the world, who confess not that Jesus Christ is come [coming] in the flesh. This is a deceiver and an Antichrist." The correct rendering of ἐρχόμενον (*erchomenon*) is *coming*. Jesus was especially called the "Coming One."[5] But these deceivers denied the incarnation—the coming of Christ in the flesh—either past or future. (See Alford, also Jamieson, Fausset and Brown.)

This, then, is of special significance. He that denies Jesus Christ's coming in the flesh is a deceiver and an antichrist. That is, he is possessed of the same spirit which will ultimately find its personification in the great personal Antichrist.

It is lamentable that this passage has been so improperly translated in our version. It is such a strong assertion that Jesus is coming in the flesh, that it would undoubtably have prevented much of the unwarrantable

---

3. *Isaiah 55:6.* Seek ye the LORD while he may be found, call ye upon him while he is near. See also *2 Corinthians 6:2.*

4. *Matthew 3:7.* But when he saw many of the Pharisees and Sadducees come to his baptism, he said unto them, O generation of vipers, who hath warned you to flee from the wrath to come?

5. *Matthew 11:3.* And said unto him, Art thou he that cometh, or look we for another?

Hebrews 10:37. For yet a very little while, he that cometh shall come, and shall not tarry.

Revelation 1:7-8. Behold, he cometh with clouds; and every eye shall see him, and they also which pierced him: and all kindreds of the earth shall wail because of him. Even so, Amen. I am Alpha and Omega, the beginning and the ending, saith the Lord, which is, and which was, and which is to come, the Almighty.

Revelation 4:8. And the four living creatures, having each one of them six wings, are full of eyes round about and within: and they have no rest day and night, saying, Holy, holy, holy, is the Lord God, the Almighty, who was and who is and who is to come.

John 6:14. Then those men, when they had seen the miracle that Jesus did, said, This is of a truth that Prophet that should come into the world.

"spiritualizing" of Scripture which has so largely prevailed.

Jesus *Himself* is coming at the Rapture[6] to receive us unto *Himself*.[7] And He is coming to this earth again, at the Revelation,[8] the *same Jesus*, and in *like manner* as He went away.*[9]

> Lo! He comes, with clouds descending,
> Once for favored sinner slain;
> Thousand thousand saints attending,
> Swell the triumphs of His train; Hallelujah!
> God appears on earth to reign.

But while there is such fearful foreboding of impending judgment and just retribution to those who do not love the Lord Jesus, there is, on the other hand, the sweetest comfort for those who do love our Lord's appearing.

Comfort

This is apparent when we understand the true position of the church. We have seen that it is not to be confused with the coming kingdom, nor does it include the Old Testament saints, for it was founded after Christ came.[10] It was begun on the day of Pentecost (Acts 2) and will be

---

* That is corporally, in the flesh.

6. *1 Thessalonians 4:16-18*. For the Lord himself shall descend from heaven, with a shout, with the voice of the archangel, and with the trump of God: and the dead in Christ shall rise first; then we that are alive, that are left, shall together with them be caught up in the clouds, to meet the Lord in the air: and so shall we ever be with the Lord. Wherefore comfort one another with these words.

7. *John 14:3*. And if I go and prepare a place for you, I will come again, and receive you unto myself; that where I am, there ye may be also.

8. *2 Thessalonians 2:7-10*. For the mystery of iniquity doth already work: only he who now letteth will let, until he be taken out of the way. And then shall that Wicked be revealed, whom the Lord shall consume with the spirit of his mouth, and shall destroy with the brightness of his coming: even him, whose coming is after the working of Satan with all power and signs and lying wonders. And with all deceivableness of unrighteousness in them that perish; because they received not the love of the truth, that they might be saved.

9. *Acts 1:11*. Which also said, Ye men of Galilee, why stand ye gazing up into heaven? this same Jesus, which is taken up from you into heaven, shall so come in like manner as ye have seen him go into heaven.

10. *Matthew 16:18*. And I say also unto thee, That thou art Peter, and upon this rock I will build my church; and the gates of hell shall not prevail against it.

complete at the Rapture (1 Thessalonians 4:17). It is like a parenthesis in God's dealing with His people, Israel. While they are broken off because of unbelief, the church is grafted in.[11]

And being a companion in suffering with her Lord,[12] the church follows His example.[13] Walking in humility (Philippians 2:2–8; 1 John 2:6) during His humiliation,[14] she will "be counted worthy"[15] of the greatest blessing in her exaltation with Him.[16]

The Bride of Christ

Jesus is the Bridegroom, and the church is His Bride. John the Baptist stood as the last representative of the Mosaic dispensation. He said, "I am not the Christ . . . He that hath the Bride is the Bridegroom, but the friend of the Bridegroom which standeth and heareth Him, rejoiceth greatly because of the Bridegroom's voice; this, my joy, therefore, is fulfilled" (John 3:28–29). Here we

---

11. *Romans 11:17*. And if some of the branches be broken off, and thou, being a wild olive tree, wert graffed in among them, and with them partakest of the root and fatness of the olive tree.

12. *Acts 5:41*. And they departed from the presence of the council, rejoicing that they were counted worthy to suffer shame for his name.

Philippians 1:29. For unto you it is given in the behalf of Christ, not only to believe on him, but also to suffer for his sake. See also *Hebrews 10:34*.

13. *John 13:15*. For I have given you an example, that ye should do as I have done to you.

1 Peter 2:21. For even hereunto were ye called: because Christ also suffered for us, leaving us an example, that ye should follow his steps.

14. *Acts 8:33*. In his humiliation his judgment was taken away: and who shall declare his generation? for his life is taken from the earth.

15. *2 Thessalonians 1:5*. Which is a manifest token of the righteous judgment of God, that ye may be counted worthy of the kingdom of God, for which ye also suffer.

Romans 8:17. And if children, then theirs; heirs of God, and joint heirs with Christ; if so be that we suffer with him, that we may be also glorified together.

16. *Philippians 2:5-11*. Let this mind be in you, which was also in Christ Jesus: who, being in the form of God, thought it not robbery to be equal with God: but made himself of no reputation, and took upon him the form of a servant, and was made in the likeness of men: and being found in fashion as a man, he humbled himself, and became obedient unto death, even the death of the cross. Wherefore God also hath highly exalted him, and given him a name which is above every name: that at the name of Jesus every knee should bow, of things in heaven, and things in earth, and things under the earth; and that every tongue should confess that Jesus Christ is Lord, to the glory of God the Father.

have a clear distinction between the Old Testament saints and the Bride of Christ.

They will be perfected, but God has "provided some better thing for us, that they without us should not be made perfect" (Hebrews 11:40). Not that the church is more worthy, but because in the overflowing grace of God[17] He has chosen the church to be the heavenly Bride of Christ.*

The church is the body of Christ,[18] and her precious union with Him is most clearly described in the epistle to the Ephesians. She is there regarded as spiritually quickened[19] and seated in the heavenlies[20] with her risen Lord,[21] having been "chosen in Him before the foundation of the world" to "be holy and without blame before Him in love."[22] She is to be "to the praise of the glory of His grace . . . accepted in the Beloved,"[22] being "sealed with that Holy Spirit of promise, which is the earnest of her inheritance until the redemption of the purchased possession."[23]

---

* Israel was an earthly bride, comforted with temporal blessings, and to these she will be restored. Though now through unbelief she is desolate, her children will still be as the sand of the sea (Isaiah 54; Jeremiah 3:1–18; 31:32; Ezekiel 16; Hosea 1:10, 11; 2; 3. See page 161).

---

17. *Ephesians 2:7*. That in the ages to come he might show the exceeding riches of his grace, in his kindness toward us, through Christ Jesus.

18. *1 Corinthians 12:27*. Now ye are the body of Christ, and members in particular.

19. *Ephesians 2:1*. And you hath he quickened, who were dead in trespasses and sins.

20. *Ephesians 1:3*. Blessed be the God and Father of our Lord Jesus Christ, who hath blessed us with all spiritual belssings in heavenly places in Christ.

Ephesians 2:6. And hath raised us up together, and made us sit together in heavenly places in Christ Jesus.

21. *Ephesians 1:20*. Which he wrought in Christ, when he raised him from the dead, and set him at his own right hand in the heavenly places.

22. *Ephesians 1:4-6*. According as he hath chosen us in him before the foundation of the world, that we should be holy and without blame before him in love: having predestined us unto the adoption of children by Jesus Christ to himself, according to the good pleasure of his will. To the praise of the glory of his grace, wherein he hath made us accepted in the beloved.

23. *Ephesians 1:13-14*. In whom ye also trusted, after that ye heard the word of truth, the gospel of your salvation: in whom also, after that ye believed, ye were sealed with that Holy Spirit of promise. Which is the earnest of our inheritance until the redemption of the purchased possession, unto the praise of his glory.

Oh! that we might receive "the spirit of wisdom and revelation in the knowledge of Him" to "know what is the hope of His calling and what the riches of the glory of His inheritance in the saints" (1:17–18). We should not walk "as other Gentiles walk," "but speaking the truth in love," grow up into Christ our living head, working together for the "increase of the body" and edification "in love" (4:15–17) "till we all come into the unity of the faith and of the knowledge of the Son of God, unto *a perfect man*, unto the measure of the stature of the fulness of Christ" (4:13). That is, Christ as the head, and the church as the body, will make one perfect man. "They twain shall be one flesh,[24] "the *new man* which is created in righteousness and true holiness" (4:24)—the true seed of the woman, which shall bruise the serpent's head.[25]

Wherefore, the church is exhorted to "grieve not the Holy Spirit of God whereby" she is "sealed unto the day of redemption" (Ephesians 4:30), but to be "kind one to another, tender-hearted" (4:32), "walking in love" (5:2) "as children of light" (5:8), "circumspectly" and "wise, redeeming the time" (5:15–16), "filled with the Spirit" (5:18), nourished and cherished (5:29) until sanctified and cleansed, she is presented unto the Lord "Himself a glorious church, not having spot, or wrinkle, or any such thing," but "holy and without blemish" the Bride of Christ. "For we are members of His body."[26]

Can there be anything more precious than the thought of Jesus coming to take unto Himself His Bride? It is full

---

24. *Matthew 19:4-6*. And he answered and said unto them, Have ye not read, that he which made them at the beginning made them male and female, and said, For this cause shall a man leave father and mother, and shall cleave to his wife: and they twain shall be one flesh? Wherefore they are no more twain, but one flesh. What therefore God hath joined together, let not man put asunder.

Ephesians 5:31. For this cause shall a man leave his father and mother, and shall be joined unto his wife, and they two shall be one flesh.

25. *Genesis 3:15*. And I will put enmity between thee and the woman, and between thy seed and her seed; it shall bruise thy head, and thou shalt bruise his heel.

Romans 16:20. And the God of peace shall bruise Satan under your feet shortly. The grace of our Lord Jesus Christ be with you. Amen.

26. *Ephesians 5:25-27, 30-32*. Husbands, love your wives, even as Christ also loved the church, and gave himself up for it; that he might sanctify it, having

of tenderness and love. What will He not do for her when He presents her unto Himself! The ecstasy of that meeting is above the power of description by tongue or pen. "Eye hath not seen, nor ear heard; neither have entered into the heart of man, the things which God hath prepared for them that love Him" (1 Corinthians 2:9). We have indeed "an earnest" "by His Spirit"—the "first fruits"—a foretaste of the joys to come. But *then* will the church experience the rest of love—the fulness of communion— the rapture of her Lord's embrace, and be satisfied in the sweetness of His love.

The comfort of this truth is all lost if we fail to make the proper distinction between the church and the kingdom. The church is not to be reigned over, but is to reign with Christ.[27]

No more heart-pangs nor sadness
When Jesus comes;
All peace and joy and gladness
When Jesus comes.

He'll know the way was dreary,
When Jesus comes;
He'll know the feet grew weary,
When Jesus comes.

He'll know what griefs oppressed me,
When Jesus comes;
Oh, how His arms will rest me!
When Jesus comes.

This subject of our Lord's coming again is of such vital importance and is so largely interwoven with the whole of Scripture, that it provides a boundless field of investi-

---

cleansed it by the washing of water with the word, that he might present the church to himself a glorious church, not having spot or wrinkle or any such thing; but that it should be holy and without blemish. Because we are members of his body. For this cause shall a man leave his father and mother, and shall cleave to his wife; and the two shall become one flesh. This mystery is great: but I speak in regard of Christ and of the church.

27. *2 Timothy 2:11-12*. It is a faithful saying: For if we be dead with him, we shall also live with him: if we suffer, we shall also reign with him: if we deny him, he also will deny us.

gation and an exhaustless mine of truth. There is much more I would be glad to say about it, but this book has already exceeded the intended limit, and I will only add a few words in regard to the time.

20

THE TIME

First, let us make a clear distinction between the time of the Rapture and the time of the Revelation* (see diagram, page 229). The principal thought in regard to the former is that it may happen *now*. Nothing is given us in Scripture so definite as to form a sign of or date for the Rapture. We are to be always watching and waiting for it, and expecting it at any moment.

It is true that the church may see the "fig tree signs" *begin* to come to pass[1] before she will be taken out of the world to escape the Tribulation.[2] But these signs are of such a nature, especially the "wars and earthquakes," "distress of nations, sea and waves roaring," that the church in each of the past 18 centuries might consistently have believed that the signs were *beginning*.

---

* Failure to do this has led many to make serious errors in setting dates for our Lord's return.

---

1. *Luke 21:25-31.* And there shall be signs in the sun, and in the moon, and in the stars; and upon the earth distress of nations, with perplexity; the sea and the waves roaring; men's hearts failing them for fear, and for looking after those things which are coming on the earth: for the powers of heaven shall be shaken. And then shall they see the Son of man coming in a cloud with power and great glory. And when these things begin to come to pass, then look up, and lift up your heads; for your redemption draweth nigh. And he spake to them a parable; Behold the fig tree, and all the trees; when they now shoot forth, ye see and know of your own selves that summer is now nigh at hand. So likewise ye, when ye see these things come to pass, know ye that the kingdom of God is nigh at hand.

2. *Luke 21:34-36.* But take heed to yourselves, lest haply your hearts be overcharged with surfeiting, and drunkenness, and cares of this life, and that day come on you suddenly as a snare: for so shall it come upon all them that dwell on the face of all the earth. But watch ye at every season, making supplication, that ye may prevail to escape all these things that shall come to pass, and to stand before the Son of man.

So we have no date for the Rapture, *only* that it will precede the Revelation. That is, Christ will come for His church[3] before He comes with His church,[4] the period of the Tribulation lying between the two.

The time of the Revelation, I believe, is designated by many prophetic periods: in Leviticus 26, Daniel and Revelation. But their symbolical character and our imperfect chronology render the interpretation of them difficult and uncertain. I must not take space here to consider them, but I venture to state that earnest and prayerful study of them has given me an assured conviction that they are rapidly drawing to a close.

Two events must precede the Revelation which will indicate its proximity; the restoration (partial at least) of Israel,[5] and the rise of Antichrist.[6]

But Antichrist will not be revealed, as we understand from 2 Thessalonians 2:7, until after the Rapture. Neither is it probable that the restoration of Israel (except partially in unbelief, Zephaniah 2:1–2) will take place until after that event. For "Jerusalem shall be trodden down . . .

---

3. *1 Thessalonians 4:16-17*. For the Lord himself shall descend from heaven, with a shout, with the voice of the archangel, and with the trump of God: and the dead in Christ shall rise first: then we that are alive, that are left, shall together with them be caught up in the clouds, to meet the Lord in the air: and so shall we ever be with the Lord.

4. *Jude 14*. And Enoch also, the seventh from Adam, prophesied of these, saying, Behold, the Lord cometh with ten thousand of his saints.

5. *Ezekiel 22:19-20*. Therefore thus saith the LORD God; Because ye are all become dross, behold, therefore I will gather you into the midst of Jerusalem. As they gather silver, and brass, and iron, and lead, and tin, into the midst of the furnace, to blow the fire upon it, to melt it; so will I gather you in mine anger and in my fury, and I will leave you there, and melt you. Yea, I will gather you, and blow upon you in the fire of my wrath, and ye shall be melted in the midst thereof. As silver is melted in the midst of the furnace, so shall ye be melted in the midst thereof; and ye shall know that I the LORD have poured out my fury upon you.

6. *Zechariah 13:8-9*. And it shall come to pass, that in all the land, saith the LORD, two parts therein shall be cut off and die; but the third shall be left therein. And I will bring the third part through the fire, and will refine them as silver is refined, and will try them as gold is tried: they shall call on my name, and I will hear them: I will say, It is my people; and they shall say, The LORD is my God.

2 *Thessalonians 2:7-8*. For the mystery of iniquity doth already work: only he who now letteth will let, until he be taken out of the way. And then shall that Wicked be revealed, whom the Lord shall consume with the spirit of his mouth, and shall destroy with the brightness of his coming.

until the times of the Gentiles be fulfilled" (Luke 21:24), and the tabernacle of David will not be rebuilt until He has taken out of the Gentiles a people to His name (Acts 15:14–16).

It has pleased God to give signs, or evidences, of the approach of these events and by which we might know that the day was drawing near,[7] but, as we have before said, they have been of such a character that the church could see them repeated in each generation. And this we believe was purposely designed, in order to give the church *no date* and *no sign* which might so definitely indicate the time of her Rapture, that she would in any interval stop being vigilant. It was evidently all planned so that the unfolding of events would be, to her, a constant incentive to watchfulness.

The High Priest went into the Holy of Holies alone, and the whole congregation waited in expectation outside until he had made the offering and came out to bless them (Leviticus 16; Numbers 6:23–26; Luke 1:10). So has our High Priest entered once for all into the *true holy place*, and the church should look for Him in fervent expectation until He appears the second time not to bear sin, but to bring salvation.[8] She must watch, dressed for service and with lamps burning, like men waiting for their Lord (Luke 12:35, 36).

Yet we have the blessed assurance that every passing day brings our salvation nearer than when we first believed.[9] And, while it is true that the church, during all

7. *Hebrews 10:25*. Not forsaking the assembling of ourselves together, as the manner of some is; but exhorting one another: and so much the more as ye see the day approaching.

8. *Hebrews 9:24-28*. For Christ is not entered into the holy places made with hands, which are the figures of the true; but into heaven itself, now to appear in the presence of God for us: nor yet that he should offer himself often, as the high priest entereth into the holy place every year with blood of others; for then must he often have suffered since the foundation of the world: but now once in the end of the world hath he appeared to put away sin by the sacrifice of himself. And as it is appointed unto men once to die, but after this the judgment: so Christ was once offered to bear the sins of many: and unto them that look for him shall he appear the second time without sin unto salvation.

9. *Romans 13:11*. And that, knowing the time, that now it is high time to awake out of sleep; for now is our salvation nearer than we believed.

her history, has had repeated evidence that the day was approaching, I ask, what are these evidences in our time? Surely they are of special significance.

I believe, if I can rightly read the signs of the times, that the godless, lawless trio of communism, nihilism and anarchy, so alarmingly permeating the nations today, are unclean spirits preparing the way for Antichrist.

The Jews Returning

And, again, the Jews are, even now, returning to Jerusalem.

It is said that at the beginning of the nineteenth century the Porte allowed no more than 300 of the hated people to live in the city. Forty years later that restriction was removed, but another still remained, by virtue of which they were permitted only to reside in a particular quarter of the town, which was much too small for them. It was in the year 1867 this last regulation was removed and since then the progress made by the Jews in populating their ancient capital has been extraordinary. Almost every one of the old houses as it fell vacant has been bought by them while they have built a prodigious number of new ones in all parts of the town. Schools, hospitals and religious associations have been started on a grand scale, as also a school for manual training and of agriculture.

At the time of writing, 1908, the city of Jerusalem has spread over a large extent of ground outside the walls. Great hospices, hotels, churches, stores, etc., have been erected, but most notable of all, a multitude of dwellings for the Jews.

The number of Jews now residing in the inner and outer city is estimated at from 40,000 to 50,000, being more than half the entire population. Besides these, there are large colonies at Tiberias, Safed, Joppa and Hebron, and several other smaller ones in various parts of the country. The entire Jewish population of Palestine is said to be more than 80,000, so that a greater number have already returned than the 49,697 who went up with Zerubbabel from Babylon (Ezra 2:64–65).

The anti-semitic agitations in Germany, Austria and France, and the fierce persecutions in Russia and Romania, have stirred up the Jews of the world as the eagle does its nest (Deuteronomy 32:11).

National hopes and aspirations have found vent in the organization of *Chovevi Zion* (Lovers of Zion) societies, and *Shova Zion* (colonization) societies throughout Europe and America. Land is being purchased and funds raised, on installment plans, to send back the members by lot.

A railroad has been completed from Joppa, and the engine speeds up to Jerusalem like one of Nahum's "flaming torches" (Nahum 2:3) which, the prophet says, "shall be in the day of His preparation," over the roadway which the Arabs call *Trek el Kods*, significantly coinciding with the Hebrew *Derech Hakodesh* (Way of Holiness) of Isaiah 35:8. This "highway," cast up as the Hebrew *Maslol* indicates, is a special preparation for the return of the people to Zion (Isaiah 35:10). Other lines of railway are projected or actually under construction to Hebron, Jericho, Acre, Tiberias and Damascus.

The Turkish hold on the country is continually weakening, and there is considerable talk of a Jewish state.* May we not conclude that the Lord is even now setting "His hand again the second time" for the restoration of His people?[10] "He that scattereth Israel will gather him, and keep him as a shepherd doth his flock" (Jeremiah 31:10).

Besides these, we have other evidences. Many are running to and fro on the highways of travel, or searching diligently throughout the prophetic Word, which is doubtless the true meaning of the passage (Daniel 12:4) and which is a sign of "the time of the end."

---

* The State of Israel became a reality in 1948 (publisher's note).

---

10. *Isaiah 11:11*. And it shall come to pass in that day, that the LORD shall set his hand again the second time to recover the remnant of his people, which shall be left, from Assyria, and from Egypt, and from Pathros, and from Cush, and from Elam, and from Shinar, and from Hamath, and from the islands of the sea.

The awful dearth of spiritual life in the great nominal church is another evidence. The restless and perplexed condition of the nations is also suggestive. And there are several other evidences of which I could speak, all of which substantiate the fact that the day is "approaching" (Hebrews 10:25).

And lastly, while it is entirely unscriptural and wrong to put the second coming of our Lord any distance into the future, and likewise unscriptural and wrong to fix a date, or name the time when He will come for His bride; yet there will be a privileged company of saints living on the earth[11] at the time when He will descend from heaven,[12] and who will say that they will *all* be taken by surprise? Every generation that has lived since He went away, however dark and unspiritual it may have been, has had its band of faithful watching ones.

Shortly prior to the first coming of Christ, the Holy Spirit, although He had given through Daniel the definite prophecy of the seventy weeks, gave a special revelation unto the devout Simeon, who was "waiting for the consolation of Israel;" that is, "that he should not see death before he had seen the Lord's Christ (Luke 2:26). And this leads us to ask: May not the same blessed Spirit, who revealed this mighty event to Simeon of old (and probably to the aged Anna, also)[13] likewise give to a favored one, or a chosen few of the faithful watching ones, to know that their glad eyes will see His appearing, and that they will never taste of death.[14] Even so now,

11. *1 Corinthians 15:51-52.* Behold, I show you a mystery; we shall not all sleep, but we shall all be changed. In a moment, in the twinkling of an eye, at the last trump: for the trumpet shall sound, and the dead shall be raised incorruptible, and we shall be changed.

12. *1 Thessalonians 4:16.* For the Lord himself shall descend from heaven, with a shout, with the voice of the archangel, and with the trump of God: and the dead in Christ shall rise first.

13. *Luke 2:36-38.* And there was one Anna, a prophetess, the daughter of Phanuel, of the tribe of Aser: she was of a great age, and had lived with a husband seven years from her virginity; and she was a widow of about fourscore and four years, which departed not from the temple, but served God with fastings and prayers night and day. And she coming in that instant gave thanks likewise unto the Lord, and spake of him to all them that looked for redemption in Jerusalem.

14. *John 11:26.* And whosoever liveth and believeth in me shall never die. Believest thou this?

many of the most devout and faithful of God's people, in all denominations, both in this and foreign lands, are seriously impressed with the conviction that the coming of the Lord is near.

These are certainly sufficient evidences to enforce the apostle's injunction, that we should exhort one another *and so much the more as we see the day approaching* (Hebrews 10:25).

For, if the day, or Revelation, is near, the Rapture is still nearer. And again the general conviction among Bible students and earnest Christians—that the great prophetic periods which point to the Revelation are nearly ended, and the deep conviction expressed by many, including even statesmen and scientists, that some great event is near—may well lead us to enquire,

Watchman, What of the Night?

Ever since the sin of Adam and Eve this world has been a *dark place*,[15] a moral "night."[16] By faith the believer looks forward, through prophecy, to the glorious day[15] that is coming, when salvation, which is now by faith and hope,[17] will be revealed[18] in all its grandeur and glory.[19] For this day the hearts of God's people yearn with earnest desire.

---

15. *2 Peter 1:19.* We have also a more sure word of prophecy; whereunto ye do well that ye take heed, as unto a light that shineth in a dark place, until the day dawn, and the daystar arise in your hearts.

16. *John 1:5, 10.* And the light shineth in darkness; and the darkness comprehended it not. He was in the world, and the world was made by him, and the world knew him not.

   John 3:19-20. And this is the condemnation, that light is come into the world, and men loved darkness rather than light, because their deeds were evil. For every one that doeth evil hateth the light, neither cometh to the light, lest his deeds should be reproved.

17. *Romans 8:24-25.* For we are saved by hope: but hope that is seen is not hope: for what a man seeth, why doth he yet hope for? But if we hope for that we see not, then do we with patience wait for it.

18. *1 Peter 1:5-7.* Who are kept by the power of God through faith unto salvation ready to be revealed in the last time. Wherein ye greatly rejoice, though now for a season, if need be, ye are in heaviness through manifold temptations: that the trial of your faith, being much more precious than of gold that perisheth, though it be tried with fire, might be found unto praise and honor and glory at the appearing of Jesus Christ.

19. *1 Corinthians 2:9.* But as it is written, Eye hath not seen, nor ear heard,

"Watchman, what of the night?" "Watchman, what of the night?" The watchman said: "The *morning* cometh, and also the *night*" (Isaiah 21:11–12). To the believer it will be Morning; to the ungodly it will be Night.

Jesus is the Morning Star,[20] and He is also the Sun of Righteousness.[21] Only those who are up early and watching see the morning star. So it will be only the true and faithful church that will see Christ at the Rapture as the Bright and Morning Star. As the Sun of Righteousness He will appear to Israel, and all the world, at the Revelation.

Several centuries of the night were past when Paul wrote, "the night is far spent, the day is at hand" (Romans 13:12). And surely, as many more centuries have since passed, it must now be *almost morning*.

O! then, dear reader, "let us who are of the day, be sober, putting on the breastplate of faith and love; and for an helmet, the *hope of salvation*. For God hath not appointed us to wrath, but to obtain salvation by our Lord Jesus Christ" (1 Thessalonians 5:8–9). "Therefore let us not sleep, as do others, but let us watch and be sober" (1 Thessalonians 5:6).

A dear brother writes us as follows: "I find so many who are willing to receive the truth of the Second Coming, but it is generally those who are passing through affliction, or those living very near the Lord. Those who are enjoying the well-watered plains of this world seem to care very little about seeing the Owner of the estate. *But He will come*. Hallelujah! He will come. Yes! He is coming. The bride who knows the Bridegroom, and is true, says, He is coming. Come Lord Jesus, Come! Come! Come!! Come!!! Come!!!! A poor cursed earth (Romans 8:19–22) groans out, Come! Thank heaven, He speaks:

---

neither have entered into the heart of man, the things which God hath prepared for them that love him.

20. *Revelation 22:16*. I Jesus have sent mine angel to testify unto you these things in the churches. I am the root and the offspring of David, and the bright and morning star.

21. *Malachi 4:2*. But unto you that fear my name shall the Son of righteousness arise with healing in his wings; and ye shall go forth, and grow up as calves of the stall.

"SURELY I COME QUICKLY"
(Revelation 22:20)

I'm waiting for Thee, Lord,
Thy beauty to see, Lord,
I'm waiting for Thee,
For Thy coming again.

Thou'rt gone over there, Lord,
A place to prepare, Lord,
Thy home I shall share
At Thy coming again.

'Mid danger and fear, Lord,
I'm oft weary here, Lord,
The time must be near
Of Thy coming again.

Whilst Thou art away, Lord,
I stumble and stray, Lord,
Oh hasten the day
Of Thy coming again.

"Blessed are those servants, whom the Lord, when he cometh, shall find watching: verily I say unto you, that He shall gird Himself and make them to sit down to meat, and will come forth and serve them" (Luke 12:37).

"OCCUPY TILL I COME"
Waiting for the Morning
(Revelation 19:7)

There is no roof in all the world, of palace or of cot,
That hideth not some burdened heart, nigh breaking for its lot;
The earth is sunk in pain and tears, and closer draws the gloom;
And balm for cure there can be none, till Christ, the Lord, shall
  come.

O morn, when like a summer bird, my spirit shall go free,
When I shall see Thee as Thou art, and be, my God, like Thee!
Like Thee! Like Thee! All spotless white—this heart, this will, as
  Thine!
O love of God, O blood of Christ, O grace and power divine!

My Savior, who doth know the thirst the longing spirit feels,
O Bridegroom, now so long afar, why stay thy chariotwheels?
Were ever eyes so dim with grief, breasts so oppressed with care?
Did ever hearts so yearn to catch Thy whisper from the air?

Thou lonely one, lift up thy head, array thee for the feast;
He that hath tarried long is near—the glow is in the East!
O Morning Star, so soon to lead Thy chosen one away—
O Sun of Righteousness, bring in the everlasting day!

"REDEMPTION DRAWETH NIGH"
(Luke 21:28)

My soul crieth out for a jubilee song!
There is joy in my heart, let me praise with my tongue;
For I know, though the darkness of Egypt still lowers,
That the time ere release is not ages, but hours.

As sailors, not yet within sight of the strand,
Know well their approach by the "loom of the land;"
So they, who will bend but a listening ear,
Can now catch the whisper that tells He is near.

He is near—the stars in their courses prepare
To utter the sign He hath bid them declare!
The world in its guilt waxeth haggard and grim,
And its cup of iniquity fills to the brim!

The curse so long camped upon Bosphorus' side,
And she that sits queen upon Tiber's foul tide,
And famine and pestilence stalk in the band
Of witness, attesting the Lord is at hand.

Spent at last the long cycle of wilderness dearth,
Once again sounds of latter-rain gladden the earth
In the land, still despised, but preparing e'en now
For the feet that shall stand upon Olivet's brow.

And thither to gather the tribes have begun,
From the East and the West, from the climes of the sun
For the times of the Gentiles have answered their need,
And the hiss has gone forth unto Israel's seed.

The world as of yore, naught of all doth divine,
Saith again that believers are filled with new wine,
Suffers warning to pass all unseen and unheard,
And, like Herod, fulfills while opposing His word.

Then welcome, thrice welcome, ye tokens of God!
What else but His coming can comfort afford?
What presence but His set this prisoned earth free?
O Star of the Morning, our hope is in Thee!

—From *Waiting for the Morning and Other Poems*

21

PLAN OF THE *AIŌNS* (AGES)

The diagram on page 229 is intended to illustrate the chronological arrangement of the dispensations and some of the principal events of Bible history.

The division of time into days, months, and years, is fixed by the movements of the earth and moon. The term *century* is not used in the Scriptures, but the next greater measure of time above the year (Sabbatic year and Jubilee year) is the Greek term *aiōn* or English *eon*, from which comes our word *age*. This word is used 124 times in the New Testament and is translated by eight different English words, that is *"world"* 35 times:

Matthew 12:32	Luke 1:70	1 Corinthians 1:20	2 Corinthians 4:4
Matthew 13:22	Luke 16:8	1 Corinthians 2:6	Galatians 1:4
Matthew 13:39	Luke 18:30	1 Corinthians 2:6	Ephesians 1:21
Matthew 13:40	Luke 20:34	1 Corinthians 2:7	Ephesians 3:9
Matthew 13:49	Luke 20:35	1 Corinthians 2:8	Ephesians 3:21
Matthew 24:3	John 9:32	1 Corinthians 3:18	1 Timothy 6:17
Matthew 28:20	Acts 3:21	1 Corinthians 8:13	2 Timothy 4:10
Mark 4:19	Acts 15:18	1 Corinthians	Titus 2:12
Mark 10:30	Romans 12:2	10:11	Hebrews 6:5

"Worlds," twice (Hebrews 1:2 and 11:13).

"Course," once (Ephesians 2:2).

"Eternal" twice (Ephesians 3:11 and 1 Timothy 1:17).

"End," once (Ephesians 3:21).

"Ages," twice (Ephesians 2:7 and Colossians 1:26).

"Ever," 30 times:

Matthew 6:13	John 6:51	John 14:16	2 Corinthians 9:9
Matthew 21:19	John 6:58	Romans 1:25	Hebrews 5:6
Mark 11:14	John 8:35	Romans 9:5	Hebrews 6:20
Luke 1:33	John 8:35	Romans 11:36	Hebrews 7:17
Luke 1:55	John 12:34	Romans 16:27	Hebrews 7:21

Hebrews 7:24	1 Peter 1:25	1 John 2:17	Jude 25
Hebrews 13:8	2 Peter 2:17	2 John 2	
1 Peter 1:23	2 Peter 3:18	Jude 13	

With a negative *"Never"* 7 times:

Mark 3:29	John 8:51	John 10:28	John 13:8
John 4:14	John 8:52	John 11:26	

"Evermore," 3 times:

2 Corinthians 11:31	Hebrews 7:28	Revelation 1:18

"Ever and ever," 21 times:

Galatians 1:5	1 Peter 4:11	Revelation 5:14	Revelation 19:5
Philippians 4:20	1 Peter 5:11	Revelation 7:12	Revelation 20:10
1 Timothy 1:17	Revelation 1:6	Revelation 10:6	Revelation 22:7
2 Timothy 4:18	Revelation 4:9	Revelation 11:15	
Hebrews 1:8	Revelation 4:10	Revelation 14:11	
Hebrews 13:21	Revelation 5:13	Revelation 15:3	

42 times, for in each of these above 21 passages, it is used twice, and, in all but Hebrews 1:8, it is in the plural and multiplied form, *aiōns of aiōns*. It is also plural in:

Luke 1:33	1 Corinthians 10:11	Ephesians 3:11	Hebrews 11:3
Romans 1:25		Ephesians 3:21	Hebrews 13:8
Romans 9:5	2 Corinthians 11:31	Colossians 1:26	Jude 25
Romans 11:36		1 Timothy 1:17	
Romans 16:27	Ephesians 2:7	Hebrews 1:2	
1 Corinthians 2:7	Ephesians 3:9	Hebrews 9:26	

If you will carefully examine these passages, and substitute the original word *aiōn* or *aiōns,* you will at once see that it is used not to indicate the material or physical world, but as a measurement of time.

"It shall not be forgiven him, neither in this *aiōn,* neither in the *aiōn* to come" (Matthew 12:32).

"The harvest is the end of the *aiōn*."—"So shall it be at the end of this *aiōn*" (Matthew 13:39–40).

"Let no fruit grow on thee henceforward for an *aiōn*" (Matthew 21:19).

"What shall be the sign of thy coming and of the end of the *aiōn*" (Matthew 24:3).

"Hath not forgiveness to [or for] the *aiōn,* but is in danger of *aiōnian** sin" (Mark 3:29).

---

* The adjective *"aiōnios"* is used 70 times, as follows:

Matthew 18:8	Matthew 19:29	Matthew 25:46	Mark 10:17
Matthew 19:16	Matthew 25:41	Mark 3:29	Mark 10:30

"But he shall receive . . . in the *aiōn* to come eternal life" (Mark 10:30).

"For ever," *i.e.* for the *aiōns* (Luke 1:33; Romans 1:25; 9:5; 11:36; 2 Corinthians 11:31; Hebrews 13:8).

"For ever," *i.e.* for the *aiōn* (Luke 1:55; John 6:51–58; 8:35; 12:34; 14:16; 2 Corinthians 9:9; Hebrews 5:6; 6:20; 7:17; 21, 24, 28; 1 Peter 1:25; 1 John 2:17; 2 John 2; Jude 13).

"The children of this *aiōn* are . . . wiser than the children of light" (Luke 16:8).

"The children of this *aiōn* marry . . . but they which shall be accounted worthy to obtain that *aiōn* and the resurrection from the dead, neither marry nor are given in marriage" (Luke 20:34–35).

"Shall thirst not for the *aiōn*" (John 4:14).

"Not for the *aiōn*" (John 8:51–52; 10:28; 11:26; 13:8; 1 Corinthians 8:13).

"Known unto God are all his works from the beginning of the *aiōn*" (lit. from an *aiōn*" Acts 15:18).

"To God only wise, be glory through Jesus Christ for the *aiōn*" (Romans 16:27).

"Not the wisdom of this *aiōn*, nor of the princes of this *aiōn* . . . but we speak . . .even the hidden wisdom which God ordained before the *aiōns*" (1 Corinthians 2:6–7).

"For our admonition upon whom the ends of the *aiōns* are come" (1 Corinthians 10:11).

"In whom the God of this *aiōn*" (2 Corinthians 4:4).

Luke 10:25	John 10:28	Galatians 6:8	Hebrews 9:12
Luke 16:9	John 12:25	2 Thessalonians	Hebrews 9:14
Luke 18:18	John 12:50	1:9	Hebrews 9:15
Luke 18:30	John 17:2	2 Thessalonians	Hebrews 13:20
John 3:15	John 17:3	2:16	1 Peter 5:10
John 3:16	Acts 13:46	1 Timothy 1:16	2 Peter 1:11
John 3:36	Acts 13:48	1 Timothy 6:12	1 John 1:2
John 4:14	Romans 2:7	1 Timothy 6:16	1 John 2:25
John 4:36	Romans 5:21	1 Timothy 6:19	1 John 3:15
John 5:24	Romans 6:22	2 Timothy 1:9	1 John 5:11
John 5:39	Romans 6:23	2 Timothy 2:10	1 John 5:13
John 6:27	Romans 16:25	Titus 1:2	1 John 5:20
John 6:40	Romans 16:26	Titus 3:7	Jude 7
John 6:47	2 Corinthians 4:17	Philemon 15	Jude 21
John 6:54	2 Corinthians 4:18	Hebrews 5:9	Revelation 14:6
John 6:68	2 Corinthians 5:1	Hebrews 6:2	

It is translated *everlasting, eternal* or *forever* except in three passages, where it is *world* (Romans 16:25, *aiōnian times,* 2 Timothy 1:9, and Titus 1:2, *before aiōnian times*).

"Who gave himself . . . that He might deliver us from this present evil *aiōn*" (Galatians 1:4).

"Not only in this *aiōn*, but also in that which is to come" (Ephesians 1:21).

"That in the *aiōns* to come" (Ephesians 2:7).

"The mystery which from the *aiōns* hath been hid" (Ephesians 3:9).

"According to the purpose [plan] of the *aiōns*" (Ephesians 3:11).

"Unto him be glory . . . throughout all the generations of the *aiōn* of the *aiōns*" (Ephesians 3:21).

"Now unto the king of the *aiōns*" (1 Timothy 1:17).

"Demas hath forsaken me having loved this present *aiōn*" (2 Timothy 4:10).

"By whom also he made the *aiōn*" (Hebrews 1:2).

"Thy throne, O God, is for the *aiōn*" ("of the aiōn" not authentic, Hebrews 1:8).

"And have tasted . . .the powers of the *aiōn* to come" (Hebrews 6:5).

"But now once in the end [lit. conjunction] of the *aiōns*" (overlapped, Hebrews 9:26).

"Through faith we understand that the *aiōns* were framed" (adjusted, Hebrews 11:3).

"Both now and for the day of the *aiōn*" (2 Peter 3:18).

"Both now and throughout all the *aiōns*" (Jude 25).

"The smoke of their torment ascendeth up for *aiōns* of *aiōns*" (Revelation 14:11).

"Her smoke rose up for the *aiōns* of the *aiōns* (Revelation 19:3).

"Shall be tormented day and night for the *aiōns* of the *aiōns*" (Revelation 20:10).

"They shall reign for the *aiōns* of the *aiōns*" (Revelation 22:5).

Notice that we have the singular *aiōn*, the plural *aiōns* and *aiōn* of *aiōns* (a great *aiōn* composed of *aiōns*), and the multiplied form *aiōns* of *aiōns*. An *aiōn* has an end (see Matthew 13:39, 40, 49; 24:3; 28:20), and as another follows (see Matthew 12:32; Mark 10:30; Luke 18:30 and 20:35; Ephesians 1:21), it must have a beginning. The end of one and beginning of another overlap so that Paul could say, "the ends of the *aiōns* have come upon us" (1 Corinthians 10:11). There are many *aiōns*,[1] both in the past[2] and in the future.[3] Jesus is the King of the *aiōns*,[4] and they are all made by Him[5] according to a Divine Plan, see Greek, "*purpose* [or plan] of the *aiōns*."[6]

The diagram on page 229 is intended to illustrate a minute section of this infinite plan, showing seven of the *aiōns*. The diverging lines represent the increase of population suddenly cut down to eight at the flood and to be again greatly reduced at the close of the present dispensation.[7]

1. Eden, the *aiōn* of *innocence* terminating in the explusion.
2. Antediluvian, the *aiōn* of *freedom* (conscience the only restraint) terminating in the flood and reduction of the race to the eight persons of Noah and his family. During this *aiōn* Enoch is caught up, a type of the coming rapture of the church.
3. Postdiluvian, the *aiōn* of *government,* man put under civil authority,[8] terminating in the destruction of Sodom.

---

1. *Hebrews 11:3.* Through faith we understand that the worlds [*aiōns*] were framed by the word of God, so that things which are seen were not made of things which do appear.

2. *Colossians 1:26.* Even the mystery which hath been hid from ages [*aiōns*] and from generations, but now is made manifest to his saints.

3. *Ephesians 2:7.* That in the ages [*aiōns*] to come he might show the exceeding riches of his grace, in his kindness toward us, through Christ Jesus.

4. *1 Timothy 1:17.* Now unto the King eternal [*of the aiōns*], immortal, invisible, the only wise God, be honor and glory for ever and ever. Amen.

5. *Hebrews 1:2.* Hath in these last days spoken unto us by his Son, whom he hath appointed heir of all things, by whom also he made the worlds [*aiōns*]. See also *Hebrews 11:3.*

6. *Ephesians 3:11.* According to the eternal purpose which he purposed in Christ Jesus our Lord.

7. *Revelation 9:18.* By these three was the third part of men killed, by the fire, and by the smoke, and by the brimstone, which issued out of their mouths. See also *Zechariah 13:8; 14:12–13; Revelation 14:18–20; 19:19–21.*

8. *Genesis 9:5-6.* And surely your blood of your lives will I require; at the hand of every beast will I require it, and at the hand of man; at the hand of every man's brother will I require the life of man. Whoso sheddeth man's blood, by man shall his blood be shed: for in the image of God made he man.

4. Patriarchal, the *pilgrim aiōn*,[9] terminating in the
   overthrow of Pharaoh and his host in the Red Sea.
5. Mosaic, the *Israelitish aiōn*, terminating in the
   crucifixion and the destruction of Jerusalem. In
   this Elijah becomes another type of the Rapture.
6. Christian, the *aiōn* of *mystery,* terminating in the
   great tribulation,[10] the coming of the Lord, the
   judgment of nations,[11] and another great reduction
   of the world's population. During this *aiōn* the
   Jews are scattered among all nations.[12]
7. Millennium, the *aiōn* of *manifestation* (Romans
   8:19), terminating in Satan's last deception and
   the judgment of the great white throne.[13]

Beyond this is the new heavens and the new earth
where righteousness dwells,[14] probably the beginning of
another series of *aiōns*. For these seven make a week of
aiōns, corresponding to the expression in Ephesians 3:21,
aiōn of *aiōns,* or one great *aiōn* composed of these seven
aiōns. And, in harmony with the *weeks of years* appointed
to Israel (Leviticus 25:8–11), other great *aiōns* are to follow
corresponding to the expression *aiōns* of *aiōns*. (See

---

9. *Hebrews 11:13*. These all died in faith, not having received the promises,
but having seen them afar off, and were persuaded of them, and embraced
them, and confessed that they were strangers and pilgrims on the earth.

10. *Matthew 24:21*. For then shall be great tribulation, such as was not since
the beginning of the world to this time, no, nor ever shall be.

11. *Matthew 25:31-32*. When the Son of man shall come in his glory, and all
the holy angels with him, then shall he sit upon the throne of his glory: and
before him shall be gathered all nations: and he shall separate them one from
another, as a shepherd divideth his sheep from the goats.

12. *Amos 9:9*. For, lo, I will command, and I will sift the house of Israel
among all nations, like as corn is sifted in a sieve, yet shall not the least grain
fall upon the earth.

   Luke 21:24. And they shall fall by the edge of the sword, and shall be led
away captive into all nations: and Jerusalem shall be trodden down of the
Gentiles, until the times of the Gentiles be fulfilled.

13. *Revelation 20:11*. And I saw a great white throne, and him that sat on it,
from whose face the earth and the heaven fled away; and there was found no
place for them.

   12–15. See page 105 for verses 12–15.

14. *Isaiah 65:17*. For, behold, I create new heavens, and a new earth: and the
former shall not be remembered, nor come into mind.

   2 Peter 3:13. Nevertheless we, according to his promise, look for new
heavens and a new earth, wherein dwelleth righteousness. See also *Isaiah
66:22; Revelation 21:1*.

Galatians 1:5 and the other passages cited above.) Possibly the fiftieth *aiōn* may be like the Jubilee of Leviticus 25 and then again, *aiōns* of *aiōns*. (See lower section of diagram on page 229.)

But, says one, if *aiōns* are measured periods then all *aiōns* are measured, and there will be an end to the sorrows of the ungodly,[15] and the glory and dominion of the Lamb and his saints.[16] No, beloved! For the best idea we mortals can have of infinity or eternity is that of continual measurement, and this is exactly the idea conveyed by the indefinite expression *aiōns* of *aiōns*.

It will be noticed in the diagram that the *aiōns* are not of the same duration, but each marks a change in God's method of dealing with mankind. Probably the *aiōns* of the past—the Hebrew *olams* of the Old Testament—mark the geological periods of the earth and the various eras in the development of the universe. And as the past has been an orderly unfolding of creation and revelation of the Creator, so will the future—be not a limitless *aiōn* called eternity, but a limitless succession of *aiōns* measuring infinite duration. Time is the measure of eternity and eternity is the continued measurement of time. Take for instance a yard stick, and it measures only 3 feet. But turn it over and over and over, and you pass around the world, out to the moon, the sun, the stars, the farthermost nebula, and all the limits of imagination, and still the little measure goes on and on

15. *Revelation 14:11*. And the smoke of their torment ascendeth up for ever and ever [*aiōns of aiōns*]: and they have no rest day nor night, who worship the beast and his image, and whosoever receiveth the mark of his name.
   Revelation 20:10. And the devil, that deceived them, was cast into the lake of fire and brimstone, where the beast and the false prophet are, and shall be tormented day and night for ever and ever [*aiōns of aiōns*].
16. *Revelation 1:6*. And hath made us kings and priests unto God and his Father; to him be glory and dominion for ever and ever. Amen.
   Revelation 11:15. And the seventh angel sounded; and there were great voices in heaven, saying, The kingdoms of this world are become the kingdoms of our Lord, and of his Christ; and he shall reign for ever and ever [*aiōns of aiōns*].
   Revelation 22:5. And there shall be no night there; and they need no candle, neither light of the sun; for the Lord God giveth them light: and they shall reign for ever and ever [*aiōns of aiōns*].

into the unthinkable. In the same way the Scriptural succession of *aiōns* measures eternity.

The events at the beginning of this present *aiōn*, that is, the crucifixion and ascension of our Lord and the descent of the Holy Spirit, are well understood. The events at its close constitute the time of the end.

The Time of the End

The events are briefly as follows: The descent of the Lord with a shout; the resurrection of those who sleep in Jesus; the change in a moment of those believers who are alive (1 Corinthians 15); their rapture, or being caught up to meet the Lord in the air (1 Thessalonians 4:13–18) to enjoy the marriage feast of the King's Son, the Lamb of God (Matthew 22:2, etc.; 25:10; 2 Corinthians 11:2; Ephesians 5:25–32; Revelation 19:7, and Song of Solomon).

While this is occurring in the air, Israelites are gathered to Palestine in unbelief;[17] they rebuild their temple, establish their ancient sacrifices, and plunge from bad to worse until Antichrist arises; and they make a covenant with him[18] which the prophet calls a covenant with death and sheol.[19] Terrible persecution willl follow, called "the time of Jacob's trouble."[20]

---

17. *Zephaniah 2:1-2.* Gather yourselves together, yea, gather together, O nation not desired; before the decree bring forth, before the day pass as the chaff, before the fierce anger of the LORD come upon you, before the day of the LORD's anger come upon you.

18. *Daniel 9:27.* And he shall confirm the covenant with many for one week: and in the midst of the week he shall cause the sacrifice and the oblation to cease, and for the overspreading of abominations he shall make it desolate, even until the consummation, and that determined shall be poured upon the desolate.

John 5:43. I am come in my Father's name, and ye receive me not; if another shall come in his own name, him ye will receive.

19. *Isaiah 28:15.* Because ye have said, We have made a covenant with death, and with hell are we at agreement; when the overflowing scourge shall pass through, it shall not come unto us: for we have made lies our refuge, and under falsehood have we hid ourselves.

20. *Jeremiah 30:5-7.* For thus saith the LORD; We have heard a voice of trembling, of fear, and not of peace. Ask ye now, and see whether a man doth travail with child? wherefore do I see every man with his hands on his loins, as a woman in travail, and all faces are turned into paleness? Alas! for that day is great, so that none is like it: it is even the time of Jacob's trouble. But he shall be saved out of it.

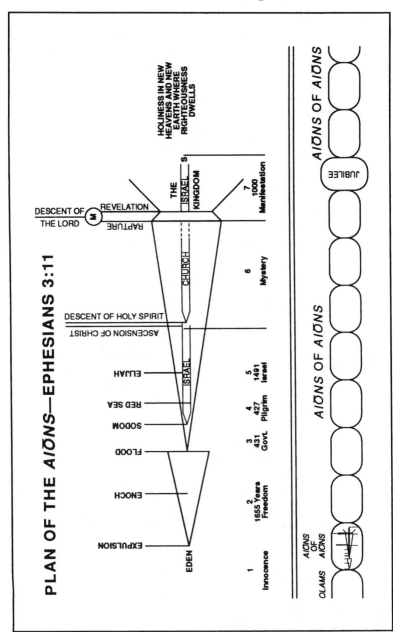

When it would seem that all was lost,[21] then the Lord will come with His saints down to the earth, destroy this lawless Antichrist, and deliver Israel, who will then look on "Him they have pierced,"[22] and a nation will be born in a day, or at once.[23] He will judge the living nations and establish His millennial kingdom (Psalm 2; Daniel 2:44; Revelation 11:15).

But let it be distinctly remembered that we have no date for the Rapture, the coming of our Lord to the meeting place in the air.[24] We are to live dressed for service and our lamps burning like men waiting for their Lord (Luke 12:35–40). And yet, in the unfolding of events we may see the day approaching,[25] the beginnings that will cause us to lift up our heads.[26]

---

21. *Zechariah 14:1-3*. Behold, the day of the LORD cometh, and thy spoil shall be divided in the midst of thee. For I will gather all nations against Jerusalem to battle; and the city shall be taken, and the houses rifled, and the women ravished; and half of the city shall go forth into captivity, and the residue of the people shall not be cut off from the city. Then shall the LORD go forth, and fight against those nations, as when he fought in the day of battle. See also verses 4 and 5. See also *Jude 14*; *2 Thessalonians 2:8*.

22. *Zechariah 12:9-14*. And it shall come to pass in that day, that I will seek to destroy all the nations that come against Jerusalem. And I will pour upon the house of David, and upon the inhabitants of Jerusalem, the spirit of grace and of supplications; and they shall look upon me whom they have pierced, and they shall mourn for him, as one mourneth for his only son, and shall be in bitterness for him, as one that is in bitterness for his first-born. In that day shall there be a great mourning in Jerusalem, as the mourning of Hadadrimmon in the valley of Megiddon. And the land shall mourn, every family apart; the family of the house of David apart, and their wives apart; the family of the house of Nathan apart, and their wives apart; the family of the house of Levi apart, and their wives apart; the family of Shimei apart, and their wives apart; all the families that remain, every family apart, and their wives apart.

23. *Isaiah 66:8*. Who hath heard such a thing? who hath seen such things? Shall the earth be made to bring forth in one day? or shall a nation be born at once? for as soon as Zion travailed, she brought forth her children.

24. *Mark 13:32-37*. But of that day and that hour knoweth no man, no, not the angels which are in heaven, neither the Son, but the Father. Take ye heed, watch and pray: for ye know not when the time is. For the Son of man is as a man taking a far journey, who left his house, and gave authority to his servants, and to every man his work, and commanded the porter to watch. Watch ye therefore: for ye know not when the master of the house cometh, at even, or at midnight, or at the cockcrowing, or in the morning: Lest coming suddenly he find you sleeping. And what I say unto you I say unto all, Watch.

25. *Hebrews 10:25*. Not forsaking the assembling of ourselves together, as the manner of some is; but exhorting one another: and so much the more as ye see the day approaching.

26. *Luke 21:28*. And when these things begin to come to pass, then look up, and lift up your heads; for your redemption draweth nigh.

22

SIGNS OF CHRIST'S IMMINENT COMING

I believe that the coming of our Lord is to be personal, premillennial, and also, that it is imminent. Let us remember the admonition that we must distinguish between the Rapture—His coming into the air to receive His saints (1 Thessalonians 4) which may occur at any moment—and the Revelation—His coming down to the earth with His saints, which will not occur until after the preaching of the gospel as a witness;[1] the gathering of Israel, in unbelief; the manifestation of Antichrist; and other prophesied events. Now we will consider what the evidences are for also believing that His coming, the Rapture, is near. Out of many reasons we will give seven, as follows:

The Prevalence of Travel and Knowledge

"Shut up the words and seal the book even to the time of the end: many shall run to and fro and knowledge shall be increased" (Daniel 12:4).

A comparison of recent years with the present shows a marvelous increase in both travel and knowledge.*

An incident is told of a woman in England who, after long consideration, had decided on a journey. Friends gathered to assist her departure and walked by the

---

* Written in 1908 (publisher's note).

1. *Matthew 24:14.* And this gospel of the kingdom shall be preached in all the world for a witness unto all nations; and then shall the end come.

conveyance a mile or more to bid her God-speed, but actually, her entire journey was only 50 miles.

Now invention has chained the mighty forces of steam and electricity to palatial tranporters by land and sea, so that one can go round the world, with comfort and ease, in 60 days. Railways cover the earth and steamers track the sea like a mighty spider's web.

Our text says *"many* will run to and fro." In the year 1896 the number of passengers carried on the railroads in the United States was 535,120,756 and the mileage was 13,054,840,243. In the whole world the railroad passengers were 2,384,000,000 and the mileage 28,677,000,000. Add to this the travel by ships and private vehicles, the explorations into every conceivable corner of the earth, from the equator to the poles, and the enormous aggregate is surely a literal fulfilment of this sign of the end.

"And *knowledge* shall be increased." The unprecedented educational facilities are a remarkable feature of our time. We have public schools for our youth, colleges and universities for higher education, and denominational schools for religious education. The public press, with its ceaseless streams of news and information, covers the earth with its ever increasing circulation, like falling leaves from some mighty tree of knowledge. And, of the making of many books, there is truly no end.

The means of communication by the mail, telegraph and telephone have been multiplied in geometrical progression. By the Universal Postal Union, printed matter is carried as cheaply to Iceland or China as to the next street in Chicago.

But perhaps the prediction of our text refers more specifically to the increase of Bible study, and here again we have a wonderful fulfillment. Since the year 1804 over 230,000,000 Bibles, Testaments, and portions have been distributed by the Bible societies alone, and millions more by private publication agencies. The Bible has been translated into over 287 languages, and parts into 340.

Over nine-tenths of the human race have the Bible to read in their own language.

Religious papers and periodicals are issued by the millions. The great system of universal Sunday school lessons, the Bible institutes, the Chautauqua summer schools and Bible conferences, have developed a world-wide study of the Word of God.

With this there has come a widespread study of the prophetic Word, especially concerning Israel and our Lord's return. While the skeptic and destructive critic, are studying about the Word, trying to undermine and tear it down, the reverent students by the thousand are looking into the sure Word of prophecy as to a light that shines in a dark place.

Perilous Times

"This know also that in the last days perilous times shall come" (2 Timothy 3:1).

Physically: Pestilence, famine, earthquakes, cyclones, etc.

Possibly the recently vented oil and gases of the earth are a preparation for some mighty conflagration to be aided by newly manifested heat and electrical forces from the sun.[2]

Politically and Socially

Under this heading I need only refer to the progress of Nihilism, Socialism, Communism and Anarchy. Could there be anything worse than the creed of the latter, that is, the first lie is God and the second is Law. They openly avow that their mission is to destroy the present social structure, and they prophesy (perhaps with the accuracy of Caiphas), that something better will come.

---

2. *2 Thessalonians 1:8*. In flaming fire taking vengeance on them that know not God, and that obey not the gospel of our Lord Jesus Christ.

2 Peter 3:7. But the heavens that now are, and the earth, by the same word have been stored up for fire, being reserved against the day of judgment and destruction of ungodly men.

Distress of Nations

National jealousies have caused offensive and defensive preparations on a scale of such magnitude as to literally grind out the life of the people with oppressive taxation. All Europe is practically a soldiers' camp, with 23,000,000 trained men ready to fly at each other in a universal war, with weapons so ingenious and deadly as to put all the past record beneath the shadow of comparison.

Governments vie with each other in the suicidal policy of adding corps to corps and ships to ships, piling up their national debts in the fact of absolute bankruptcy. It is appalling to contemplate the woe and carnage that would follow in the wake of these forces, if once let loose. No wonder the statesmen strain every nerve to defer that day by their struggle to preserve the peace of Europe.

In the very midst of the scene, *lawlessness* lifts its hydrahead. Capital cringes before the coming revenge of labor (James 5). Men's hearts fail them for fear of the things that be coming on the earth. And well they may, for Satan will combine all these forces in his mighty culminating effort to stamp out the name of God from the earth. He will head them up in his masterpiece, the atheistic Antichrist, who will deny both the Father and the Son.

Spiritualism

"Now the Spirit speaketh expressly that in the latter times some shall depart from the faith, giving heed to seducing spirits and doctrines of devils" (1 Timothy 4:1).

Modern Spiritualism is by no means mere trickery. There is plenty of fraud and deception that requires darkened rooms and suspicious cabinets, but there are also unquestionable mysteries and spirit manifestations, demons that long to possess the bodies of men, wicked spirits which love darkness rather than light. It is a definite sign of the times.

So also is Christian Science a doctrine of devils, for, like Theosophy, it denies the atonement of Christ, and asserts that every man is his own savior. There are said to be more esoteric Buddhists in and around Boston than there are natives in Australia. Christian Science has swept over the country like a prairie fire, and Spiritualism has its myriads of adherents. This surprising prevalence of these three delusions is, like a cloud of darkness, a sign that the end is near.

Apostasy

The day of the Lord [the revelation] shall not come, "except there come a falling away first" (2 Thessalonians 2:3).

The Laodicean, or the last state of the church, is one so sickening that the Lord says He will spue it out of His mouth.[3] There is to be a dearth of faith especially in regard to the coming of the Lord. "Nevertheless, when the Son of Man cometh shall He find the faith on the earth?" (Luke 18:8). An aged minister once said that he did not believe the Lord was coming for 60,000 years. I concluded that he could not be watching for it.

Postmillennialists say very little about the coming of the Lord. An elderly Methodist clergyman in Florida said that he had heard only five sermons on the Lord's coming, and he preached them all himself. In many large audiences where a survey has been taken it is surprising to see what a great majority have never heard a single sermon on this blessed hope, which finds so large a place in the Holy Scriptures. There is a notable dearth of power in the preaching of the Word today! Men discourse on how to reach the masses but the masses go on unreached.

Every period of hard times and business depression until now, has been followed by a wonderful revival. But not so this last time. Why so few conversions during this last era of hard times? There is evidently one answer. The attacks by Higher Critics on the inspiration of the Bible have found so many adherents in the ranks of the

---

3. *Revelation 3:16.* So then because thou art lukewarm, and neither cold nor hot, I will spew thee out of my mouth.

clergy and theological professors who proclaim their *doubts*, that the faith of the masses has been undermined. The great truths of the Bible no longer have that firm hold on their consciences which has up to now stimulated the disciples to faithful service, and brought sinners to repentance. With the great Greek church wedded to politics; the Catholic church worshiping Mary in the place of Christ and pronouncing blessing upon those who idolatrously kiss the toe of the image of Agrippina and Nero;* and the Protestant churches so largely stiffened with formalism and honeycombed with infidelity; we see the apostasy moving forward with such rapid strides that we again conclude the end is near.

Worldwide Evangelism

"This gospel of the kingdom shall be preached in all the world for a witness to all nations, than shall the end come" (Matthew 24:14).

It is important here to explain that while the church is the present agent for the world's evangelization, she may be caught away at any moment. Then the Tribulation saints—those who will believe by the very fact of the church being caught away—may become the agents, for God will always have a witness in the earth. Later it may be converted Israel. Lastly, it is to be a heavenly messenger.[4]

So we are simply to work while the day lasts, watching and waiting because we have no sign nor event that stands

---

* In the church of Saint Augustino, in Rome, is a marble statue of a woman and child, which, it is generally claimed represents Agrippina and Nero. This is denied by the Roman Church, but it appears to be evidenced by the fact that the latter is crushing a bird against his breast, showing the ferocious cruelty of his nature. This image has been consecrated by the highest authorities of the Catholic Church to represent the virgin Mary and the Child Jesus. On the pedestal underneath is this inscription in Latin: "Our Lord, the Pope Pius 7th, concedes perpetually 100 days of indulgence, to be used once a day, to all those who devoutly kiss the foot of this holy image, reciting one Ave Maria for the needs of the Holy Church. June 7, 1822."

---

4. *Revelation 14:6.* And I saw another angel fly in the midst of heaven having the everlasting gospel to preach unto them that dwell on the earth, and to every nation, and kindred, and tongue, and people.

between us and the coming of the Lord. But let us see what has been accomplished. What is a witness? We have only one example or illustration in the Word, and that is Jonah's three days of preaching in the streets of Nineveh.

Every nation in the world today has a testimony comparatively as great, with the exception of Tibet, Nepal and Bhutan and the Mohammedan countries of Afghanistan and the Sudan, and into the former the Bible has already gone in great numbers, and missionaries stand at the doors waiting for the privilege of entering in.

Is it not impressively significant that the missionaries sent forth during this century have seemingly without any human supervision, been impelled to go to every land, island, nation and tribe of the earth?

> "Oh, Church of Christ, behold at last
> The promised sign appear;
> The gospel preached in all the world,
> And lo! the King draws near."

Rich Men

"Go to now, ye rich men, weep and howl for your miseries that shall come upon you . . . Ye have heaped treasures together for [in] the last days" (James 5:1, 8).

The accummulation of riches, in the hands of a few men, is specially characteristic of the present times. It is needless to mention the financial kings who, through trusts and various manipulations, continue to add to their enormous estates. If Adam had lived to the present time and accummulated $10,000 additional wealth each year of his life, this vast aggregate would not equal several individual fortunes which have been amassed in recent years.

What extent these colossal estates will attain by joining "house to house" and "field to field," none can tell. But we know that *woe* has been uttered concerning it,[5] and that it is distinctively a sign of the last days.

Israel

Israel is God's sundial. If we want to know our place in chronology, our position in the march of events, look at Israel. God says of Israel: "I will make a full end of all the nations whither I have scattered thee, but I will not make a full end of thee" (Jeremiah 30:11).

Like Tennyson's brook they can sing, "Nations come and nations go, but I go on forever." They are the generation that does not pass away. Israel will be restored to Palestine and no more be pulled up our of their land.[6] Hundreds of prophecies affirm this dispensational truth. Like the red thread in the British rigging, it runs through the whole Bible: prophecies to the people like Ezekiel 37, and prophecies to the land like Ezekiel 36.

The title deed to Palestine is recorded, not in the Mohammedan Serai of Jerusalem nor the Serglio of Constantinople, but in hundreds of millions of Bibles now extant in more than 300 languages of the earth. The restoration was summed up at the first council of the apostles in Jerusalem, as their conclusion based upon the words of the prophets.[7]

As the fig tree which Jesus found bearing nothing but leaves, Israel has been set aside for a whole (*aiōn*) dispensation.[8] Jerusalem was to be trodden down until

---

5. *Isaiah 5:8.* Woe unto them that join house to house, that lay field to field, till there be no place, that they may be placed alone in the midst of the earth! In mine ears said the Lord of hosts, Of a truth many houses shall be desolate, even great and fair, without inhabitant.

6. *Amos 9:15.* And I will plant them upon their land, and they shall no more be pulled up out of their land which I have given them, saith the Lord thy God.

7. *Acts 15:13-18.* And after they had held their peace, James answered, saying, Men and brethren, hearken unto me: Simeon hath declared how God at the first did visit the Gentiles, to take out of them a people for his name. And to this agree the words of the prophets; as it is written, after this I will return, and will build again the tabernacle of David, which is fallen down; and I will build again the ruins thereof, and I will set it up: that the residue of men might seek after the Lord, and all the Gentiles, upon whom my name is called, saith the Lord, who doeth all these things. Known unto God are all his works from the beginning of the world.

8. *Mark 11:13-14.* And seeing a fig-tree afar off having leaves, he came, if haply he might find any thing thereon: and when he came to it, he found nothing but leaves; for the time of figs was not yet. And Jesus answered and said unto it, No man eat fruit of thee hereafter for ever [an aion]. And his disciples heard it.

the times of the Gentiles is fulfilled.[9] But note carefully that a little later Jesus said, "Now learn a parable of the fig tree [and all the trees]: when her branch is yet tender, and putteth forth leaves, ye know that summer is near. So likewise, ye, in like manner, when ye shall see these things come to pass, know that it is nigh, even at the doors" (Mark 13:28; Luke 21:29).

In Ezekiel 31 the trees are used as symbols of the nations. "The fig-tree was the *Jewish people* full of the leaves of an useless profession, but without fruit," writes Dean Alford. Now if Israel is beginning to show signs of national life and is actually returning to Palestine, then surely the end of this dispensation "is nigh, even at the doors."

Zionism

Zionism is the present movement of the Jews to return to the land of their fathers. Zionsim is a modern term expressing the national hopes and sentiments of the Jews. These sentiments, however, are based on widely different views, as held by the most extreme sections of the parties into which the Jews are divided.

As is well-known the Jews have, in the past 50 years, become divided into three great sections: the orthodox, the status quo, and the reformed. The orthodox hold to the Old Testament Scriptures, as interpreted by the Talmud, as the literal Word of God, and also to the hopes and heritage of their ancestors founded thereon. They believe in the frequent repeated utterances of the prophets, that some day they will return to Palestine and become permanently settled as a holy and happy nation, under the sovereignty of their coming Messiah.

These hopes are the very core of their intensely religious life, and are embedded in the most solemn devotions of their prayer-book. Every morning, throughout every nation and climate, wherever they are scattered over this

9. *Luke 21:24.* And they shall fall by the edge of the sword, and shall be led away captive into all nations: and Jerusalem shall be trodden down of the Gentiles, until the times of the Gentiles by fulfilled.

whole world, the orthodox Jew lifts up his prayer: "Save us, O God of our salvation, and gather us together and deliver us from the nations. May it be acceptable unto thee, Eternal; our God and the God of our Fathers, that the sanctuary may be rebuilt speedily in our days and our portion assigned us in thy law. There will we serve thee in reverence as of old, in days of yore."

In that solemn service of the Passover they cry out: "At present we celebrate it here, but the next year we hope to celebrate it in the land of Israel," and again, "O build Jerusalem the holy city speedily in our days. Blessed art Thou, O Lord!"

With such faithful and earnest prayers have these orthodox Jews have kept alive the fires of devotion and the glorious hopes of restoration, while being driven up and down the earth with the rods of enmity, ostracism and banishment. But for over 17 centuries, while they have thus fervently prayed, they have made no effort to return to Palestine, believing that they should wait until God Himself brought about their restoration by supernatural means.

About 200 years ago the persecutions began to abate, and in the eighteenth century they were gradually emancipated from these various disabilities. With this coming of liberty, there was a noise and a shaking and the dry bones of Ezekiel 37 began to come together.[10]

The Universelle Israelite Alliance was organized in Paris in 1860, and later the Anglo-Jewish Association in England. Through these powerful organizations the Jews

---

10. *Ezekiel 37:1-7.* The hand of the LORD was upon me, and carried me out in the Spirit of the LORD, and set me down in the midst of the valley which was full of bones. And caused me to pass by them round about: and, behold, there were very many in the open valley; and, lo, they were very dry. And he said unto me, Son of man, can these bones live? And I answered, O LORD God, thou knowest. Again he said unto me, Prophesy upon these bones, and say unto them, O ye dry bones, hear the word of the LORD. Thus saith the LORD GOD unto these bones, Behold, I will cause breath to enter into you, and ye shall live: and I will lay sinews upon you, and will bring up flesh upon you, and cover you with skin, and put breath in you, and ye shall live; and ye shall know that I am the LORD. So I prophesied as I was commanded: and as I prophesied, there was a noise, and behold a shaking and the bones come together, bone to his bone. See also verses 8 to 14.

can make themselves felt throughout the world. And now, within a few years, there have been organized *Chovevi* (lover of) *Zion* and *Shova* (colonizers of) *Zion* societies, mostly among the orthodox Jews of Russia, Romania, Germany, and even in England and the United States. This is really the first practical effort they have made to regain their home in Palestine.

In a few words, followers of the status quo are striving to reconcile the genius of Judaism with the requirements of modern times, and in Western Europe are in a great majority.

The reformed Jews or Neologists have rapidly thrown away their faith in the inspiration of the Scriptures. They have flung to the wind all national and Messianic hopes. Their rabbis preach rapturously about the mission of Judaism, while joining with the most radical higher critics in the destruction of its very basis, the inspiration of the Word of God. Some have gone clear over into agnosticism.

Strange to say, from these agnostics now comes the other wing of the Zionist party. And not only have they joined this party, but they furnished the leaders, such as: Dr. Max Nordau of Paris, and Dr. Theodore Herzl of Vienna.

The orthodox Jews who have enlisted under the Zionist banner are animated by the most devout religious motives. But the agnostics declare that this is not a religious movement at all. It is purely economic and nationalistic. Dr. Herzl, its founder and principal leader, espoused it as a *dernier resort,* to escape the persecutions of anti-semitism, which has taken such a firm hold of the masses of the Austrian people. He conceived the idea that if the Jews could regain Palestine and establish a government, even under the power of the Sultan, it would give them a naional standing which would expunge anti-semitism from the other nations of the world, and make it possible for all Jews to live comfortably in any nation they may desire. Not all the orthodox Jews have joined this movement. Indeed, the leaders of the *Chovei Zion* Societies hold aloof.

The call, issued by Dr. Herzl for the Zionist Congress, held in Basle, Switzerland in 1897, met with severe opposition from the German rabbis and also a large portion of the Jewish press, as well as the mass of rich reformed Jews. Nevertheless, over 200 delegates from all over Europe and the Orient and some from the United States, met and carried through the program of the congress with tremendous enthusiasm.

Memorials, approving the object of the congress, came in from all sections, signed by tens of thousands of Jews. The congress elected a central committee and authorized the raising of $50,00,000 capital. It has certainly marked a wonderful innovation in the attitude of the Jews and a closer gathering of the dry bones of Ezekiel.

And now, after ten years of wonderful growth and progress, it remains to be seen what the providential openings in the Ottoman Empire may be that shall give opportunity to realize its object. Zionism is now the subject of the most acrimonious debate among the Jews. Many of the orthodox criticize it as an attempt to seize the prerogatives of their God. While others say that God will not work miracles to accomplish that which they can do themselves.

Most of the reformed Jews, now that they can no longer ridicule the movement, decry it as an egregious blunder that will increase instead of diminishing anti-semitism. They have no desire to return to Palestine. They are like the man in Kansas, who, in a revival meeting said he did not want to go to heaven, nor did he wish to go to hell but he said he wanted to stay right there in Kansas.

In the same way these reformed Jews are content to renounce all the prophesied glory of a messianic kingdom in the land of their ancestors, preferring the palatial homes and gathered riches which they have acquired in Western Europe and the United States. They coolly advise their persecuted brethren in Russia, Romania, Persia and North Africa, to patiently endure their grievous persecutions until anti-semitism dies out.

But these brethren retort that their prudent advisers would think very differently if they lived in Morocco or Russia, and that even in Western Europe anti-semitism instead of dying out, is rather on the increase. In the midst of these disputes, the Zionists have seized the reins and eschewing the help of Abraham's God they have accepted agnostics as leaders and are plunging madly into this scheme for the erection of a Godless state.

But the Bible student will surely say, this godless national gathering of Israel is not the fulfillment of the glorious divine restoration, so glowingly described by the prophets.

No, indeed! Let it be carefully noted that God has repeatedly promised to gather Israel with such a magnificent display of *His* miraculous power that it will no more be said, "The LORD liveth that brought up the children of Israel out of the land of Egypt; but the Lord liveth, that brought up the children of Israel from the land of the north and from all the lands whither he had driven them" (Jeremiah 16:14). Yet He has also said, "Gather yourselves together, yea, gather together, O nation that hath no longing, before the decree bring forth, before the day pass as the chaff, before the fierce anger of the LORD come upon you" (Zephaniah 2:1, 2). Could this prophecy be more literally fulfilled than by this present Zionist movement?

One of the speakers at the first congress said of the Sultan, "If His majesty will now receive us, we will accept Him as our Messiah." God says, "Ye have sold yourselves for nought and ye shall be redeemed without money" (Isaiah 52:3). But Dr. Herzl is reported to have said, "We must buy our way back to Palestine, salvation is to be by money."

What a sign is this that the end of this dispensation is near. If it stood alone we might well give heed to it. But when we find it supported by all these other signs set forth in the Word, how can we refuse to believe it? Will we Christians condemn the Jews for not accepting the cumulative evidence that Jesus is the Messiah; and ourselves refuse this other cumulative evidence that His second coming is near?

It is significant that this first Zionist congress assembled just 1,260 years after the capture of Jerusalem by the Mohammedans in A.D. 637 (Daniel 12:7). It is probable that "the times of the Gentiles" are nearing their end, and that the nations are soon to plunge into the mighty whirl of events connected with Israel's godless gathering, "Jacob's trouble" (Jeremiah 30:6, 7), that awful time of tribulation, like which there has been none in the past, nor will be in the future (Matthew 24:21).

But we, brethren, are not of the night. We are to watch and pray always that we may escape all these things that will come to pass and stand before the Son of Man (Luke 21:36).

Oh! glorious Hope. No wonder the Spirit and the Bride say come. No wonder the Bridegroom says, "Surely I come quickly," and will not we all join with the enraptured apostle, "Even so come, Lord Jesus"? *I must work the works of Him that sent me while it is day: the night cometh when no man can work"* (John 9:4).

All the worldwide mission fields demand increased consecration of ourselves, our time, and our substance. O fellow servants, let us improve the wonderful opportunities of our day to make investments for eternity.

Jesus Is Coming Again

"WATCH
therefore; for ye know not what
hour your Lord doth come."
Matthew 24:42.

"WATCH
therefore; for ye know neither the day nor the hour."
Matthew 25:13.

"Take Ye Heed,
WATCH
and pray; for ye know not when the time is."

"WATCH
ye therefore; for ye know not when
the Master of the house cometh, at even,
or at midnight, or at the cock crowing, or
in the morning, lest, coming suddenly,
He find you sleeping. And what I say
unto you I say unto all,

WATCH."
Mark 13:33–37.

"Blessed is he that WATCHETH, and keepeth his
garments." *Revelation 16:15.*

"If therefore thou shalt not
WATCH
I will come on thee as a thief."

"BEHOLD, I COME QUICKLY."
Revelation 3:3, 11.

"YE SHALL BE WITNESSES"

Reader, what will our occupation be, as disciples of the Lord Jesus, while we watch and wait for His return? It is not enough that we have a personal experience of repentance, faith, forgiveness, adoption and sanctification; it is not enough that we study the Word to search out the deep things of Providence and prophecy. We must join heart and hand in the great practical work of world evangelization.

EVANGELIZING THE WORLD

For this is our Lord's command: "Go ye into all the world, and preach the Gospel to every creature" (Matthew 28:19); and He has said, "This Gospel of the kingdom shall be preached in all the world, for a witness to all nations, and then shall the end come" (Matthew 24:14.) While the church remains on earth (see page 88) she is certainly the agent to accomplish this purpose, because

Jesus said: "Ye shall be witnesses unto me . . . unto the uttermost part of the earth" (Acts 1:8; Luke 24:47–48.)

Let us engage, with all our might, in this worldwide mission work. Let us give of our means, our prayers and our words of encouragement to those who go to preach in the by-ways and hedges and in distant lands (Romans 10:15), and, if possible, let us go ourselves, thereby insuring ourselves of His fellowship who said, "and lo, I am with you alway."

This is how we best please the Master. This is how we hasten the day of God (2 Peter 3:12; Matthew 24:14.)

The progress already made inspires us to greater effort. The world is belted with centers of evangelization. From Greenland to Patagonia, from Norway to Good Hope, from Siberia to Tasmania, and throughout the Islands of the sea, multitudes of Gospel messengers are proclaiming the Word of Life. Only a few strongholds of Satan are still without any witness, and of these Nepal and Tibet are opening their doors to waiting missionaries, while Central Africa unbars her millennial fastness to advancing heroes from every quarter. Read the missionary periodicals, especially those giving general news, and your soul will rejoice in the hope that even now the witness is almost complete. Then arouse yourselves brothers, and let us obey our marching orders, until we hear the welcome "well done" when the "ambassadors" are called home.

SCRIPTURE INDEX

Note: In some instances a brief text is paged under the reference to a larger one which includes it. Example: 2 Thessalonians 1:10 may be found under 2 Thessalonians 1:7–10, etc.

The Church in Prophecy
Exploring God's Purpose for the Present Age

by John F. Walvoord

What part will the church play in the end times? Has it replaced the nation of Israel in God's plan? Are Old Testament prophecies being fulfilled spiritually in the church? These and many other questions are answered in this comprehensive look at the church and God's prophetic plan.

Some of the chapters included in this work are:
- The Church in the Old Testament
- The Church in the End of the Age
- The Importance of the Rapture
- The Church and the Tribulation
- The Church in Eternity

ISBN 0-8254-3968-x

The Final Drama
Fourteen Keys to Understanding the Prophetic Scriptures

by John F. Walvoord

As the world anxiously moves toward a new century and a new millennium, one of America's leading experts in the field of biblical prophecy, John F. Walvoord, offers a detailed and fascinating explanation of how specific events in the late 1980s and early 1990s relate to biblical prophecy.

"About one-fourth of the Bible is predictive prophecy. About half of these prophecies have already been fulfilled," Walvoord observes in the Introduction. "Therefore, a study of the prophecy concerning events of the past will give many guidelines for understanding the fulfillment of the prophecy of events in the future."

This is a foundational book for understanding end-time Scripture, the future of the church, Israel, Satan, and the world.

ISBN 0-8254-3971-x

ALSO FROM KREGEL PUBLICATIONS

The Return
Christ's Second Coming and the End Times

Thomas Ice and Timothy Demy, general editors

As the turn of the millennium nears, sensational-ism abounds concerning the return of Christ and the end times. What does the Bible teach about Christ's return?

This work presents a Bible-based, reasoned examination of the Second Coming. Contributors to this work include:

- Larry Crutchfield
- Edward E. Hindson
- H. Wayne House
- Thomas Ice
- Tim LaHaye
- J. Randall Price
- Gerald B. Stanton
- Stanley Toussaint
- John F. Walvoord

ISBN 0-8254-2904-8

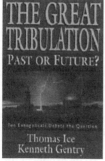

The Great Tribulation—Past or Future?
Two Evangelicals Debate the Question

by Thomas Ice and Kenneth L. Gentry

Thomas Ice, director of the Pre-Trib Research Center, and Ken Gentry, author and teacher, address an issue at the heart of the current interest in the end times: Are the events of the book of Revelation yet to be fulfilled or have they already been fulfilled in the first century experience of the church?

Ice presents a premillennial view that Revelation contains prophetic events yet to be fulfilled while Gentry presents an amillennial position that there are no end-time catastrophes yet to come.

Presented in a friendly debate format with responses by each author to the other's position, this work will inform readers who hold either of these positions.

ISBN 0-8254-2901-3